The Arcana of Reproduction

Leopoldina Fortunati was a core member of Lotta Femminsta and the Wages for Housework Movement internationally. Along with Mariarosa Dalla Costa, Selma James and Silvia Federici, she composed many of the group's core theoretical and political texts. Her early work continues to inform movements concerned with struggles over reproduction globally, and in subsequent work as a theorist of media and technology, Fortunati has been at the vanguard of contemporary theory addressing the relation between gendered labour and technology.

The Arcana of Reproduction

Housewives, Prostitutes, Workers and Capital

Leopoldina Fortunati

Foreword by Silvia Federici

Translated by Arlen Austin and Sara Colantuono

VERSO

London • New York

This English-language edition first published by Verso 2025
Translation © Arlen Austin and Sara Colantuono 2025
First published as *L'arcano della riproduzione. Casalinghe,
prostitute, operai e capitale* (Venice: Marsilio, 1981)
© Leopoldina Fortunati 1981
Foreword © Silvia Federici 2024
Afterword © Leopoldina Fortunati 2025

1 3 5 7 9 10 8 6 4 2

Verso
UK: 6 Meard Street, London W1F 0EG
US: 207 East 32nd Street, New York, NY 10016
versobooks.com

Verso is the imprint of New Left Books

ISBN-13: 978-1-83976-740-1
ISBN-13: 978-1-83976-741-8 (UK EBK)
ISBN-13: 978-1-83976-742-5 (US EBK)

British Library Cataloguing in Publication Data
A catalogue record for this book is available from the British Library

Library of Congress Cataloging-in-Publication Data
A catalog record for this book is available from the Library of Congress

Typeset in Minion by Biblichor Ltd, Scotland
Printed and bound by CPI Group (UK) Ltd, Croydon CR0 4YY

Contents

Foreword

Silvia Federici

The Arcana of Reproduction is a unique book in the world of Marxist feminism. Generally, Marxist feminists have elaborated on the methodological significance of Marx's work for understanding the specific historical forms of oppression that women have experienced in capitalist society, or they have extended Marx's analysis of the exploitation of women workers. Fortunati breaks with these trends, demonstrating how our understanding of the activities by which our everyday life is reproduced can be radically transformed if we apply to them the very same categories that Marx developed to analyse the process of commodity production. The result is a true *tour de force* exploring the similarities and differences of these two interlocking spheres of the capitalist organisation of work. Her painstaking analysis unsettles our common notions concerning reproduction as well as Marx's own work.

As Fortunati explained in an interview with *Viewpoint*, the idea of the book originated from 'the practical needs of the feminist struggle': that is, the need to explain – both to feminists and the wider movement – why it has been necessary to rethink Marxism, and how feminism relates to class and the capitalist exploitation of labour.[1] These were the issues at the centre of the campaign for Wages for Housework and the endeavours

---

1   Leopoldina Fortunati, 'Learning to Struggle: My Story Between Workerism and Feminism', *Viewpoint*, 15 September 2013, viewpointmag.com.

of the Padua-based Triveneto Committee, of which Fortunati was a founding member.[2]

At a strategically important moment for the development of the feminist movement, Wages for Housework (WFH) provided an alternative to the dominant feminist tendency to view entrance into wage labour as the key step on the path to women's emancipation. Partly inspired by the *operaismo* movement in Italy, as well as anticolonial struggles and the struggle against racism in the US, WFH embraced an anti-capitalist perspective.[3] At the same time, however, it faulted Marxism for ignoring the exploitation that takes place in the sphere of reproduction – that is, the exploitation of women's labour in the home, the family, the sphere of domestic activities – this being the 'nerve centre' (as Fortunati was to define it) of the production of labour power: that precious commodity on which all capitalist accumulation depends.

A key document, in this context, was Mariarosa Dalla Costa's essay *Women and the Subversion of the Community*, originally published in Italian in 1972. It revolutionised Marx's theory in arguing that, far from being a personal service or a vestigial remnant of a pre-capitalist world, 'domestic work' is a specific form of capitalist production that produces not commodities but the workers' capacity to work.[4] Dalla Costa's now classic essay, together with Selma James's *Sex, Race and Class* from 1975, was the theoretical foundation of both the WFH campaign in the 1970s, and of a feminist critique of Marx that was much needed both to respond to the attacks by the male left, and to articulate a new understanding, produced by the struggle, of the specific reality of women's lives.[5]

---

2   On the founding of Lotta Femminista, see Louise Toupin, *Wages for Housework: A History of an International Feminist Movement* (London: Pluto Press, 2018), 83–6. See also Silvia Federici and Arlen Austin, eds, *The New York Wages for Housework Committee: History, Theory, Documents, 1972–1977* (New York: Autonomedia, 2018). The final section of this book is dedicated to documents from the Triveneto Committee, which was the leading organisation in Italy in the campaign, and a centre for the campaign internationally.

3   Here, I prefer to use the Italian term *operaismo* rather than its American translation as 'Workerism' because the latter somewhat changes and distorts its meaning, since *operaio* is the iconic term that was used in all political discourse in Italy to characterise the key contributor to capitalist accumulation and protagonist of the class struggle.

4   Mariarosa Dalla Costa, *Potere femminile e sovversione sociale con 'Il posto della donna' di Selma James* (Venice: Marsilio Editori, 1972).

5   Selma James, *Sex, Race and Class, with contributions from Barbara Reese, Mala Dhondy, Darcus Howe and Correspondents to Race Today* (Bristol: Falling Wall Press, 1975).

In this context, it is Fortunati's work that, more than any other, has tested to what extent Marx's analysis of the logic of capitalist production can be recuperated and extended to the sphere of domestic work, and thrown light on the principles by which the latter operates and is integrated in the process of capital accumulation.

Fortunati builds upon Dalla Costa's thesis, but expands it. On the one hand, she dissects reproductive work to bring to light those elements that make it an aspect of the capitalist work-machine; on the other, she offers a historical overview of the context in which the capitalist restructuring of housework has taken place and the changes that it has undergone under the impact of women's struggle.[6]

Like Dalla Costa and James, Fortunati is critical of Marx's exclusion of reproductive work from the process of value creation, but her unique contribution is to demonstrate that, if consistently applied, Marx's categories lead to a different understanding of this work – indeed a different understanding of the entire sphere of family, life, parental and sexual relations – that denaturalises and fully reveals its capitalist function.

Housework, she shows, may appear to be a personal service and an individual activity, but in reality it is a form of social labour, as it is generalised and only modified by the kind of labour power to be produced. It is also a value-generating activity, in the Marxian sense of the term, as it makes it possible for capitalists to extract more labour power from workers, who are strengthened by their incorporation of the houseworkers' labour. She further shows that the home is a factory, that familial and sexual relations are relations of production, that marriage is a labour contract, and that conjugal and parental love hide unequal, hierarchical power relations.

In particular, Fortunati dissects the function of the wage as the means by which the hegemonic role of the male worker in the family is constituted, as he becomes the representative of the state and supervisor of his wife's work, as well as of his children's formation as future workers. It is through the wage and the disciplining of the male worker (as Fortunati

---

6   The need to rethink the political history of capitalist development from the viewpoint of women and reproduction led to our collaboration in the production of *Il Grande Calibano. Storia del corpo sociale ribelle nella prima fase del capitale* (Milan: Franco Angeli editore, 1984). On the relation between *Il Grande Calibano* and *Caliban and the Witch*, see the Introduction to *Caliban and the Witch: Women, the Body, and Primitive Accumulation* (New York: Autonomedia, 2004).

demonstrates) that capital also disciplines the houseworker, who does not confront capital directly but through the mediation of her husband or lover – an arrangement that inevitably hides the exploitation involved and undermines the woman's struggle. This, Fortunati argues, is a necessary strategic condition imposed by capital and the state, since the illusion of a loving relation powerfully binds male and female workers to the marriage contract, enabling them to accept the servitude of the factory and the home, while providing the capitalist class two workers for the price of one.

As in Marx, the contrast between formal appearance and reality is a key principle in Fortunati's analysis of the production/reproduction relation, powerfully confirming that what appears as capitalist economics is always, in fact, highly political, insofar as it is structured in such a way to guarantee not only maximum profit, but also maximum control over the workforce. She observes, for instance, that the way capital operates in the sphere of reproduction is diametrically opposed to its organisation of production. Whereas in production workers cooperate in the labour process, in reproduction they are isolated, disaggregated from each other, and work is highly individualised. This is because the illusion of *uniqueness* – the essential ingredient in the ideology of love— is a potent drug, necessary to keep the male worker bonded to his job. It hides the fact that neither husbands and wives, nor parents and children truly relate to each other directly, but always through the mediation of capital, which is the *deus absconditus*, the hidden agent, of familial relations.

As I will demonstrate, Fortunati's insistence on the dominance of capitalist relations in the world of reproduction does not extinguish the possibility of autonomy and refusal. Schooled in the principle of *operaismo* as originally articulated in Mario Tronti's *Operai e Capitale*, according to which 'the struggle comes first' – meaning that it is the workers' struggle that explains capital's movements – Fortunati alerts us to the power of even subterranean acts of refusal.[7] She points out, for example, that women's increasing refusal to carry the burden of bearing many children, although visible only in the fall of the birth rate, was yet powerful enough to force the capitalist class since the 1960s and 1970s to open the doors to migration from abroad and, in time, construct a global labour-market.

---

7   See the recent translation of this work: Mario Tronti, *Workers and Capital*, trans. David Broder (London: Verso, 2019).

While not foreclosing the possibility of resistance, Fortunati's account of the ways in which capital's logic permeates our private life has great de-fetishising effect. Today, thanks to the feminist movement, the decon-secration of domestic work and the family that results from her analysis is more readily accepted. But, in the late 1970s, when Fortunati was working on *The Arcana of Reproduction*, her approach was iconoclastic – for, as the title of the book suggests, few social realities have been so manipulated as the sphere of reproduction, especially in Italy where years of Fascism had turned maternity into a religion.

Undoubtedly, what has driven Fortunati's relentless demythologising of a world of activities that generations have considered the *other* of work – her insistent call to characterise such activities as *labour* – is a profound reflection on Marx's political theory, at a time when, before the fall of the Berlin Wall, the new left in Italy was rediscovering Marx's radical critique of capitalist society. But what has most motivated and shaped the book has undoubtedly been the power of women's revolt against the family form and domestic work. In a previous text, *Brutto ciao* (1976, co-authored with Dalla Costa), Fortunati had traced the beginning of this revolt in Italy to the period after the war, when women, especially in rural areas, broke with the patriarchal family, beginning a process of migration into cities that allowed them to gain more equality with men and started to democratise family relations.[8]

The Arcana of Reproduction follows the evolution of this struggle, marked by gaining a new mobility in marriage, as well as women's refusal to have many children or to have children at all, the refusal of heterosex-uality, and women's insistence on a new familial use of the male wage. These – she argues – should be considered not as changes of custom but as forms of class struggle, as each represents a subversion of capital's plan for women.

The Arcana of Reproduction was published first in 1981. Since then, the process of social reproduction has undergone significant trans-formations. With the massive entry of women, both in Europe and the US, into the wage labour-market, domestic work has increasingly been performed by immigrant women coming from parts of the world which

---

8   See, in particular, Fortunati's essay 'La famiglia: verso la ricostruzione', in Maria-rosa Dalla Costa and Leopoldina Fortunati, *Brutto ciao. Direzione di marcia delle donne negli ultimi trent'anni* (Roma: Edizioni delle donne, 1976), 71–118.

the expansion of capitalist relations has recolonised and impoverished. There have also been attempts to fill the vacuum produced by the exit of women from the home through the mechanisation of care work; though so far it has remained an extremely limited phenomenon, unaffordable by the majority and to a great extent not desirable.[9] A good proportion of the work once done in the home has also been taken out of the home and commercialised. Yet the problems at the root of the feminist revolt of the 1970s have still not been resolved.

As the crisis of the COVID epidemic demonstrated, working outside the home has failed to liberate women from housework. Reinvesting in domestic work and the family, governments across the world brought women back to a home that was now also an office and a school, where they were expected to act as a buffer and compensate for the tensions generated by the pandemic. Meanwhile, as is clear from the uphill battle fought by migrant domestic workers to be recognised as workers, reproductive work continues to be devalued. As for a technological solution to the problem of reproduction, this has proven chimeric, for the very technologies that have been devised to enable women to take a paying job have most often expanded the task houseworkers expected to perform, or have created new problems. For instance, *Telecommunicando in Europa*, a collection edited by Fortunati, shows that the invasion of the home by communicative technologies has added to the breakdown of communication among family members, whose relations are increasingly instrumental.[10]

Constructed over five centuries of capitalist hegemony, the devaluation and naturalisation of reproductive work, in all its different (and constantly expanding) aspects, are clearly not amenable to any particular solution, nor can they be addressed by any reform of this work – though both reforms and changes giving women and all non-conforming subjects more power must be an object of struggle. The devaluation of reproduction, which, in essence, is the devaluation of our life, is a structural condition of capitalist accumulation. Fortunati's analysis in *The Arcana of Reproduction* – of the capitalist structuring of the

---

9   On the mechanisation of care work, see in particular Leopoldina Fortunati, 'Robotization and the Domestic Sphere', *New Media and Society* 20, no. 8 (2018): 2673–90.

10   Leopoldina Fortunati, 'Introduzione', in Leopoldina Fortunati, ed., *Telecomunicando in Europa* (Milan: Franco Angeli, 1998), 13–41.

family and reproductive work thus continues to be both relevant and necessary.

As in the 1970s, revealing the extent to which capitalism dominates our lives – and revealing all the unpaid labour that it has extracted from women through the organisation of marriage and the family – is an essential step for forging a feminist political agenda: an agenda not limited to the quest for equality, equal rights or opportunities, but driven by the conviction that, as Fortunati argues throughout *The Arcana of Reproduction*, women's liberation can be obtained only through the construction of a society beyond capitalism.

Acknowledgements

Leopoldina Fortunati

Just as *L'arcano della riproduzione* was a collaborative work, so its republication by Verso is the fruit of a collective effort that deserves to be reported. I would like to thank first of all Arlen Austin and Sara Colantuono, who translated the manuscript with great expertise. I would also like to thank Sebastian Budgen of Verso, who decided to republish this book. Natalie Hume has all my gratitude and admiration for the deep and thorough job she did in the copy-editing, demonstrating a rare ability to constantly improve the text. Heartfelt thanks also go to Jeanne Tao, the book's production editor at Verso, and to Melissa Weiss, who spent a great deal of time and energy coordinating the design of a cover that faithfully expressed the content.

Furthermore, I would like to thank Silvia Federici for finding the time within her busy agenda to write the foreword to the book, and all the contributors to the crowdfunding campaign which was organised to support translation of the book – special thanks go to Ron Day, Kathi Weeks and Steve Wright for the substantial donations they made. Finally, thanks also to all the study groups that have formed over the years around this book and pressed for its new publication in English.

Translators' Note

Arlen Austin and Sara Colantuono

The Arcana of Reproduction moves rigorously through foundational categories of Marxism, subjecting them each in turn to a feminist analysis that centres questions of reproduction and reproductive labour. However, the work is not a mechanical, corrective exercise – one that would simply add the gendered division of labour to supplement stale Marxian categories; rather, the work builds on categories already thrown into flux in 1970s upheavals of both Italian feminist and Marxian traditions to construct a systematic analysis of global import.

The first, foundational move in this process is the decentring of (male) waged, advanced industrial labor as the protagonist of value production: enter the housewife, and then the prostitute, figures through which, for Fortunati, a broader system of exploitation can be understood. None of this would have been possible without the radical rethinking of the female subject generated by more than a decade of multifaceted feminist theorisation and practice. From institutional organisations affiliated with political parties such as the Unione Donne Italiane closely associated with the Communist Party to radical separatist groups that required a complete withdrawal from the world of men, as did Rivolta Femminile, Italian feminism exemplified how the process of women's liberation can and should be simultaneously organic and oppositional.

Fortunati's own collective, Lotta Femminista, affiliated with both the Wages for Housework movement internationally and critically engaged Italian extra-parliamentarian discourses of the era. The tradition of

operaismo had formulated theses of the primacy of factory workers'
revolts and work refusal to the development of capitalism, while subsequent groups of autonomia, influenced by tendencies of the New Left
and movements of 1968, had multiplied the subjects and spaces of leftist
political discourse. In this constellation of revolutionary possibilities,
Fortunati's system distils the unique, often clandestine, forms of women's
refusal, and stands out as one of the most coherent and implacable theories of the social and economic origin of women's subjugation.

Although it emerged in and through such political and theoretical
upheavals, this text, unlike other contemporaneous works of the author,
restricts its references primarily to the works of Marx and Engels. The
primary texts of operaist feminists of the Wages for Housework movement that most directly inform its argument are invoked in its
introduction, but the subsequent chapters exhibit an extreme economy
of reference. Such an approach was not uncharacteristic of the great
programmatic texts of *operaismo* or other tendencies in Marxism and
Third Worldism of the era but is much less familiar today.

Attending its restriction of reference is a careful structuring in the
unfolding of the argument that is necessary given the radical nature of
the project of subjecting Marxian categories to scrutiny through their
very unorthodox application to the sphere of reproduction. Though
Fortunati's arguments build gradually in intricacy, the guiding questions remain implacable: what are the implications of re-examining
primary categories of political economy through a feminist lens focused
on the ideological denial, obfuscation and devaluation of reproductive
labour?

In translating the text, we were compelled to balance aspirations to
idiomatic precision with the desire to place the work in dialogue with
both its own implicit historical engagements and current concerns.
Fortunately, this new, collaborative translation was generously aided by
the author herself, who was particularly helpful in offering advice and
encouragement and granting license as we have attempted to remain
faithful to the original's rigour while simultaneously trying to increase
its accessibility through explanatory notes, the occasional stylistic
liberty and minor rewordings where we agreed that such would not
significantly compromise the intentions of the original.

In this regard, we attempted to conserve the clear structure of the
work's core argument: one developed along the axis of the gendered

division of labour in the variegated context of Italian feminism and politics of the 1970s. Here, the silent negation of the labour of women, achieved through its categorisation as a 'natural disposition', its constitutively unwaged and unacknowledged position, joins with the labour of the colonised and the extraction of value from nature itself to condition the entire socio-economic field.

Throughout *The Arcana of Reproduction*, the spatial division that reciprocally co-determines such a gendered division of labour (the *operaio* or worker in the factory and the *casalinga* or houseworker in the home) is analysed in terms of a specific historical process culminating in the Fordist organisation of labour. As Fortunati discusses in a new afterword to this edition, much has certainly changed in the past half century since the work was written – and almost as much as has remained horrifyingly the same. The division of labour has only intensified, largely along traditional gendered lines, under COVID, and, in nations where the increase in waged industrial labour requires a nuclear family form, this old Fordist model has increased or retained relative dominance even as family and kinship structures are dismantled and destroyed through forced migration. In translation we found it important to maintain the gendered terms for work and labour deployed in the original – though to attempt to do so in English can present specific difficulties, as noted below.

The articulation and analysis of a system that discriminates on the basis of gender was certainly a historical necessity for the feminist movement in 1970s Italy, as it was elsewhere and more often than not remains today. The text precedes explicit critiques by subsequent post-structuralist feminisms of the binarism and potential structural biases inherent in such discourse. That said, the text was in many ways ahead of its time and the broader movement in which it participated, in developing a methodology for describing the work of producing, reproducing and transforming gendered roles in relation to their status as labour power available for exploitation – processes rigorously engaged also by recent developments in queer and (trans)feminist theory that address the work and labour of producing and reproducing gendered identities.[1]

---

1   See, in particular, Jules Joanne Gleeson and Elle O'Rourke, eds, *Transgender Marxism* (London: Pluto Press, 2021).

The Arcana of Reproduction describes a social field constituted by the gendered division of work and labour: first and foremost, the complexities generated by the status of reproductive labour. Among the primary challenges we encountered as translators was simply what to do with the word *lavoro*, which serves as a root or base term for constant elaboration, a centre of gravity around which the original text develops. In Italian, as in Marx's original German, the term may indicate both *work* and *labour*, where the latter can specify homogeneous, abstract and socialised work generative of exchange value, while the former indicates a diversity of specific sensuous material activities generative of use value.[2] Engels famously claimed, in a note for the fourth edition of *Capital*, that English had the advantage of offering the distinction between work and labour that were lacking in the univocality of the German *Arbeit*, potentially 'solving' a problem shared by any translator of Marx and Marxian discourse in multiple languages more generally: 'Just as the word "*Arbeit*" can be rendered both as "work" and as "labour", so also the word "*Arbeiter*" can be rendered as "worker" and as "labourer".'[3]

Such a distinction becomes increasingly complex, however, as it is refracted through considerations of reproductive labour due to its status as a form of work/labour which is devalued in an ideological and economic sense as it is not mediated by the wage or money form – unless performed outside family or kinship structures. The definition, description, categorisation and analysis of the different types of *lavoro* performed by women (and other workers outside the realm of strictly defined commodity production but within and beyond what might be defined strictly as the realm of reproduction) is the undeniable foundation of the book: *lavoro domestico, lavoro di riproduzione, lavoro di prostituzione, secondo lavoro, doppio lavoro, lavoro direttamente e non direttamente salariato, lavoro extradomestico, lavoro nero o del sesso, lavoro produttivo o improduttivo, lavoro femminile* are only some of the various iterations of such typologies of work invoked in the volume. It should be noted as well that Fortunati refers, from the introduction onwards, to *lavoro domestico immateriale* and its affective aspects, long

---

2   See Engels's note to Chapter 1, Section 3 of the fourth German edition in Karl Marx, *Capital*, vol. 1, *A Critique of Political Economy*, trans. Ben Fowkes (London: Penguin, New Left Review, 1990 [1976]), 137–8.

3   Ibid., 271.

before terms such as *immaterial* and *affective* labour held wide currency in an Anglo-American academic context.[4]

Due in large part simply to its belated translation into English in 1995, the specific arguments of Fortunati's work can be considered only by proxy in relation to the notorious domestic labour debates of the 1970s and '80s, which largely unfolded in Anglo-American academia and movement groups.[5] The work will, however, certainly have relevance to a subsequent elaboration of social reproduction theory and its inheritance of the perennial question of the relation between reproductive labour, exploitation, value production and accumulation.[6] In this context, the decision to render the term *lavoro domestico* as 'housework' as we have generally done here is a difficult one, as other options ('domestic labour' or 'domestic work') might more clearly connect the argument to debates in Anglo-American Marxian and socialist feminisms. The decision, however, is appropriate given the use of the term within the broader Wages for Housework movement, where it operates in the articulation of what Kathi Weeks points out is a capacious demand that attempts to synthesise political analysis and polemic.[7]

This is one of the few instances where a type of unwaged *lavoro* is

---

4   For a thoughtful consideration of the specific neglect of Fortunati's work and that of debates over domestic labour in feminisms of the 1970s more generally in contemporary discussions of 'immaterial' and 'affective' labour see Kylie Jarrett, 'The Relevance of "Women's Work": Social Reproduction and Immaterial Labor in Digital Media', *Television and New Media* 15, no. 1 (2013), 14–29.

5   For one of the early English-language collections that attempted to condense and present the domestic labour controversies unfolding in 1970s feminism, see Ellen Malos, *The Politics of Housework* (New York: Shocken Books, 1980). Better known to an Anglophone readership perhaps is the 'unhappy marriage between Marxism and Feminism' debate galvanised by Heidi Hartmann's eponymous essay and anthologised the following year in a collection which did not take domestic or reproductive labour as a specific object of analysis and included no contributions from authors affiliated with the Wages for Housework movement. See Lydia Sargent, ed., *Women and Revolution: A Discussion of the Unhappy Marriage of Marxism and Feminism* (Montréal: Black Rose Books, 1981).

6   Tithi Bhattacharya ed., *Social Reproduction Theory: Remapping Class, Re-centering Oppression*, (London: Pluto Press, 2017). For an overview of the value-producing nature of informal and reproductive work in the majority world see Alessandra Mezzadri, 'On the value of social reproduction: Informal labour, the majority world and the need for inclusive theories and politics', *Radical Philosophy* 204 (Spring 2019), 33–41.

7   Kathi Weeks, *The Problem with Work: Feminism, Marxism, Antiwork Politics, and Postwork Imaginaries* (Durham, NC: Duke University Press, 2011), 119–20.

rendered as 'work' rather than 'labour', though Fortunati makes it clear that such work is essential for creating the labour power commodity that appears in production and has the qualities of simple and abstract labour socially mediated by exchange. Maintaining the term 'housework' also attempts to remain faithful to the Wages for Housework claim for such work as a potential site of the creation of use values that might be wrested from a gendered social distribution of labour based on capitalist accumulation. Though degraded, it was claimed as a 'lever of power' that did not require women to enter wage labour to become worthy political subjects.[8] Mindful that the term 'housework' performs a complex mediation of analysis and polemic, unwaged work and labour power, we accentuate and mark the differentiation made throughout the text between these terms and their various permutations as specifically as possible, but it should be kept in mind that a certain ambiguity is inherent to the argument.

If the English language multiplies the possible meanings of *lavoro*, thanks to its double heritage of Latin and Saxon derivation, the words *operaio* and *operaia* are, on the other hand, erased in their specificity, and, regrettably for the translation of this project and the literature of *operaismo* and the Italian left more generally, the English term 'worker' lacks the strong correlation between *operai* and the industrial factory as a locus of struggle. As for the common translation of *classe operaia* as 'working class', and *operaismo* as 'workerism', the translation of *operaio* as 'worker' generalises and nullifies the political and historical significance of the term, as Federici mentions above in her preface to this edition. *Operaio* designates a worker in a factory, a worker more or less specialised in the repetitive tasks of manual labour he is assigned, and both dependent on and subordinated to someone else within a strict distribution of tasks. He – the term is intrinsically gendered in its historical conception – works for a wage, and is, for example, distinguishable from the *impiegato*, a worker who directly invests in the enterprise of his employer, usually taking on some form of administrative role. To retain something of the sense of the original *operaio*, we often specify 'factory worker'. We also add male or female whenever the gendering of the term

---

8   Louise Toupin, 'A Wage as a Lever of Power: The Political Perspective', in *Wages for Housework: A History of an International Feminist Movement* (London: Pluto Press, 2018), 46–82.

seems crucial for the argument, or when the opposition between such roles, divided and defined according to gender, is intentionally highlighted. In accordance with the translation of *lavoro domestico* as 'housework', we also render the key figure of the *operaia della casa* as a 'houseworker', though the gendering of the term is, once again, lost.

Relatedly, the terminology characterising work defined as *sociale* or socialised can lead to certain misunderstandings in translation. The labour of reproduction is defined by Fortunati in the first chapter as a kind of labour that 'appears', in a superficial sense, as a *forza naturale del lavoro sociale*. In this characterisation, the author effectively pairs two of the main *apparent* characteristics of reproductive labour: that of its alleged naturalness and that of its intrinsic social necessity. Importantly, Fortunati is also engaging with Marx and Marxism's tendency to use definitions of the *socialised* character of labour exclusively to define work performed in the realm of production, arguing that such analysis of the socialisation of labour should also be extended, at least as rigorously, to the realm of reproduction. The Italian *forza* indicates strength or power and in this context could be read as a provocative reference to *forza lavoro*, that is, labour power understood as the product of reproductive labour. As such, we generally translate the phrase simply as 'the natural power of social labour', though of course it suggests a profoundly *unnatural* and contested process.

The original Italian phrase would have had resonance, for the reader of Marx in Italian translation, with the great descriptions of capital's power to appropriate the forces of social production such that they appear not as subject to exploitation but as an inherent outgrowth of capital's own self-valorisation process. For example, Delio Cantimori, whose 1968 translation of *Capital* was widely used by the *operaisti* and Fortunati herself, renders Marx's great description (in Chapter 24, on the transformation of surplus value into capital) of the encounter between labour and capital as one in which labour comes to appear as the 'forze produttive sociali del lavoro'. Such productive social forces in this transformation process 'present' themselves as qualities inherent to the 'autovalorizzazione costante del capitale'.[9]

---

9   Karl Marx, *Il Capitale*, vol. 1, trans. Delio Cantimori (Rome: Editori Riuniti, 1968), 664. For the English rendering by Ben Fowkes, see Marx, *Capital*, vol. 1, 755–6. For use of the passage from Marx cited here, see Mario Tronti, *Workers and Capital*,

Alhough Fortunati's work clearly bears the influence of famous texts of the Italian extra-parliamentary left of the time, particularly Mario Tronti's concept of the working class's power to refuse work and thus deny itself as labour power, the complex *duplice carattere* or *duplicità* of reproductive labour, as Fortunati analyses it, greatly complicates the situation. These terms draw on Marx's *Doppelcharakter* of labour – which had made its dramatic entrance in the 1859 preface to the *Grundrisse*, and was more fully developed in the second chapter of *Capital* where it takes pride of place – which he claimed as his own unique and foundational contribution to political economy.[10] In this context, labour is understood as infinitely diverse and specific in its creation of use values, and at the same time abstracted, simple and average in the social field produced by exchange. In Fortunati, of course, this dual character is refracted through the complications of reproductive labour, which remains largely unwaged, unacknowledged and generally only indirectly paid unless performed outside family and kinship structures.

Devaluation and invisibilisation – processes that deny reproductive labour as a realm of experience and contribution to the economy, broadly speaking – reverberate across the entire social field, and indeed are constitutive of the social itself. The implications are countless and operate on what Fortunati describes (in terminology borrowing from *operaismo* and Hegelian Marxism) as the levels of the *piano formale* and the *piano reale* (the formal and real planes), which in turn draw on concepts of essence and appearance that emerge from Marx's own critical engagement with German Idealism. In Fortunati's work, as with any of these traditions, there is no reliance on a simple set of complementary, binary or stable hierarchies, and particularly not when it comes to Fortunati's own

---

trans. David Broder (London: Verso, 2019), especially the classic essay 'The Factory and Society', 13–14. The naturalisation of labour as a productive force available for capitalist expropriation as distinct from simply living labour power was crucial to the analysis of the *operaisti*. For an analysis of this triangulation between living labour, labour power and the worker in Tronti and its subsequent decline and simplification in the discourse of *operaismo*, see Massimiliano Tomba and Riccardo Bellofiore, 'The "Fragment on Machines" and the *Grundrisse*: The Workerist Reading in Question', in Marcel van der Linden and Karl Heinz Roth, eds, *Beyond Marx* (Leiden: Brill, 2014), 345–68.

10   Karl Marx, *Grundrisse: Foundations of the Critique of Political Economy*, trans. Martin Nicolaus (London: Penguin, New Left Review: 1993 [1973]), 81–114; Marx, *Capital*, vol. 1, 131–7.

analysis of reproductive labour. This is to say that, if reproductive labour *appears* to be without value on a formal plane, while actually producing value on the plane of the real, this does not necessarily indicate the latter's more essentially stable constitution. The two realms or planes remain co-constituting, relative and subject to political struggle.

In the feminist tradition from which Fortunati emerged, these categories are specifically subject to feminist struggle. The mass refusal of housework, broadly speaking, from lowering birth rates to refusals of marriage, to increases in abortion, divorce, non-normative sexualities and relationship structures, and sex work, for example, profoundly destabilise capital's attempts to devalue reproductive labour. If the term *performance* would become central to Anglo-American feminist and queer theory in the decade following the publication of *The Arcana of Reproduction* – as indicating a re-instantiation, repetition and potential transformation of gendered norms and roles – a similarly complex process was described in Fortunati's text, albeit in a different political discourse and historical context.

Fortunati herself adopts a metaphor of optical reversal to articulate the simultaneously dialectical and co-constitutive relationship of the visible with respect to value as a more or less invisible support mapped along the axis of gender: 'Reproduction is governed *by laws that are very different*, if not opposed to those that govern production. *Reproduction* appears as *the mirror image*, the photographic negative of *production*.'[11] Indeed, the cascading implications that proceed from the simultaneous devaluation and naturalisation of reproductive labour inform everything from the most general structure to the most minute aspects of daily life, from broad social conventions to individual perceptions, affects and exchanges. While we have often evoked the concept of such *duplicità* with terms such as 'duplicity', 'twofold' or 'double' (and preserved Marx's own *Doppelcharakter* when Fortunati does the same in the original), it should be kept in mind that specific language concerning the real and apparent planes, the formal organisation of labour as paid or unpaid and its real role in generating value, has sometimes been glossed for readability and that the original Italian text carries a theoretical and historical baggage impossible to render with total clarity or fidelity.

There are certain references that remain unmarked in Fortunati's text,

---

11   See p. 5.

which, save for its initial citation of works central to the Lotta Femminista and Salario per il Lavoro Domestico/Wages for Housework
movements, restricts notes to the works of Marx and Engels. Other references, though implicit, would have been unmistakable to members of
the Italian feminist movement versed in debates of *operaismo*. The third
chapter, for example, begins with a plea that the labour of reproduction
be reappropriated, transformed and reinvented. This includes a radical
call for the 'abolition of love' itself with its 'macabre face of exploitation',
which, insofar as it serves the capitalist form of heterosexual masculine
dominance and accumulation, negates the potential specificity of individual relations. For members of Lotta Femminista, such a passage
would have clear resonance with key texts of their own movement: Silvia
Federici's great adage 'They call it love. We call it unpaid labour'; Mariarosa Dalla Costa's discussion of the 'capitalist function of the uterus' that
negates autonomous sexuality; or, Giovanna Franca Dalla Costa's analysis of the 'ideology of love' or 'love pact' that compels women to perform
duties out of love or face violent retribution.[12]

In general, a critical reception of *operaismo* informs the work's development of the housewife as precondition of the 'mass worker' of advanced
industrial production that the tradition had glorified. However, the final
chapter in particular takes up another trend in *operaismo*, invoking the
possibility of a 'workers' history of reproduction' and asking how such a
history might be represented in light of the inverse processes that determine the development, or rather 'underdevelopment', of reproduction in
capitalist terms. Such a workers' history is unmistakably related to claims
of the *operaisti* that the working class was engaged in a process of its own
self-negation as labour power, as well as attempts in the Italian extra-
parliamentary tradition to compose collective histories of movement
struggles.[13]

---

12   Silvia Federici, 'Wages against Housework', in *Revolution at Point Zero: House-
work, Reproduction and Feminist Struggle* (Oakland, CA: PM Press, 2020), 32; Mariarosa
Dalla Costa, 'Women and the Subversion of the Community', in *Women and the Subver-
sion of the Community: A Mariarosa Dalla Costa Reader*, ed. Camille Barbagallo
(Oakland, CA: PM Press, 2019), 17–51; Giovanna Franca Dalla Costa, *The Work of Love:
Unpaid Housework, Poverty and Sexual Violence at the Dawn of the 21st Century* (New
York: Autonomia, 2008).

13   In the Italian context specifically see Mario Tronti's classic essay 'The Strategy
of Refusal', originally published in 1966 (Tronti, *Workers and Capital*, 241–62), as well as
his call for a 'worker's newspaper' to chronicle the refusal of the mass worker on the

Fortunati's work, however, should not be reduced to her critical engagement with the Italian extra-parliamentary left and its political repression, or even the segment of the feminist movement in which she was most involved. Rooted in and simultaneously critical of (post-) Marxist structures of thought – different but not totally divergent from attempts to rethink the world undertaken by other feminists who, like Carla Lonzi, insisted on articulating an uncompromising autonomous discourse for a feminist project even as their work remained inextricably embedded in the lifeworlds of 1970s Italy – this book was intended as a practical manual for struggle against unpaid domestic labour: one of the great historically specific struggles initiated with particular intensity and brilliance by Italian feminism from the 1970s onwards.

A thorough historical-theoretical overview of the work's terminology cannot be accommodated here. Lengthy exposition aside, we have to be faithful in some sense to Gayatri Spivak's important injunction to consider the project of translation not as a foreclosure, an attempt to make a work easily consumable by a contemporary readership (particularly since English is the lingua franca for *Capital*) but as an invitation to participate in an 'active practice . . . something one never stops (not) translating'.[14] The importance of this text as a provocation and resource for the current debate on social reproduction and for today's global feminist activism and theory has been well remarked by scholars and activists alike, and we do not need to reiterate it here.

A wealth of recent literature has engaged the Wages for Housework movement, through both publications from original members and a growing secondary literature exploring its history and theoretical-political provocations.[15] We would mention however, that *The Arcana of*

---

factory floor in 'A New Type of Political Experiment: Lenin in England' (in Tronti, *Workers and Capital*, 65–72). For a nuanced history of the print cultures of the Italian extra-parliamentary left, see Steve Wright, *The Weight of the Printed Word: Text, Context and Militancy in Operaismo* (London: Brill, 2021); Nanni Balestrini and Primo Moroni, *The Golden Horde: Revolutionary Italy 1960–1977*, trans. Richard Braude (London: Seagull Books, 2021).

14   See Gayatri Spivak, 'Translating in a World of Languages', *Profession* (2010), 39.

15   For a detailed history of these movements throughout the 1970s written by a feminist historian and former member of a Canadian branch of the movement, see Toupin, *Wages for Housework*. Central to bringing renewed contemporary consideration to the work has been Weeks, *The Problem with Work*. Important publications of collected essays from the movement have been released by Selma James, Mariarosa Dalla Costa

Reproduction is not only one of the central texts of a particularly influential strain of the Italian feminist movement, but can also be read as one of its critical condensations. It is our hope that, in re-translating such a canonical text, we offer Anglophone readers the resources to resist reading Italian feminism – or any feminism associated with particular nation-states – as a form of exoticism, a danger of representing particular strands of the 1970s feminist movement in Italy as exceptional and radical rather than in dialogue with the broad array of movements of the era.[16]

Indeed Fortunati's own project is one of ongoing translation, in the sense that she has both preserved and developed the wealth of interpretive insight in *The Arcana of Reproduction* and other iconic works to which she contributed, many of which remain untranslated in English to this day.[17] The 'arcane' analysis of the sexual division of labour unique to capitalist development that she conducted as one of the younger members of the Lotta Femminista and subsequent Wages for Housework movements, gradually transformed into a radical sociology of media and technology as her career as scholar and activist progressed. In a sense, it is not surprising that Fortunati's work made such a turn, given that her early texts had intensively analysed the mediation between labour and capital performed by reproductive labour itself, as well as women as the primary agent of such mediation. Unsurprisingly, Fortunati's work has been particularly influential in contemporary fields ranging from media studies to art history, and her recent work has focused both on attempts

---

and Silvia Federici: Selma James, *Sex, Race, and Class – The Perspective of Winning: A Selection of Writings 1952–2011* (London: Pluto Press, 2012); Mariarosa Dalla Costa, *Women and the Subversion of the Community*; Federici, *Revolution at Point Zero*.

16   For an important study of Wages for Housework in the context of Italian feminisms, see Maud Anne Bracke, 'Between the Transnational and the Local: Mapping the Trajectories and Contexts of the Wages for Housework Campaign in 1970s Italian Feminism', in Lucy Bland and Katharina Rowold, eds, *Reconsidering Women's History* (London: Routledge, 2016), 105–22. See also the discussion of Italian Marxian feminisms in historical context in Anna Curcio, ed., *Introduzione ai femminismi. Genere, razza, classe, riproduzione: dal marxismo al queer* (Roma: DeriveApprodi, 2021).

17   Among Fortunati's important 1970s essays that remain untranslated in English should be included her extensive study of women's refusal in Italy during and after the Second World War, 'La famiglia: verso la ricostruzione'. See also her lengthy essays on the transition to capitalism in Silvia Federici and Leopoldina Fortunati, *Il Grande Calibano. Storia del corpo sociale ribelle nella prima fase del capitale* (Milan: Franco Angeli editore, 1984).

to extract value from reproductive labour that have been enabled by digital media technologies as well as on the possibilities of resistance and reappropriation that such technologies afford.[18]

To conclude these brief introductory notes, it is useful to remark on the untranslatability of the book's title itself – *L'arcano della riproduzione. Casalinghe, prostitute, operai e capitale* – as it represents something of the work's multifaceted programme. The original English-language translation of the text, one made in the 1990s with admirable urgency by a member of the movement, rendered the first part of the title as 'The Arcane of Reproduction.'[19] Here the English *arcane*, generally used in adjectival form to mean mysterious or obscure, although technically faithful in a certain sense, can also obscure something of the primary associations of the original. On the one hand, *l'arcano* is the term consistently used in Italian translation to render Marx's *Geheimnis*, a term that bookends *Capital* as indicating the 'mystery' associated with the expression of value and fetish character of commodities in the opening chapters of the work, as well as the 'mystery' of surplus value and of primitive accumulation itself that structure the work's conclusion.

The basic associations of *l'arcano* therefore invoke both Marx's most innovative observations on the commodity form and the origin story of accumulation itself: histories that must be told and retold to combat attempts to naturalise the emergence of capitalism. The analysis of capitalist temporality through the figure of originary accumulation as both a foundational and ongoing violence structuring the sphere of reproduction has obvious resonance with the great critical engagements with anticolonial theories of primitive accumulation: these would complement or displace the specific context focused on by Marx (the formation of a working class in England) with histories of colonial violence and slavery,

---

18   For a particularly generative use of Fortunati's early work in relation to contemporary media studies and questions of digital media and its mediation of labour see Kylie Jarret, *Feminism, Labour and Digital Media: The Digital Housewife* (London: Routledge, 2016). For samplings of Fortunati's extensive work on the relation between reproductive technologies from telecommunications to fashion see the extensive collections edited or co-edited by the author: Leopoldina Fortunati, ed., *Telecomunicando in Europa* (Milan: Franco Angeli, 1988); Leopoldina Fortunati, James E. Katz and Raimonda Riccini, eds, *Mediating the Human Body: Technology, Communication, and Fashion* (Mahwah, NJ: Lawrence Erlbaum, 2003).

19   See the translation released in abridged form by Autonomedia in 1995. Leopoldina Fortunati, *The Arcane of Reproduction: Housework, Prostitution, Labour and Capital*, trans. Hillary Creek (New York: Autonomedia, 1995).

and with classic second-wave invocations of 'women's time' as both an unending workday and potential temporality of resistance. The triangulation of 'Casalinghe, prostitute, operai e capitale' in the title alternately invokes the primary and secondary subjects of reproductive labour as analysed in the text (that of the housewife and sex worker respectively) relative to the subject most idealised in much Marxian tradition as the vanguard subject uniquely capable of revolutionary consciousness and struggle. All three now stand in contradiction to capital but in the light of the 'arcane' and contradictory structure of reproduction.

In a more playful sense, Fortunati's title was simultaneously an invocation of the major arcana of the tarot deck. To make such a reference inescapable, the original Italian edition carried on its cover reproductions of two of the tarot cards drawn from the major arcana, trump cards which took on occult significance in the eighteenth century. In a witty visual pun, the inverse development and mystification of reproductive labour is presented as an occult game of early modernity, specifically using cards suggesting women's power: the card for Strength (*La forza*) and that for the World (*Il mondo*) – the former showing a woman taming a lion, and the latter a naked woman astride four symbols of the cosmos.

It should be evident that there can be no definitively *correct* translation of the references at work here. We hope we have been able to indicate however, some of the complexities of the original in its analysis of reproductive labour as both a site of division and potential political unification. Our translation, at best, offers an opportunity to engage critically with the text and its mission, one that is historically specific as much as it is timeless and timely.

Introduction

This essay is an attempt to systematise, on the theoretical plane, the analysis of the process of reproduction (domestic work and prostitution specifically) with respect to Marxian categories and beyond them.[1] In relation to the Marxian categories, this essay deals with the analysis of the relations of production between women and capital, and the many institutional, economic and political aspects this relationship implies, situating it within the Marxian corpus. It also extends beyond the Marxian categories – since we must assume that Marx's methodology can extend *beyond* his own work in the analysis of reproduction, a problem that he touched upon only briefly at various points. The analysis goes a*gainst* Marx, when his partial vision of the capitalist cycle of accumulation leads to errors.

This new interpretation of the Marxian theoretical corpus, starting from the feminist critique of political economy, is historically and politically necessitated by at least two factors. First, the orthodox application of Marxian categories to reproduction has led to the Leninist assumption

---

1   In this essay, by 'reproduction' we mean that part of the capitalist accumulation process concerning the production and reproduction of individuals as the commodity labour power. That is, the process of production and reproduction of the workforce is primarily undertaken by the houseworker, in the family and in the process of sexual reproduction of male labour power that takes place in prostitution. These two processes coalesce as the nerve centre of the process of reproduction itself. Unless otherwise specified, 'production' here indicates that part of the capitalist accumulation cycle that concerns the production of other commodities.

that domestic work is unproductive. Second, it was necessary to test whether Marxian methodology can be used innovatively in the analysis of reproduction.

As for the first point, in the Leninist theory of organisation, the central moment of political strategy for women's liberation is the resort to a second job outside the home, to which might be added a timid request for more or better social services. Women, like underdevelopment itself in the Leninist schema, suffer from insufficient capitalist investment.[2] The exhortation is therefore to a sort of migration: from the home to the factory, the only place where an effective fight against the extraction of surplus value is possible. This is the well-known path of so-called emancipation, along which women have not been spared political blindness, the ferocious repression of their organisational skills and potential, nor the atrocious mockery of performing twice the work for a single discriminatory salary. Here we take the opposite path, one which centres feminist political strategy starting from domestic work and prostitution, for the definitive destruction of unwaged labour as well as waged labour.

The Leninist assumption, incorrect even in Lenin's time, became even more ridiculous in its persistence within the political thought of the male left in the early 1970s, against and despite the international explosion of the feminist movement. This explosion of a feminist movement, which emerged from the crises of the 1970s, inspired in thousands of women from the Western metropoles to the Global South a great awareness that, through the increasingly massive organisation of their struggles against reproductive work ranging from domestic work to prostitution, they were inflicting fatal blows to the production of surplus value and to the process of capital accumulation.[3] The 1970s were a decade of struggles

---

2   Here Fortunati draws on an analysis that had developed within the Lotta Femminista groups and subsequently the Wages for Housework movement internationally, one which saw a Leninist analysis and policy inherited and realised in the post-war era by core capitalist nations. In the Italian context, an analysis of Lenin's New Economic Policy developed in 1921 and resonated with the faith in technological investment, work discipline and austerity advocated by both the PCI and elements of the extra-parliamentary left in the late 1970s. See in particular Lotta Femminista, 'Mille fiori sbocciano appassiti', *Le operaie della casa*, special issue, April 1977.

3   For an example of the Wages for Housework analysis of the 'crises' of the 1970s broadly speaking see Silvia Federici, 'Wages for Housework and the Crisis', in Arlen

that – like a powerful earthquake – reshaped even the landscape of reproduction, disrupting every state policy in this regard. In contrast to this explosion, international capital, aware of the centrality of reproductive labour in the process of valorisation, but also of the formidable struggles that now arose against this work, has taken up the Leninist strategy of pushing for a second job for women.

The 1970s saw the increased *sovietisation* of capitalist politics towards women. It was now capital itself that increasingly acknowledged, in the US and Europe, women's demand for extra-domestic work to such an extent that it forcefully pushed the supply of female labour power into the extra-domestic market. Obviously, in this case, the purpose was exactly the opposite of the Leninist one. While, under the 'communist' programme, the Leninist strategy represented the illusion that exploitation of women would become equal to that of men through their liberation from domestic work, capital's aim was more realistic: the intensification of the exploitation of women, a social subject who, in the reproductive sphere, had learned to become more and more undisciplined and unmanageable. They could only be blackmailed by the need for income, lacking money of their own from the work of reproduction.

Having struggled to free themselves from a large share of domestic work while demanding higher and higher quotas of the male wage, women were forced by the crisis to switch increasingly to extra-domestic work. From the second job as a demand – for liberation from domestic work – it has become an obligation, a lengthening of women's working day and an intensification of its rhythms. The age-old assumption that extra-domestic work is a goal for which women struggle has become increasingly muted. Of that political strategy, however, a confused discourse persists regarding demands for social services as an objective of struggle for the destruction of domestic work, given that its presence in women's working day is now considered the greatest impediment to equality with men. This is a strategy that, whether made in a tone of violent appropriation or of demand, addresses only a part of women's

---

Austin and Silvia Federici, eds, *The New York Wages for Housework Committee 1972–1977: History, Theory and Documents* (New York: Autonomedia, 2019), 137–43. Antonio Negri's major essays of the 70s help to contextualise such arguments in the context of *operaismo* and related movements. See Antonio Negri, *Books for Burning: Between Civil War and Democracy in 1970s Italy* (London: Verso, 2005).

exploitation; it provides no weapons to attack capital's domination over women at the roots.

We are not interested in becoming liberated from domestic work only in order to assimilate ourselves to the exploitation of the waged worker. Nor are we interested in emancipating ourselves by changing the type of exploitation to which we are subject. Such an approach minimises what women can achieve: wealth, liberation from both factory and house-work, as well as social services. However they are rebranded, discourses on social services remain confused, because they mistake a partial goal of struggle for the political strategy of women's liberation, and, we would add, they are illusory, because they assume that the socialised reproduction of labour power can succeed in replacing that which is performed at the individual level. This assumption is incorrect because social services (kindergarten, hospital, school and so on) not only presuppose domestic work but constantly demand it: for example, the vital assistance provided by (usually female) relatives to the sick for the successful functioning of hospitals. Finally, the assumptions of such discourses cannot be true because large shares of domestic work cannot be social-ised, nor can they be eliminated through the development of technology. They can only – and must be – destroyed as capitalist labour and freed to the richness of a creativity released from the yoke of exploitation. Here we allude particularly to the immaterial aspects of domestic work (including affection, love, consolation and, above all, sexuality) that, among other things, constitute an increasingly important part of domestic work.[4]

Would we socialise sexuality? In such a case, socialisation becomes mass prostitution, such that prostitution becomes the general form of sexuality, organised and managed by the state. Could this be our goal? Nor can the objective of a totally socialised reproduction of labour power make sense as a political programme. In fact, it would entail the libera-tion of women from domestic work that is indirectly waged, but at the cost of the seizure by the state of all aspects of life, including compulsory factory work for every woman, and preschool and edu-factory for every child from birth. This is the opposite of what we aim for. Of course, the

---

4   For context see, in particular, the discussion of day care, early-childhood educa-tion and hospitals in Mariarosa Dalla Costa's 'Women and the Subversion of the Community', one of the sources on which Fortunati draws here. Mariarosa Dalla Costa and Selma James, *The Power of Women and the Subversion of the Community*, 37–40.

struggle regarding social services is a very important political issue within a feminist strategy, because in capitalist countries, as indeed in supposedly communist ones, the presence of women in the factory has never automatically led to investment in the social reproduction of labour power. Indeed, the level of struggle has always been the measure of the quantity and quality of social services instituted by the state.

How weak our struggle has been on this ground is demonstrated by the scarcity and poor quality of social services everywhere, from the USSR to the USA. It is therefore necessary to strengthen our attack on this ground, but with the awareness that it is only a partial objective, because what we can achieve today is infinitely more. It is the rupture of capital's domination over us, and therefore over the class as a whole.

Passing through Marx to oppose Lenin thus becomes a necessary operation not only for our own struggles, but also for the men's movement and class struggle in general. This operation, which was carried out on the wave of the new class composition of the 1970s, in which – we repeat – not just proletarian housewives but also prostitutes should be included, not only makes it possible to analyse reproduction anew through the Marxian categories, but also allows us to make Marx's work function in light of feminist struggle.[5] It takes us along the opposite path to that of Lenin, leading us to the understanding that domestic work and prostitution are productive labour. From this point of view, the feminist struggle emerges as a fundamental struggle of the working class for its potential and proven ability to undermine the mechanisms of surplus value extraction.

In terms of strategy, this operation leads us to start on and follow the paths that unite, holding together, in the vice of a shared and violent demand for money and power, the woman as factory worker and the woman as housewife, the worker or metropolitan housewife and the proletarian of the Global South. It leads us to listen to and support the slogans

---

5   For a discussion of the term 'class composition' (*composizione di classe*) as a central category of analysis in *operaismo*, as it informed Fortunati's use here, see Steve Wright, *The Weight of the Printed Word: Text, Context and Militancy in Operaismo* (London: Pluto Press, 2021). Fortunati, of course, adds the feminist figures of housewife and sex worker to those established figures of *operaismo* that included the factory worker, student, unemployed person and migrant worker. Important distinctions between the 'organic', 'technical' and 'political' aspects of class composition play out in the literature of *operaismo* and are addressed in the discussion below.

that spring from women's struggles: enough with the misery – appropriation of social wealth; enough with the crumbs of the salary of others – we want money in our hands; enough with the economic, psychological and sexual dependence on men – women's freedom will be our self-determination.

The political programme is already here, expressed in a thousand ways, in the articulations of the new forms of mass behaviour, in the refusal of domestic and extra-domestic work. The central problem is that of labour time, the struggle for the reduction of overall working time (domestic and extra-domestic), which is a struggle that concerns not only the organisation of the working day, but above all the capitalist organisation of work. This is clear if we observe the extraordinarily innovative effects of women's autonomous struggles over the organisation of reproduction. Everything has been literally turned upside down: the form and function of the family; the man/woman relationship and its relative exchanges; the relationship between woman/woman and man/man and their related exchanges; marriage, birth, maternity and paternity; and so on. These effects, however, have not manifested in a great pressure for a scientific and technological revolution in the domestic labour process. There is still a large material aspect of reproductive labour that remains to be revolutionised. It is our political problem to force science to take up this task. This must be the expression of our new level of power, but to do so with the awareness that, for a large part of domestic labour – the immaterial part specifically – the way out does not pass so much through science as through the liberation from the obligation to perform directly or indirectly waged work. The emotional, sexual, sentimental and affective potential – the potential to love, to reproduce and be reproduced – that an individual is able to express today, be it man or woman, child, adult or older person, is enormous. However, this potential capacity is frozen, diminished, repressed and distorted, because the individual is forced to become a commodity. Destroying the command of exchange value over use value also means freeing these innumerable creative forces and energies of reproduction in order to reproduce ourselves as individuals and no longer as commodities.

How much the innovation produced by such struggles can constitute a *radical break* and how much our critique of science manages not to fall prey to capitalist exploitation will depend on how they are integrated with the struggle for our own income, as well as with the organisational deepening of the struggle against domestic and extra-domestic work. Without money in the hands of women, it is not possible for women and the whole class to exercise command over the process of reproduction. Today, an increasingly large number of women have their own wages: as factory workers, workers in social services or in the world of illegal work or sex work. But this is a discriminatory wage earned at the cost of a practically unlimited working day, a ferociously extended and intensified exploitation.

In addition, a large proportion of women who carry out only domestic work still have no money of their own. This is a price it is possible not to pay today, given the level of social wealth produced by women and, more importantly, the political strength that the new class composition is able to express internationally. It is, therefore, a cost that we women must refuse to pay. We want enough money, and therefore wealth, to stop working, to reproduce ourselves as free individuals, and to be free from the chain of capitalist exploitation. With respect to our second point, this strategy is necessary because, after the initial explosion of the feminist movement, in which we explored and weeded the terrain of reproduction with our autonomous struggles, we had to verify whether it was possible to use Marxism to dig and sow anew in its soil.

The feminist movement in recent years has accumulated a large body of analyses and reflections on reproduction, also using Marx in those instances when it affirmed that domestic work was the work of production and reproduction of the commodity labour power, that the woman as domestic worker was the primary subject of this work, that the family was the centre of this production, and that domestic work was productive work. This discourse has used Marx only in an empirical and fragmentary fashion, however, and did not build an organic and systematic analysis of reproduction using Marxian categories; this opened up many unresolved contradictions with respect to the Marxian corpus and the political projects of the left, without offering a solution. For example, we asserted that housework and prostitution were productive work without demonstrating it theoretically, even if, in practice, the struggles in these sectors of reproduction shook the capitalist cycle with such a virulence that this fact alone should have sufficed to disprove those who argued otherwise. The theoretical demonstration of this discourse is nevertheless necessary because we applied the Marxian analysis of productive work to labour (housework and prostitution) that, according to Marxian categories, cannot strictly be considered as such. In fact, such work did not, apparently, conform to the necessary criteria, since it was not directly waged, it was performed outside a work structure organised according to capitalist canons, it was determined in a way that did not involve the development of either cooperation or the division of labour, and it was organised in such a way as to imply a very limited development of technology (to the point that there has been much confused talk of the 'underdevelopment' of the house as compared to the factory).

These unresolved contradictions not only carried weight in the debate that we had managed to open within the male left, but also continually removed the possibility of shifting from an empirical analysis to a political theory of our working relationships and therefore of our living conditions. At that point, it became essential to collect, organise and attempt to systematise organically all the observations, considerations and indications that women through these years of organisation and struggle had expressed regarding the function of reproduction, and to revisit the Marxian theoretical corpus in the light of the feminist experience.

This process yielded at least two results. The first is that the characteristics of reproduction, which seemed to mark it as irremediably irrelevant with respect to an analysis based on the Marxian corpus, have instead found their place, explanation and *raison d'être* within this feminist examination of Marxism. Second, it has allowed us to tackle with newfound insights many issues related to the problem of reproduction, such as the family, the relationship between technology and domestic work, the female labour-market, the functions of the state with respect to reproduction, the domestic work cycle, the history of struggle over the working day and the shift from the production of absolute surplus value to that of relative surplus value.

In moving from theory to practice, the problems on the table are many – primary among them the problem of the feminist organisation. The coming decades can and must see the strengthening of feminist organisation in terms of class composition and capacity for organised attack. It is possible and necessary to pursue the path of our political and organisational autonomy to victory. The stakes are high: they are wealth, freedom, and happiness – in other words, our very life.

*

In order not to burden the development of the argument, I have cited only key Marxian works. The bibliography to which I could refer is in fact enormous: there are now numerous works (essays, articles, pamphlets) on domestic work, the condition of women, productive work, feelings, sexuality, the family. Therefore, in the various topics treated below, many of these connections remain tacit. But I would be betraying my integrity and my feminist identity if I did not mention, at least here, a few of the fundamental contributions that the Wages for Housework movement has made to the debate on the topics covered here, and upon which I draw deeply below: Mariarosa Dalla Costa's essay 'Women and the Subversion of the Community', published with 'A Woman's Place' by Selma James; the two pamphlet collections of materials from Lotta Femminista, 'L'offensiva' and 'Il personale è politico'; the collection *Brutto ciao* with essays by Mariarosa Dalla Costa and myself; Gisela Bock and Barbara Duden's essay 'Arbeit als Liebe. Liebe als Arbeit'; Giovanna Franca Dalla Costa's *Un lavoro d'amore*, whose first chapter describing the exchanges between housewife and worker has particularly influenced the account here; and finally, Silvia Federici and Nicole Cox's pamphlet 'Counter-planning from the Kitchen'.[6]

---

6   The first edition of Mariarosa Dalla Costa's essay 'Women and the Subversion of the Community' was released in Italian in 1972 and in English translation the same year as a pamphlet from Falling Wall Press (see Mariarosa Dalla Costa, *Potere femminile e sovversione sociale con 'Il posto di donna' di Selma James* [Venice: Marsilio Editori, 1972]; and Dalla Costa and James, *The Power of Women and the Subversion of the Community*). Lotta Femminista released two booklets containing formative texts from the group and the Wages for Housework movement internationally: Lotta Femminista, *Quaderni di Lotta Femminista N. 1. L'offensiva* (Turin: Musolini Editori, 1972), and Lotta Femminista, *Quaderni di Lotta Femminista N. 2. Il personale è politico* (Turin: Musolini Editori, 1973). The collection *Brutto ciao* was released in 1975 (see Mariarosa Dalla Costa and Leopoldina Fortunati, *Brutto ciao. Direzione di marcia delle donne negli ultimi trent'anni* [Rome: edizioni delle donne, 1976]). The original edition of the essay by Bock and Duden, see Gisela Bock and Barbara Duden, 'Arbeit als Liebe – Liebe als Arbeit: Zur Entstehung der Hausarbeit im Kapitalismus', in *Frauen und Wissenschaft: Beiträge zur Berliner Sommeruniversität für Frauen*, July 1976 (Berlin: Courage Verlag, 1977), 118–99. A co-founder of Lotta Femminista and sister of Mariarosa, Giovanna Franca Dalla Costa published her influential work in 1978: *Un lavoro d'amore la violenza fisica componente essenziale del trattamento maschile nei confronti delle donne* (Rome: Edizione delle donne, 1978). Finally, the pamphlet by Federici and Cox was first published by Bristol's Falling Wall Press, which carried many publications by the International Wages for Housework movement through the 1970s and into the 1980s; see Silvia Federici and Nicole Cox, 'Counter-planning from the Kitchen' (Bristol: Falling Wall Press, 1975).

PART I

1

Production and Reproduction: The Apparent Antithesis of the Capitalist Mode of Production

We begin our analysis of reproduction by examining the transition from the pre-capitalist to the capitalist mode of production. This examination is crucial not only to understand the destiny of reproduction in the new mode of production – the privileged object of our analysis – but ultimately to understand how the entire cycle of capitalist production is articulated. The transition from pre-capitalist to capitalist modes of production is characterised by the fact that *the economic purpose* in capitalism is radically different from that of previous modes of production. If, in previous modes of production, the economic purpose is 'the production of use values, i.e., the *reproduction of the individual* within the specific relation to the community in which he is its basis', in capitalism it becomes the production of exchange values, the creation *of value*.[1] This means that 'production appears as the aim of mankind and wealth as the aim of production', such that the 'unhappiness of society' and no longer the reproduction of the individual becomes 'the purpose of political economy'.[2]

---

1 Karl Marx, *Grundrisse: Foundations of the Critique of Political Economy*, trans. Martin Nicolaus (London: Penguin Books, 1993 [1973]), 485.

2 Karl Marx, 'Economic and Political Manuscripts (1844)', in *Early Writings*, trans. Rodney Livingstone and Gregor Benton (New York and London: Penguin, 1992), 286. There is a significant difference between the Italian translation in this context, where

Obviously, this upheaval of economic purpose has precise consequences both for the premises and the conditions of existence of
capitalist accumulation, and for reproduction. In the first place, this
means that exchange value comes to take precedence over the individual's use value. This process occurs even though the individual is the
sole source capable of creating value. Indeed, it happens precisely
because of this fact. Because it is only by positioning individuals as
devoid of value, as pure use value, that capital is able to transform their
labour power into exchange value, to force them to sell their capacity to
work and thus to realise their exchange value. But the devaluation of the
free worker is not merely an effect of the new mode of production. The
devaluation of the free worker is also the premise and the condition of
existence of the new mode of production. Capital cannot exist, it cannot
become a social relationship, if it cannot confront an individual devoid
of any value, and thus forced to sell the only commodity they possess –
their labour power.

The second consequence of the transition to capitalism is that *reproduction is separated from production*. The unity existing in pre-capitalist
modes of production between production of use values and reproduction of the individual – in which production is not production of use
values subordinate to exchange value – has disappeared. The general
process of commodity production is now separated, by the dividing line
of value, from the process of reproduction, and opposed to it. While the
first process – the production of commodities – appears as the *creation
of value*, the second – reproduction – presents itself as the *creation of
non-value*.[3] Commodity production comes to be considered the site *par
excellence* of capitalist production, and the laws that govern it considered
the laws that characterise capitalist production itself. By contrast, *reproduction*, now considered the creation of *non-value*, becomes the site of
natural production. This shift corresponds to the devaluation of the

---

Marx discusses Adam Smith's admission that new capitalist political economies require
widespread immiseration in which 'l'infelicità della società' rather than the reproduction
of the individual becomes 'lo scopo dell'economia politica'. The translation of Rodney
Livingstone and Gregor Benton from the Penguin edition cited here simply renders the
passage as 'society's distress is the goal of the economic system'.

3   This phrase 'attraverso la linea del valore', used throughout the text, which we
have rendered as 'by the dividing line of value' is a complex one with rich legacies in
Italian Marxism. *Attraverso* also means 'across' or 'through', indicating not so much a
strict partition as a division through a dialectical interrelation.

individual. In production, work is paid and performed in the factory, the quintessential capitalist structure. Its organisation specifically involves developing cooperation and the division of labour, as well as high levels of technological advancement. In reproduction, work is not paid; it is carried out in the house, a structure organised in a fashion opposed to that of the factory. Its organisation requires neither the development of cooperation nor the division of labour, and it demands only limited technological development. In other words, reproduction is governed by laws that are *very different*, if not opposed to, those that govern production. *Reproduction* appears as the *mirror image*, the photographic negative of production.[4]

This difference between production and reproduction has been interpreted in multiple ways: first, as the insufficiency of development within reproduction, which is to say as the persistence of strong pre-capitalist vestiges in this sector. Second, it has been considered as a mode of production in its own right – an interpretation which would characterise reproduction as a non-capitalist world persisting at the heart of capital. Third, it is regarded as a *natural* form of production, albeit one which is recognised as increasingly incorporated into the overall capitalist cycle, or at least increasingly organised in a manner compatible with capitalist development in accordance with the rules of production. The contradictions opened by these interpretations are many: above all, that reproduction turns out not to produce value, even though it is a sector that produces commodities (specifically that of labour power). Leaving aside, for the moment, such contradictions, let us ask ourselves: what does this separation through the dividing line of value mean? Does it really mean that reproduction is relegated to the world of non-value in such a way that it is not invested by the laws of the new mode of production? In our opinion, it does not. This *separation* concerns only the formal plane and not the real one. In this context, by the term 'formal plane', we mean how things appear; while with the use of the term the 'real plane', we refer to the intrinsic nature of things.[5] Our first argument

---

4   A recurring figure throughout the text, Fortunati uses the phrase 'come l'immagine speculare, la fotografia rovesciata della produzione' (like the mirror image, the inverted photograph of production).

5   Here, Fortunati uses the terms 'piano formale' (formal plane) and 'piano reale' (real plane) in relation to the reflexive verbs *presentarsi* (to present) and *rappresentarsi* (to represent) in rapidly shifting fashion to indicate contradictions between actual value

is that although reproduction presents itself as *creation of non-value*, as *natural* production, it works, as we will demonstrate below, as *creation of value*, and is thus as an integral and crucial part of the capitalist accumulation process. The difference between the two is that, while production is presented as value creation, reproduction is also value creation, but is presented as its opposite.

In spite of the apparent separation between production and reproduction, the capitalist mode of production persists in both as a process of valorisation. As we will see later, production and reproduction are indissolubly linked and interdependent, with the former acting as the presupposition and condition of existence for the latter. Reproduction operates with more complexity as compared to production. Production is what it appears to be: *production of commodities*. Reproduction, or more precisely reproduction of the commodity that is labour power, is instead made to appear as reproduction of individuals devoid of value. This greater complexity of reproduction concerns all its aspects and elements. While in production, labour is presented as the waged production of commodities, reproductive work is presented as a natural force of social labour.[6] Although reproduction is represented as an unwaged personal service, it is, in reality, the indirectly waged labour of reproducing labour power.

In the realm of production, the exchange between worker and capital is twofold. On the formal plane, their exchange is represented as one of equivalents between equals, while, on that of the real, it is an

---

production and its appearance/representation in the organisation of a capitalist accumulation process. For brief discussion of these terms in relation to *operaismo* and their inheritance from Marx and a German Idealist tradition, see Translators' Note.

6   Here, Fortunati uses the phrase 'forza naturale del lavoro sociale' (natural force of social labour), which recurs throughout the text to describe the naturalisation of reproductive labour and its consignment under capitalism to the role of an unpaid naturally occurring force inherent in the 'social'. The phrase strongly invokes Marx's own discussions of the capacity of capitalism to represent social processes and labour as natural aspects of its own 'autovalorizzazione'. For a brief discussion on the precedents for Fortunati's use of the term, see the Translators' Note. The naturalisation of labour as a productive force available for capitalist expropriation as distinct from simply living labour power was crucial to the analysis of the *operaisti*. For a discussion of this triangulation in Tronti, see particularly Massimiliano Tomba and Riccardo Bellofiore, 'The "Fragment on Machines" and the *Grundrisse*: The Workerist Reading in Question', in Marcel van der Linden and Karl Heinz Roth, eds, *Beyond Marx* (Leiden: Brill, 2014), 345–68.

exchange of non-equivalents between unequal parties. In the realm of reproduction, the exchange between worker and capital operates on *three* different levels. This must occur such that these exchanges can simultaneously exist as exchanges of non-equivalents between unequal parties while, at the same time, they cannot appear as organised in a capitalist fashion. While an exchange appears to take place between the waged worker and the woman, in reality the exchange occurs between the woman and capital mediated by the waged worker. In terms of the objects exchanged in this labour process, while they appear as reproductive work on the one hand, and the wage on the other, in reality they consist of the relation between labour power and money operating as capital.[7]

The extreme complexity of the organisation of reproduction has greatly weakened the possibility of struggle in this arena. Moreover, this complexity is accompanied by an *ideological orchestration* far more richly articulated and vast than that which accompanies production. In the realm of production, organised workers' struggles soon demystified the formal arrangement with its claims of equal exchange between workers and capital, making evident the real level of exploitation. In the realm of reproduction, however, it has been more difficult for women's struggles to reveal the mechanisms of exploitation because of the special complexity of their relationship with capital.

Now if, on the level of the real, reproduction is an integral part of the capitalist production process – that is to say, the fact that there is a separation between production and reproduction made by the dividing line of value does not mean that there is not production of surplus value in both realms – then the question remains: how does capitalism really work? Our second thesis is that the capitalist mode of production is *formally* characterised by its dual character: production/value; reproduction/non-value. On the level of the real, however, the capitalist

---

7   Here Fortunati uses the phrase 'denaro che funziona come capitale', familiar to readers of Marx in Italian or German as indicating the role of money in mediating social labour in a transition from a currency with metallic counterpart to an increasingly abstracted and idealised form of 'coin', acquiring its own 'mirroring' of both value and commodity circulation. For example, the title for Part II of *Capital* would be translated by Delio Cantimori in the edition used by Fortunati and many of the *operaisti* as 'Transformazione del denaro in capitale': the greater complexity indicated in the text is one in which reproductive labour does not appear directly mediated by the money form.

mode of production operates as the creation of value throughout its entire production cycle, including that of reproduction. The capitalist mode of production operates formally on two different tracks with determinate laws governing the production cycle, and different laws governing the cycle of reproduction, while, on the level of the real, these two cycles share a single character. The fact that capital formally assumes a twofold nature is the very condition that allows it to work in a unified fashion, with a single logic, with a unified direction and purpose. Its twofold nature is the condition that allows capital to make use of both production and reproduction as two sides of the valorisation process: to exploit both the waged worker and the unwaged woman for the creation of value.

One can understand how capital works only by starting from the hypothesis of its duplicity. Capital operates in production and in reproduction as the valorisation of value by requiring each element to assume a twofold nature. This duplicity of value/non-value affects the entire ground of reproduction, starting from the individual. It is not only assumed by the labour of commodity production, as Marx discovered. This *Doppelcharakter* is also assumed by reproduction, but in a different fashion. In the realm of reproduction, such duplicity operates on the status of reproductive labour as both a commodity and natural force of social labour. Once the sphere of reproduction has been established as apparently creating non-value, it becomes possible to make production function as the site of value production. At the same time, once reproduction is established as a site for the apparent creation of non-value, reproduction itself can, in turn, operate to produce value.

This duplicity is played out by capital to create value. To be precise, this duplicity not only allows the capitalist mode of production to exist and function but allows it to function *far more productively* than previous modes of production. The capitalist mode of production is made more productive not only by lengthening the working day to the limit of human resistance in the production process, but also by framing reproduction as a *natural* form of production. With this operation, capital not only exploits two workers with only one salary, but also unloads onto labour power all the costs of reproduction. The elements outlined above show how the Marxian analysis of the capitalist production cycle describes only the production of commodities, and that this analysis cannot be applied to reproduction. In fact, reproduction functions very differently from production and, to understand the entire cycle of capitalist production, we must proceed through the analysis of reproduction. But what tools do we have? Is it possible to progress in this analysis within the Marxian corpus? For us, such analysis *is* possible, if we are willing to use the Marxian categories in a way that is not pedantic and to combine them with the tools of feminist criticism.

Our first argument, as mentioned above, is that reproduction, even if it presents itself as a creation of non-value, as a natural process, is, in reality, production of value, a capitalist process of production of the commodity labour power. It is evident that the double character of reproduction is linked to the destiny of the individual in the passage from pre-capitalist to capitalist modes of production. While, as a slave or serf, property of the master or feudal lord, individuals had a determined value, as free workers the individuals themselves have no inherent value. It is only their labour power that has value. The other side of their supposed freedom is their total devaluation. This is why the reproduction of the free worker can neither be the economic purpose of the capitalist mode of production, nor can it fall within the sphere of social relations directly regulated by exchange value. On the contrary, the presupposition and condition for the existence of capital and of free labour is that reproduction cannot entail the exchange between the labour of reproduction and capital, and, therefore, such labour cannot directly be part of the waged labour relationship. There is no development of social relations of production mediated by exchange value if the corresponding development of social relations of reproduction of individuals is not mediated by an exchange with capital. Reproduction must be represented as the antagonist of the production of commodities by presenting itself as reproduction of individuals, and therefore as creation of non-value. More precisely, reproduction must represent itself as a natural process, and the work of reproduction as a natural force of social labour that costs nothing to capital.

Within the individual, however, there exists a commodity – their labour power as productive capacity – that has exchange value. The individual is thus also established as *value*, even if this is true only in the moment when they exchange such a commodity with capital. The time limitation of the individual's role as value derives from the fact that 'for capital, the worker is not a condition of production, only work is', and it is not the worker that is appropriated but only work, 'not directly, but mediated through exchange'.[8] And labour, therefore, when it appears before capital, does so as a 'pure use value, which is offered by its possessor himself in exchange for it, for its exchange value'.[9]

The specific contradictory character of this co-presence of value and non-value within the individual must be understood in the context in which each characteristic seamlessly opposes the other. The individual confronts itself as both non-value and as the commodity labour power and thus exchange value. This is a contrast inherent in the fact that individuals exist both in relation to their own *reproduction* and to the production of commodities. While, as the subjects/objects of reproductive labour, individuals have no value, as the subjects of productive work they have a determined value. Given that, under capitalism, the individual's reproductive labour has no value except that given to it through production, the reproduction of individuals can only exist as the production of labour power.

This means that individuals are forced to reproduce themselves only as labour power. Since for individuals this means to reproduce themselves as a value, their own reproduction implies the *creation of value*. But value for whom? Individuals cannot create value for themselves. They can engage their labour power in production only in relation to its *exchange value*, and not its *use value*. When individuals sell their labour power, they cannot exchange it with capital as a product of their reproductive labour having innate value. To do so would be to confront capital as individuals with inherent value. In such a scenario, free workers would be a condition of production, whereas, for capital, the condition of production is only work and not the worker. The workers can present their labour power to capital only as a pure use value that capital buys in exchange for a wage. In purchasing it, capital takes possession of this use value for its own self-valorisation. Capital does not appropriate labour power through a direct exchange with the individual. To reiterate, if such an exchange took place directly, the individual would have inherent value.

Capital appropriates the use value of labour power in a more mediated fashion: indirectly, through the exchange between the individual's capacity for production and itself. For capital, therefore, it is the individual that creates value and capital's appropriation of this value occurs

---

8   Marx, *Grundrisse*, 498.
9   Ibid., 289.

indirectly because it is individuals themselves who self-expropriate. How does such expropriation occur? Initially the value of labour power belongs to the individual as a productive capacity. But, since workers can only sell their capacity of production as a use value to capital, every time workers sell such capacity, they expropriate themselves of the product of their own reproductive labour, and thus of the value of such labour power.

As a consequence, the precondition for the existence of *labour power* as capacity of production and therefore of capital itself is that labour power has *exchange value* only to the extent that the individual reproduces such labour power as valueless – only to the extent that the creation of value in the process of reproduction is represented as the creation of non-value.

This is the twofold nature that reproduction assumes within capitalism. Reproduction represents itself as a creation without value, but only for the individual and not for capital. For capital, reproduction is exclusively the creation of value. It is only by positioning the process of reproduction as a natural process, and the work of reproduction as a natural force of social labour, that reproduction costs nothing and capital can self-valorise. It is only by opposing, within the individual, the capacity of reproduction as pure use value to the capacity of production as an exchange value that capital is able simultaneously to confront labour power as use value and, in doing so, to devalue the individual.

The twofold nature of capitalist individuals is ultimately given by the co-presence within them of labour power as a capacity for production and as a capacity for reproduction. Thus, contrary to what Marx believed, there is no direct correspondence between labour power and the capacity to produce commodities. There are, rather, two opposed faces of labour power: one the capacity of commodity production and the other that of reproduction of individuals as labour power. Divided from each other by the line of value, the first face confronts capital as a commodity with exchange value. The second confronts capital as non-commodity, as pure use value, a natural force of social labour. The duplicity of the capitalist mode of production also affects labour power as reproductive capacity. On the one hand, in relation to capital, reproductive capacity appears as a natural force of social labour. On the other hand, in relation to labour power as capacity of production, reproductive capacity appears as a commodity – and therefore as exchange value.

Reproductive capacity can exist as a commodity, an exchange value, in relation to the labour power of production, only to the extent that it is represented as valueless in relation to capital. The precondition for production based on exchange value is the following: that the exchange of the labour power objectified as exchange value with the living labour of reproduction (that is the labour power of individuals as use value) *does not* take place in mediated form, as occurs between the waged worker and capital. In other words, the objects of such exchange, that is, the labour of reproduction and variable capital, cannot both be exchange values, otherwise labour power as a capacity of reproduction itself would have exchange value. At the same time, Marx specifies: 'The condition of exchange value is its measurement by labour time, and hence living labour – not its value – as measure of values.'[10] In this context, obviously, the *objective conditions* of the labour of production are *distinct* from those of reproduction.

The identity (the coincidence) of the worker's relationship with the objective conditions of the labour of reproduction of individuals is transformed by capitalism during the shift from pre-capitalist modes of production. The objective conditions of productive labour confront free workers in the form of *capital*. The objective conditions of reproductive labour confront houseworkers in the form of *variable capital*. Although existing in different forms, they confront the free worker in the same way. In the production process, 'the side which appears as capital has to possess raw materials, instruments of labour and necessaries of life so that the worker can live during production, before production is completed'.[11] The same is true in the process of reproduction. Here, too, the part that presents itself as variable capital must be able to buy raw materials, instruments of labour and other necessities of life so that the workforce can live during production. But what is more important is that capital is simultaneously valorised on two fronts: on that of reproduction and on that of production – presented as the two sides of its valorisation process. This *double face of the valorisation process*, to which we will return, is *determined by the double face of the value of labour power*, which, as we have seen, presents itself as a creative subject in both these sides of production. This

---

10   Ibid., 515.
11   Ibid., 504.

is the most precious commodity for capital, therefore, not only because it is the unique commodity able to create value in the production process, but also because it reproduces itself as value in the reproduction process.

We talked above about the separation through the dividing line of value between labour power as productive capacity and its reproductive capacity. Let us now consider another aspect of this separation: its sexual connotation. Productive capacity is developed primarily in male workers, and reproductive capacity primarily in women working as houseworkers. On the one hand, in fact, the liberation of labour power implies that, for the male worker, the possession of productive capacity is accompanied by *the expropriation of his labour power as a capacity of reproduction*. In other words, masculine labour power is fundamentally alienated from the objective condition of its own reproduction, its own labour power as a capacity of reproduction. On the other hand, the capitalist liberation of labour power implies that their capacity for reproduction is accompanied by that of production, but with the compulsion to primarily sell the former, and the latter only subordinately. There is a precise difference between the destiny of the male worker and that of the woman. For the former, the possession of labour power involves his *liberation* understood here as liberation from *the labour of self-reproduction*. This liberation has represented an advantage for male workers but also has the disadvantage that they became *alienated from the objective conditions of their reproduction*, their own labour power in its capacity for reproduction. For many men, it was convenient to free themselves from domestic work during their marriage, but, once they were widowed, for example, they found themselves vulnerable because they had lost any ability to reproduce themselves. For women, by contrast, possession of labour power as reproductive capacity *does not* imply their liberation from the labour of commodity-production.

In order to reproduce himself, the free male worker must confront, on the one hand, 'the objective conditions of production as his *not-property*, as *alien property*, as *value* for-itself, as *capital*'.[12] On the other hand, he must confront the objective conditions of his own reproduction, that is to say, labour power as the capacity for reproduction, as the property of

---

12   Ibid., 498.

others (not his own and not having value for itself – the natural force of social work has no value), rather as having value in itself.[13]

Like the free male worker, the free female worker, in her productive capacity, confronts 'the objective conditions of production as [her] *not-property*, as *alien property*, as *value* for-itself, as capital'.[14] On the other hand, in her capacity for reproduction, she confronts the objective conditions of reproduction not as capital, but as variable capital – the value of waged labour power as a capacity for production. From this it follows that, while the free male worker must necessarily confront the capacity of reproduction as the property of others, the free female worker does not necessarily do so with respect to labour power as productive capacity, because she is not expropriated of this capacity. As non-value, she can counterpose herself to variable capital both as having value of her own and in reproducing the other's capacity for production. In other words, the woman, in order to reproduce herself, can exchange her labour power as reproductive capacity either with the male salary or with her own salary if she also works in commodity production. But, in reality, this opposition of women to variable capital in its double guise is never positioned, at a general level, as an *alternative*, but rather as a *dual obligation*. The proletarian woman, in order to reproduce herself, is always forced, on a mass level, to exchange her ability to reproduce *both* with her own salary *and* with the male salary. *His* salary has rarely allowed her to go without the second job.

The woman, even when salaried, is obliged to exchange with the worker for two basic reasons: first, because the extremely low salary she receives at a mass level does not allow her to reproduce herself independently from men; second, because the possibility for the woman to reproduce herself is subordinate to the modalities of this exchange. For

---

13   Here, Fortunati uses 'non valore per se stante' (not a value for itself) to describe the reproductive labour primarily undertaken by women in the sexual division of labour and 'valore per se medesimo' (having value in itself) to mean the inherent value of reproductive labour for the waged worker. The passage from Notebook V of Marx's *Grundrisse*, referenced in this paragraph and the subsequent, describes the new conditions in which the worker confronts capital as labour power. It appears in the original as translated by Enzo Grillo as 'alle condizioni oggettive della produzione dei valori di scambio come alla sua non proprietà, come a proprietà altrui, a valore per se stante, a capitale'. Karl Marx, *Lineamenti fondamentali della critica dell'economia politica*, vol. 2, trans. Enzo Grillo (Florence: La Nuova Italia, 1968), 126.

14   Marx, *Grundrisse*, 498.

example, for a woman to have a romantic relationship with a man, she must be willing to do domestic work for him.

Therefore, the process of the so-called liberation of labour power does not historically affect men and women in a *homogeneous fashion*. The process is much more complex than Marx described in his historical treatment, in which he considered the liberation of labour power in terms of its vicissitudes in production, meaning the vicissitudes of a working class made up predominantly of men. This is a process that runs along the gender division of labour, with the so-called liberation of the worker taking different paths, depending on whether that worker is a man or a woman. The man who was a serf becomes a *salaried worker*: his liberation from feudalism also becomes the expropriation of any property other than labour power as the capacity of commodity production. The other side of his liberation is the compulsion to sell his labour power, to submit himself to the waged labour relationship. The woman has a more complex destiny: from servant of serfdom, she becomes primarily an *indirectly salaried worker*. She too is expropriated of the little property she possessed – obviously much less substantial than that of a man – except for her labour power. However the expropriation occurs in both her modes of existence: reproductive and productive. The other side of the woman's liberation is the compulsion to sell these two commodities: to submit herself to the relationship of indirectly salaried work and to that of salaried work.

The fundamental step in her liberation process is not the transition from serf as an 'accessory of the earth' to paid worker, but from serf to being a natural force of social labour. Therefore, the liberation of the woman is much more limited than that of the man. Moreover, having suffered discrimination in her liberation, as a capacity for reproductive labour, she has also heavily mortgaged her liberation process in her capacity for productive labour. Without going into detail here, it is enough to think of the sorts of jobs women are primarily assigned and the highly discriminatory wages they receive.

The complexity of reproduction is obviously reflected in the whole capitalist mode of production. Not only the functioning of reproduction, but also that of the *entire capitalist production* process is much more complex than even Marx himself grasped. Many Marxian categories, therefore, must be revised, starting from the very concept of capital.

For example, it is clear from what has been argued above that:

1. The *exchange of labour for labour* does not, in the capitalist mode of production, become only the exchange of waged work and capital, but also the exchange of variable capital and reproductive work that is indirectly waged;
2. the first exchange cannot exist without the second and *vice versa*.

As fundamental as the first may be, the need for the second exchange is established by capital at a general level for both the free male and free female worker. For the free male worker, this exchange is based on the expropriation of his labour power as a capacity for reproduction. For the free female worker, the exchange is based on the co-presence of the two working capacities in her person. In other words, it is based on the one hand, on the fact that the value of women's labour power, as productive capacity, is generally insufficient for the woman to engage with exchange value as something that she owns exclusively. The female salary is, in fact, auxiliary to that of the male. On the other hand, this exchange is based on the fact that capital as a value in-itself, as property of the objective conditions of production, deals with women, in their capacity as labour power capable of producing commodities, to a considerably lesser degree than it does so with men.

The purchase of women's labour power, as productive capacity, is regulated by capital to ensure the primacy of the purchase by the 'free' male worker of female labour power as reproductive capacity – that is, so as not to hinder capital's own simultaneous appropriation of the labour of reproduction.

The subordination of the exchange between capital and women, when the latter is a female worker, to that between her and the male worker, is determined by capital precisely in order to oblige the woman, first and foremost, to exchange her labour power, as capacity of reproduction with variable capital corresponding to the value of male labour power, and not with her own variable capital when such even exists.

Consequently, the opposition of the free woman worker to the objective conditions of production is both twofold, and of a double character. She can simultaneously oppose herself to capital and variable capital corresponding to the value of male labour power, or she can oppose only one or the other. As we have seen, however, at the general level, she can only refuse to engage the former but must necessarily engage with the latter. This means that she may encounter capital simultaneously both in her role as a natural force of social labour and as exchange value, or only as the former, but never exclusively as exchange value. She can also confront variable capital corresponding to the value of male labour power simultaneously as use value and as exchange value, or exclusively as an exchange value, but in no instance as pure exchange value.

Even *the exchange of labour with labour* in the capitalist mode of production is more complex than Marxist tradition has argued, because it too has a dual character. This exchange takes place in relation to the process of production as exchange of labour objectified as capital with living labour as use value. In relation to the process of reproduction, this exchange takes place in terms of objectified work, as the exchange value of labour power as capacity of production and living labour as use value.

Correspondingly, the *labour relationship* in the capitalist mode of production is much more complex than it has appeared. The male worker, as we have seen, is liberated both in relation to the waged labour relationship and in terms of the indirectly salaried labour relationship in reproduction. The male worker's freedom in the latter relationship in the reproduction process is a presupposition for his liberation in waged employment. The *liberation of labour power*, therefore, implies that male and female workers, positioned as owners of their productive capacity, are formally free to sell it, as a commodity, to the capitalist, just as they are formally free to pose themselves as subjects of the exchange of reproductive labour and variable capital. Therefore, under capitalism, men and women as workers have won not only the right to work freely but also to marry freely. Such freedom, however, applies only on a formal level; below the surface the *obligation to work* marches hand in hand with the *obligation to marry*.

Therefore capital is not simply a salaried labour relationship, but *a dual labour relationship*: a salaried employment relationship in the production process and an indirectly salaried employment relationship in the reproduction process.

In fact, two productive relationships take place, being both opposed to and mutually dependent on each other: the relationship of the worker with the objective conditions of productive work – a *waged labour relationship*; and the relationship of the worker with the objective conditions of reproductive work – an *indirectly salaried relationship*. In the first case, the individual's productive capacity engages with capital; in the second case, the individual as reproductive capacity relates not to capital, but to their own self as exchange value – as waged worker.

2

The 'Kingdom of Nature', or the Reproduction of the Individual as Labour Power

How is reproduction organised under capitalism, and in what manner does it function? What are its subjects, its production processes, its places?

Besides the family and prostitution, reproduction in a capitalist society comprises other branches. These branches include domestic work that is salaried and performed for a wage for a family other than the worker's own, the social reproduction of labour power established and organised by the state, and social services provided by private companies (or the state itself acting as entrepreneur). We limit our analysis here to that part of the reproduction process that takes place in the family and in so-called prostitution, because they represent the backbone, the nerve centre of the overall reproduction process.

In the family and prostitution, the fundamental production processes that generally occur are: the *production and reproduction of labour power* and the *specifically sexual reproduction of male labour power*. We should specify that the former, the production and reproduction of labour power, also entails the sexual reproduction of male labour power. While the sexual reproduction of male labour power is often presented as the primary task, it is just one of the many tasks comprising domestic labour. In fact, domestic labour encompasses the entire arc of the reproduction of the male worker, together with the production and reproduction of future workers. In prostitution, the specific process of the reproduction of male labour power is, by contrast, limited to this one task, and it is precisely such a task that defines it. We should specify, in this context, that prostitution indicates for us sexual reproduction of *male* labour power. Even though there is a growing demand from women, albeit less evident, for sexual reproduction, the recipient of this work, the client, remains, at a general level, men.

The production and reproduction of labour power is fundamental and general. The sexual reproduction of male labour power is corollary and particular. The first is fundamental and general because:

1. It presents itself simultaneously as a process of *production* and, at the same time, of *reproduction*.
2. It produces and reproduces labour power in a twofold manner, as productive/reproductive; in other words, it produces both male and female labour power.
3. It presents itself as a process of production of both the material and immaterial use values necessary for reproduction, since individuals as labour power express needs for their individual consumption of both a material and immaterial order;
4. It presents itself as a *process* that is articulated in an extremely diversified fashion throughout the production process (and therefore as a process linked to a specific production cycle); this is because labour power, in its claim over individuals, presupposes their reproduction for the whole of their life and therefore presupposes a diversified reproductive process tailored to the needs expressed in various life phases.

Prostitution, on the other hand, is a corollary and particular process of reproduction. It is corollary, because it must function as a support and complement to domestic labour – filling in where domestic sexuality is lacking. Its scope and magnitude are, consequently, more limited than domestic labour. It is particular because it is a selective process both with respect to the sphere of operations of the reproductive work it provides, which is that related to sexual reproduction, and with respect to the specific form of labour power that it reproduces – primarily that of the male workforce. Together domestic labour and prostitution, which are based on opposition but also on interdependence, describe a process of reproduction within which domestic labour presents itself as a presupposition and condition of existence for prostitution and vice versa. In both, the primary working subject is the woman, because, as we have seen, it is the woman worker who is generally forced to sell her capacity for reproduction. This remains generally the case, although there has been, in recent years, a growing masculinisation of the labour power active in prostitution, as well as in domestic labour. The rise in male prostitution is related to an increase in demand from men and, to a lesser extent, from women. The increase in the number of houseworkers who are male – single fathers, widowers and men living alone – is a reflection not only of the increasing isolation of the sexes, but also of an increase in the mass rejection of domestic work by women, leading to an attempt by the state to throw the work that women are less willing to provide on men's shoulders.

Apart from these rather recent trends, women, in their capacity for the production and reproduction of labour power, continue to be the fundamental subjects of reproduction. The woman is not, however, the only subject. The process of reproduction includes, as we explore below, a number of secondary processes that take place within the family. As subject of reproduction, the woman is necessary but insufficient. Because the production of labour power is positioned as a central and internal moment in the reproduction of both the labour power of the male worker and of the female houseworker, *the production and reproduction of labour power require a plurality of productive relations assuming a plurality of exchanges*. These relations of production are the following: the relationship between the male worker as husband and capital, mediated by the woman as houseworker; the relationship between the waged male worker and woman as houseworker in their role as parents and capital, mediated by the children as future workers; the relationship between these future workers as children and capital, mediated by the male worker and female houseworker in their role as parents; and finally, the relationship between the future workers themselves as brothers and sisters and capital, mediated by their siblings (and vice versa). With these relations we consider their corresponding exchanges.

Among all these relations of production and their relative exchanges, that between the woman as houseworker and capital, mediated through the waged male worker – and its relative form of exchange – is fundamental. The production of future workers is, in fact, not only a moment internal to the reproduction of the male worker and the woman as houseworker, but also a subsequent process on which their reproduction depends. In other words, it is fundamental, because the births and raising of children constitute not only an integral part of the reproduction of the waged worker and houseworker, but also an internal moment in their relationship and subsequently to its regulation.

The dependence of procreation on reproduction does not mean that capital has not simultaneously tried to subordinate the reproduction of the male worker and the female houseworker to the production of the future generation of workers, so as to ensure the greatest possible increase in population. The massive fall in the birth rate that has occurred in the USA, USSR and many other countries in recent decades has amply demonstrated how difficult it is for capital to achieve its desired results in this regard. In response to the expansion and intensification of areas of struggle and sabotage – a primary example being Black communities in the United States – capital has tried, often violently, to prevent demographic increases among the classes deemed dangerous (as in, for example, the forced sterilisation of Black, Puerto Rican and Indian women). This does not mean that the capitalist attempt to subordinate the reproduction of the waged worker and houseworker to the production of new workers does not proceed where possible on the terms set by capital, in the attempt to guarantee the supply of labour power.[15]

The relationship of production between the woman as houseworker and capital, mediated by the waged worker, although fundamental, is not, as we said, exclusive. It is necessary but insufficient to describe the overall process of production and reproduction of labour power, which also requires the relations of production and corresponding exchanges mentioned above. In their totality, the relationship of production between the woman as houseworker and capital – as well the relationship between the husband and capital, and those between the spouses, between parents and children and between siblings – form the core of the relations of production and of the exchanges necessary for the production and reproduction of labour power. These familial relations constitute the essential core, because the value of labour power, like that of every other

---

15   Questions of population control and family planning, including the genocidal policies of forced sterilisation, were extensively explored within the literature of Lotta Femminista and the Wages for Housework movement more broadly. See in particular, 'Mille fiori sbocciano appassiti', *Le operaie della casa*, special issue, April 1977.

commodity, is constituted by the necessary labour time required to produce and reproduce the labour force. The total labour time supplied by the working subjects engaged in these relationships constitutes the total labour time necessary for its reproduction. At the same time, these familial relations also constitute the sufficient core: the time, with its relations and exchanges, that must suffice for labour power to reproduce itself. This means that what goes beyond these limits is considered a waste, a luxury that the working class should not be allowed to indulge in. It is no coincidence that, under capitalism, the maximum formal possibility of individual relationships corresponds to the maximum isolation of individuals themselves, who are forced to produce surplus value, as we will demonstrate below, even when they reproduce themselves.

This core of productive relations represents the capitalist family, which is defined as *a unit of production and reproduction of labour power* specifically because it is composed of a plurality of productive relations. The family is, therefore, the *capitalist form* in which the reproductive relations of individuals present themselves. This does not mean that, outside of family, there are no relations of reproduction between individuals, but that the entire capitalist organisation of relations trends in this direction. Capitalist organisation tends to privilege familial relationships. These relationships, developed in either the family of origin or the family built in adulthood, or both, are the hinges on which the reproduction of the individual/labour power pivots. It must be noted, however, that the proletariat has always fought fiercely against its confinement within the family as the only safe harbour for relationships. One need only think of how the history of marriage is strewn with adulterers of all genders. The confinement of labour power within the family structure is growing ever less effective, first and foremost because the structure of the family has been modified by women's struggles. Today, many families are made up of single women with children, of lesbians and homosexuals, with or without children, and families in communes where men and women live together. In addition, the proletariat has become less willing to be confined in the family, to accept the family as their containment and isolation from the outside world. The increasing appropriation of extrafamilial relationships by the proletariat has been so explosive as to rewrite the family unit completely, such that today it is far more *temporally flexible, spatially mobile*, more *extensive* and much *less parental*.

On the other hand, capital always tries to make the family function, in its more or less emancipated versions, as the unit of individual relationships sufficient for reproduction. Similarly, capital tries to ensure that the relations of reproduction between individuals, even in their new forms, still appear as relationships between husband and wife, mother and child – as relationships between individuals who form a family, no matter of what kind. But since family relationships are actually relations of production, indirectly waged between these working individuals and capital, these roles are nothing more than representations of how these different subjects exist in relation with one another. They seem to be in a relationship with each other as individuals linked by a family bond, but in reality they relate to each other as subjects of different relations of production. The woman is the working subject necessary but insufficient for the production and reproduction of labour power, a process which also presupposes men and children as working subjects. In this process, men and children are secondary subjects. Unlike the adult woman, they do not possess the capacity to produce labour power. Men and children are only capable of reproductive labour, which is primarily immaterial, at least in the current phase of the capitalist mode of production. But this emphasis on the secondary nature of these working subjects (because they are only capable of reproducing the workforce at an immaterial level) does not mean that the female child, more than the male child, does not soon participate materially in the production process. Nor does it exclude the possibility, at the current stage of capitalist development corresponding with a high level of extra-domestic female employment, that the increasing redistribution of the material reproduction of labour power within the family could fall on the male worker.

As we have said, the sector of reproduction operates in a far more complex fashion than production specifically because its value-creating character appears as its opposite. In production the elements that are commodities are represented as such: the process of production is the production of commodities; workers are labour power – they are commodities, but they are also the working class; labour is waged labour; exchange is organised in a capitalistic fashion; the relationship of production is one of waged labour. It is not on this level that capital most mystifies its voracious appropriation of value, the violence of exploitation. In production, capital mystifies the content of the relationship that it establishes with the worker, which in reality is appropriation of surplus labour but which is represented as an exchange of equivalents between equals. In reproduction on the other hand, all the elements – from the processes through which labour power is forged, passing from waged labour to the female worker, through the exchanges and the relative relationship of production – are *denied as agents or elements of capitalist production*. Here, the mystification takes place further upstream, with the representation of the relationship between women and capital established even before its content is known, to the point that this relationship does not even appear to be between a woman and capital, but between a woman and a male worker. This relationship appears as a private affair of the proletariat, as a relationship where the issue of women's exploitation does not need to be investigated, because it appears untouched by capital. For capital, the entire sphere of reproduction is a natural process, one with spontaneously occurring forces, where relationships are innate. This is but one characteristic of reproduction; the other is that of value, of capital. This latter is a hidden character, but it is the real and dominant one.

Nature and capital: this is the binary antithesis on which reproduction is organised. Here, capital reveals a great flexibility: it was able to mould its iron laws in such a way as never to disturb the formal representation of this spectacle of nature. Unravelling the complexity of reproduction means untangling the duplicity of the different elements that describe it and revealing their hidden capitalistic nature below their natural appearance. It means discovering *the iron dominion of capitalist relations* in places where elements that seem to have little in common with them, such as feeling, sexuality or personality, seem to reign unchallenged. It means recognising in the apparent anomalies that are increasingly found on this terrain the paths of struggle against the specific exploitation of reproduction that different subjects, first and foremost women, express.

Let us examine these elements then, one by one, and dissect their duplicity, starting with labour power.

Labour power in the realm of reproduction has two faces, each opposed to the other. On its one face, reproductive labour power is the production and reproduction of waged labour power; on its other, it presents itself as the capacity of sexually reproducing male labour power. Corresponding to the different centrality and functionality of the respective production processes, the former aspect of reproductive labour power is positioned as its fundamental and general labouring capacity, and the latter as secondary and particular. Taken together, although based on contradiction but also on mutual interdependence, they describe the labour power of the reproduction process, with respect to which the former is the presupposition and condition of existence of the latter. Furthermore, labour power as a capacity of reproduction assumes a double character. On the one hand, the labour power of reproduction is represented, in its encounter with capital, as a natural force of social labour. On the other, in relation to the labour power of production, reproductive labour positions itself as a commodity to function as labour power for expropriation by capital. The labour power of reproduction assumes this double character either as capacity of production and reproduction of waged labour power or as capacity for the sexual reproduction of male labour power. The only difference between the two is that, while the former is presented as a natural force of social labour, the latter is represented as *unnatural*. The different, if not opposite, way in which these forces present themselves to capital is reflected in the different possibilities of each for representing their value monetarily. When the capacity of production and reproduction of labour power establishes its labour as a commodity in relation to the labour power of production, the exchange value of its labour cannot be represented monetarily. In fact, its monetary representation would contradict its contemporary representation as natural force of social labour. However, when the capacity to sexually reproduce male labour power is established as a commodity in relation to the waged worker, the exchange value of its labour can be represented monetarily. This does not contradict the contemporary representation of such labour power as an *unnatural force of social labour*, because the work of prostitution is already considered an unnatural commodity (even criminal), and thus is not formally recognised as a commodity by capital.

Analogously, reproductive labour, understood as *domestic labour* and *the labour of prostitution* presents a twofold nature. Domestic labour presents itself to capital as the natural force of social labour, and thus as non-labour; it presents itself to the waged worker as a personal service performed by the woman, though it is, in reality, labour that is indirectly waged. The labour of prostitution presents itself to capital as an unnatural social labour power, and thus as non-labour; it presents itself to the waged worker as a personal service, though it is in fact labour paid for with money, though not directly waged.

Likewise, the free waged female worker, as labour power in its reproductive capacity, also has a twofold nature. As labour power with the capacity to produce and reproduce labour power, the woman presents herself to capital in her role as the natural force of social labour and therefore as non-worker. In relation to the waged male worker, she positions herself in relation to capital as a *housewife*, though she is in fact an indirectly waged *houseworker*. On the other hand, as labour power capable of sexually reproducing male labour power, the woman positions herself in relation to capital as an unnatural social labour power and therefore as a non-worker. In relation to the worker, she positions herself as a prostitute, although in relation to capital, she is an indirectly waged sex worker. In reality, two classes face each other in the realm of reproduction: a class comprising capitalists; and a class comprising *houseworkers and sex workers.*[16] It is from this complex condition of the free female worker in her reproductive capacity that there derives the *particularly contradictory character of the female condition in capitalist society.* For bourgeois ideology, the woman does not work in the proper sense, but carries out a mission, that of wife and mother (more or less emancipated). For the free male worker, the woman is a housewife or prostitute, for she provides a service that remains merely personal and is given more or less out of love. For capital, she must present herself as a natural force of social labour in order to exist in reality as a houseworker or sex worker who is indirectly waged. This explains why, for the woman, trapped in this double bind, within the complexity of a productive relationship that the male worker does not recognise, and oppressed by an ideological production of extraordinary depth, it is particularly difficult to identify herself as part of a class, and therefore to organise any form of struggle. Her struggles against the labour of reproduction have never been considered as struggles against labour, since reproductive labour is not considered labour. Only when the expansion of the feminist movement resulted in a much higher level of power for all women were they able to highlight their work as such, their struggles as struggles and themselves as class subjects in struggle.

---

16   The term 'sex worker', while emblematic of the content of the work of prostitution, is not the most felicitous. On the other hand, we are forced to use it, at least until a more adequate term emerges. (Note in original.)

The exchange of variable capital and reproductive labour is also twofold. On the one hand, it is an exchange of variable capital for domestic labour, and, on the other, it is an exchange of variable capital for the labour of prostitution. Likewise, variable capital is also twofold: for the male worker, it functions as income; and for the female houseworker and for the female sex worker, it functions as capital. While variable capital formally corresponds to the value of the male worker's labour power, in reality it corresponds to the value of labour power in its twofold productive/reproductive aspects. Marx says: 'The wage-form thus extinguishes every trace of the division of the working day into necessary labour and surplus labour, into paid labour and unpaid labour. All labour appears as paid labour.'[17] It must be specified that the wage form extinguishes every trace of the division of the working day into necessary labour and surplus labour but does so only in relation to the working day of the male worker. This specification is necessary, because without it the other effect provoked by the wage form – that is the transformation of the working day of the houseworker and of the sex worker into non-labour – remains obscure, preventing a description of its effects. Contra Marx, it is not true that all labour appears as paid labour. Only the labour provided in the production process appears as paid labour. The labour provided in the reproduction process appears as non-labour, or, more specifically, it is positioned as non-labour; it is represented as a personal service and functions as indirectly waged labour.

The *relationship of domestic labour* and *the relationship of the labour of prostitution* have a twofold nature. In the relationship of domestic labour, no employment relationship appears to exist between women and capital, but only between houseworkers and male workers. The relationship of domestic labour is represented as a domestic working relationship with the purpose of mutual individual consumption. It is, in reality, a relationship of production with capital. Likewise, in prostitution, no employment relationship appears to exist between women and capital, but only between prostitutes and male workers. Here, too, the relationship is represented as one of prostitution offered for the purpose of individual consumption, while in reality it is a relationship of production with capital itself. These relations of production, which take place

---

17   Karl Marx, *Capital*, vol. 1, *A Critique of Political Economy*, trans. Ben Fowkes (London: Penguin, New Left Review, 1990 [1976]), 680.

between capital and women in the roles of houseworkers and sex workers, are mediated by the male worker and are established as indirectly waged relations of production.

We now consider the issue of reproduction starting from the relations of reproduction between individuals. Our argument is that because the individual is reduced to the labour power commodity, the individual's relationships can only exist as relations of production. In fact, the individual cannot reproduce himself or herself, nor any other individuals, except as labour power. As a commodity, his or her reproduction can only be subject to the general laws governing the production of commodities and therefore, as with the production of any other commodity, must assume commodity exchange. Given the separation between labour power as capacity of commodity production and labour power as a capacity of reproduction; given the separation by the line of value between the process of production and the process of reproduction; given the sexual separation existing between the corresponding working subjects – the fundamental exchange of reproduction is that between women and capital, mediated by the waged worker. The commodities exchanged are, on the one hand, variable capital and, on the other, domestic labour and, as its corollary, the labour of prostitution. These two forms of labour, while presenting themselves to the male worker as personal services, are, in reality, labour power commodities.

The fact that the subjects of this exchange can only be the male worker and the female houseworker, or the female sex worker, explains why, in capitalist society, adult relationships between individuals are established as heterosexual. Only the adult male has the full possession of his labour power in production and can sell it to obtain a wage. Only the adult woman has the full possession of her labour power as the capacity of production and reproduction of labour power, and as the capacity of sexual reproduction of male labour power. She can thus sell this commodity and take possession of her means of subsistence, primarily in a direct form – as in the first case, and, in the second case, in a mediated form as money. The coercive pressure towards heterosexuality in capitalist society is therefore not only an expression of its ideology or a form of social control and discipline: heterosexuality is the foundation of the capitalist organisation of individual relationships, and it is the result of specific material processes. The emergence of mass homosexuality and lesbianism in the last decade clearly cannot be understood simply as the expression of a change in sexual orientation by millions of individuals. It is the expression of mass rebellion and rejection of the capitalist organisation of social relations that has completely undermined the landscape of reproduction. This means that the functioning of the fundamental exchange relation established in reproduction has been severely undermined: that between the male worker and the female houseworker, and, what is more important, the corresponding relationship of production.

To say that lesbianism and homosexuality are expressions of mass rebellion does not mean that they automatically disrupt the functioning of reproduction. The heterosexual model, as a model of power relation, is so strong at the social level that it is often incorporated by gay and lesbian relationships. In its plans for restructuring reproduction, capital tries everything to make these new variables function. These mass behaviours and organised struggles have managed to express themselves despite harsh state repression and criminalisation, and have transformed many material processes that are at the basis of the capitalist organisation of relationships between individuals.

As far as the generational connotation of individual relationships in capitalist society is concerned, the possibility of having individual sexual relationships has always been linked to the possession of one's own money or to the assets that allow self-maintenance (as in the case of the adult woman). Those non-adults who do not work are not entitled to sex. This is not only because the sexual policy of capital has relentlessly reiterated the idea that sex should only be a reward for those who work, but also because capital has always tried to ensure that those in a position to procreate are able to support any children that might be produced. The non-adults are excluded from the possibility of fulfilling individual relationships. The struggles of children, teenagers and young people have been so constant and radical as to cast doubt on how much they have practised asexual relationships in the past. Certainly today it is very difficult for capital to impose restraints on their relationships. Perhaps this is still possible with children – but for how much longer?

As relations of production, *individual relationships* are, as we have seen, severely confined to the family. The family is the primary site of reproduction of the individual as labour power. It is only male labour power that capital allows to be reproduced in a programmatic fashion outside the family itself, at least in relation to its sexual reproduction. How does the family's reproduction of labour power take place? Some elements are already available to answer this question. In the family, labour power is produced by more than one working subject. Among these working subjects, the woman is primary and the others, the man and the children, are secondary. The production of labour power presupposes multiple segments of working time provided in different fashions and quantities by different subjects. Within it, however, they all work as *reproducers*. Labour power, as a more or less immaterial reproductive capacity, inheres in each individual, even the male and the non-adult. This capacity inheres in subjects from birth and at all times throughout their life, even if it does so in a diversely articulated fashion because it operates differently depending on age and sex. The adult woman is the only one in the family who can freely sell her reproductive labour power as a commodity, because she is its owner. As we will discuss in greater detail below, this is one of the essential conditions for the exchange between her and the worker, and consequently for the production of the family itself. Both men and children are obliged to exchange their labour power within the family. For the man, this is one of the essential conditions for his exchange with both capital and the houseworker, based on his ownership of his wage. For children this exchange of their labour power within the family is necessary because they cannot possess their own labour power. The differentiation in the marketability of the reproductive capacity of different members of the family is determined precisely to anchor them to the family as the primary centre of their reproduction.

The production of new labour power is positioned by capital in the family as necessary to the waged worker and the houseworker for the reproduction of their own labour power. It is necessitated because, paradoxically, it is the only way for them to widen the circle of fundamental relationships and to have relationships with children, with non-adults. The refusal to have children, however, cannot be explained only by the obstacles and prohibitions imposed on contraceptives and abortion, despite all the burdens these interdictions impose. It remains to be said that, despite the fact that having children is posed as a necessity by capital, more and more women and couples are not having children because of the cost in terms of domestic work and money and because of the social isolation having children entails.

It is precisely the reduction of individual relationships to relations of production (to familial relationships) that is the basis of the progressive isolation of the individual in capitalist society. The individual is isolated not only from those outside their family, but also progressively isolated even from their family members because, although familial relationships are established as fundamental, they are not unique individual relationships but relations of production which are therefore alienated. In capitalist society, the maximum formal possibilities of the relations of reproduction, given by the fact that everyone is formally free to exchange with whomever he or she wants, corresponds to the minimum possibility of real individual relationships.

3

The Capitalist Form of the Man/Woman Relationship

If the advent of capitalism signifies reproduction of individuals as production of value (even if represented as its opposite), what then of the man/woman relation?

The upheaval that the new mode of production causes throughout the sphere of reproduction determines specific transformations with respect to pre-capitalist forms of reproduction in the organisation of the man/woman relationship.

In the history of capital, the exchange between man and woman undergoes enormous transformations resulting from the development of the sexual division of labour. In this process, it changes radically: from a *working relationship with labour* in its immediately living form in the pre-capitalist societies, it becomes a *relation of production* formalised between men and women themselves. However, this transformation does not become manifest – it does not appear immediately evident as such – because, just as all reproduction is organised in a dual fashion, the man/woman relationship also takes on a twofold nature. Although it is a productive relation, it is represented as a relationship between individuals. Given the radical transformations involved, it would be more appropriate to speak of a leap – a clear break between its capitalist and pre-capitalist organisation.

We analyse the transformation of the male/female relation with regard to the development of the sexual division of labour, examining the three primary forms of servitude that, as Engels claims, distinguish the three ages of civilisation. Only in this way is it possible to address, in its essential features, the materialist history of the relationship between man and woman.

Our thesis is that:

1. The *difference in power* that emerges between the indirectly waged woman and the waged man is *incomparable* to that which existed between them in slavery or serfdom. The great leap caused by capital in the sexual division of labour means first and foremost a great leap in the division of men from women. The man is subjected to the waged working relationship, which is the capitalist relationship par excellence, and he is formally positioned as the woman's master. The woman has no formal relationship with capital, and she is positioned in a relationship of service to the man. Given this situation, not only is his social power immeasurably greater than hers, but women and men each have antagonistic interests so far as their relationship is concerned. This division between man and woman is reflected, of course, in a stratification of power and hierarchy within the proletariat. Never before, as in capitalism, has man been divided from woman by such a deep chasm. But at the same time, never until this new mode of production have the possibilities of destroying this power relationship been so great. Beyond any historical judgement about what such a relationship has represented, its persistence today is barbaric not only because it is robbery of unpaid labour from women, who are forced to live socially isolated and largely dependent on men, but also because it is functional to the robbery of unpaid labour from men. As women, we are forced to work, through those we 'love', for capital. That is why our 'love' confirms their – and our – negation as individuals: their and our status as commodities. The only alternative today is to reproduce and to be reproduced by others as individuals, not as commodities: to break, to interrupt this flow of love with its macabre face of exploitation. This is possible today. It is possible to destroy this power relationship between man and woman, to destroy the mediation of men as capital and the state in relation to us. This, today, is the only realistic programme of equality between men and women: the non-exploitation of both.

2. In pre-capitalist modes of production, the relationship between the slave or serf and the woman is established in terms of the exchange of labour with labour in its immediately living form. This relationship does

not usually include the exchange with sexual reproductive labour of prostitution. Under capitalism, the relationship between the male worker and the woman is an exchange with a twofold form. First, it is a relationship between the male waged worker and the female houseworker based on the exchange of objectified labour with the living labour of production and the reproduction of labour power. Second, it is a relationship between the male waged worker and the female sex worker, based on the exchange of objectified labour with the living labour required for the sexual reproduction of male labour power.

Since the advent of class society, the sexual division of labour within the family – a division on which the entire social division of labour is based – has involved:

> the *distribution*, and indeed the *unequal* distribution, both quantitative and qualitative, of labour and its products, hence property: the nucleus, the first form, of which lies in the family, where wife and children are the slaves of the husband. This latent slavery in the family, though still very crude, is the first property, but even at this early stage it corresponds perfectly to the definition of modern economists who call it the power of disposing of the labour-power of others. Division of labour and private property are, after all, identical expressions: in the one the same thing is affirmed with reference to activity as is affirmed in the other with reference to the product of the activity.[18]

In this context, the relationship between man and woman is not based on an exchange of any kind, because the woman herself is positioned by the man as an object of exchange between men. When slavery shifts from its very crude and latent relationship within the family to become the first of 'the three great forms of servitude characteristic of the three great epochs of civilization' – that is, when it is discovered that, like the woman within the family, the individual, divorced from a kinship structure, can be a commodity, itself an object of exchange – the class relationship between man and woman is articulated differently.[19] Slavery no longer

---

18 Karl Marx and Friedrich Engels, *The German Ideology*, in *Marx and Engels Collected Works*, vol. 5 (London: International Publishers, Progress Publishers and the Institute of Marxism-Leninism, 1976), 46.

19 Friedrich Engels, *The Origins of the Family, Private Property and the State* (London: Penguin Classics, 2010), 214.

presents itself only as a form of production characterised by the ownership of women and children by the *pater familias*. It comes to be a
perfected and therefore manifest relationship, which includes the ownership by the *pater familias* of unrelated individuals as objects of exchange:
men, women and children. Consequently, the division of power between
man and woman develops and stratifies, corresponding to the articulation of the different relationships now established: one potential
relationship is that between the woman who is apparently free, but a
latent slave within the family, and the *pater familias*; another relationship
might be that between the woman and the man as slaves; and yet another
could be the relationship between the female slave and the *pater familias*
as her master. The class struggle between women and men also develops
as does the class struggle between slaves of both sexes and their masters.
These masters, as owners, are mostly male, but can also be free women,
who, as wives of the *pater familias*, have the right of usufruct of their
husbands' property.

The extension of slavery outside the bonds of kinship not only causes
the refinement of this relationship of production, but also makes men
fundamentally equal to women in their role as slaves. The relationship
between men and women as slaves, both being commodities, work
machines and the property of their master, is no longer a relationship
of production between the two. The only relationship of production to
which they are subject is that which they both, individually, have with
their master. As property of the master, not only the use value of
what they produce but also their children and themselves, as a product
of their reproduction, belong to him. The fact that they are both commodities and property of their master makes them fundamentally
equal. This does not mean that the sexual division of labour at the social
level does not cause an unequal distribution both in quantity and
quality of labour performed by male and female slaves. However, this
unequal arrangement does not apply to the product of labour itself,
which belongs to their master. The division of power between male and
female slaves is strictly limited by the *fundamental equality of their
condition*. The master's power over them is so overwhelming that even
the relationship between them is subordinate to his consent and all the
conditions he imposes.

When this relationship is established under the conditions described
above, it is based on an *exchange of labour with labour in its immediately*

living form, because neither of them has the right to own anything in which their labour is objectified and with which they could buy the other's living labour. Their relationship is therefore based on the working cooperation of both for the purpose of mutual consumption of the products of their labour.

Serfdom implies a growing inequality between men and women: that is, it deepens the division of power between them. Although both men and women, as serfs, live in the same condition as 'accessories of the land' and property of the feudal lord, they are subject, individually, to *different relations of production* with him.[20] The male serf becomes, as Marx says, 'not only the owner of the piece of land attached to his house, although admittedly he was merely a tribute-paying owner, but also a co-proprietor of the common land', while the female serf has access to these rights only if she remains a widow; and, in that case, she exercises them in the name of her son.[21]

The lessened equality of the relations of production to which serfs are subject implies less equality in their overall condition. They become less equal, both with respect to their obligation towards the feudal lord, with respect to the number of days that they are obliged to work for him and with respect to the remaining labour time that is their own. Unlike slavery, where the sexual division of labour does not correspond to any division of the product of labour itself between male and female slave, in serfdom the sexual division of labour corresponds to a specific, unequal division of the product of labour between the male and the female serf. Obviously, this is true not in terms of *ownership* – since, by right, everything is the property of the feudal lord, including the serfs themselves – but in terms of *possession*, of that part that is due to the serfs themselves. Their lesser equality with respect to the feudal lord translates into a lesser equality in the relationship with one another. This determines a deepening of the inequality in terms of the power relationship between men and women under serfdom as compared with their relations under slavery.

---

20 Fortunati references expressions used by Marx to describe relations of feudalism. Although the original does not include a note, this phrase can be found in Karl Marx, *Grundrisse: Foundations of the Critique of Political Economy*, trans. Martin Nicolaus (London: Penguin Books, 1993 [1973]), 489.

21 Karl Marx, *Capital*, vol. 1, *A Critique of Political Economy*, trans. Ben Fowkes (London: Penguin, New Left Review: 1990 [1976]), 877, n. 2.

As in slavery, however, their relationship cannot be configured as a relation of production. They are in fact both positioned as 'accessories of the earth', and their only relation of production is that with the feudal lord. Here too, his power is so overwhelming that the relationship between them is subordinate above all to his consent – which, when given, always requires payment – and to all the limitations imposed by him. This relationship is also configured as an *exchange of labour with labour in its immediately living form*. It is based on the working cooperation of both, for the purpose of mutual consumption of the use values produced. Obviously, given the difference of power existing between male and female serfs, the quantity and quality of the work reciprocally exchanged is unequal. Also unequal are the quantity and quality of consumption of the use values produced.

What happens to the man/woman relationship with the advent of capitalism and the transformation of serfs into free workers? *Unlike slavery and serfdom, in which men and women were fundamentally subjected to an identical relationship of production, capital establishes a relationship of production with men that is formally different from the one it establishes with women.* The sexual division of labour develops to such an extent that it leads to a sexual separation of the working subject of the production process from the working subject of the reproduction process. Here, these two processes are separated through the dividing line of value. The man, as the primary working subject of production is forced into a *waged labour relationship*. The woman, as the primary subject of reproduction, is forced into an *indirectly waged labour relationship*.

Given that the relationship of production exists formally only between the male worker and capital, the difference in power between men and women in their formal relation to capital *grows to an extent never reached by men and women as slaves in relation to the master or by men and women serfs in relation to the feudal lord*. Such a difference emerges in its real amplitude if we consider that, while slaves reproduced themselves as 'work machines' because they embodied such a role and serfs reproduced themselves as 'accessories of the earth' in their role as such, the woman under capitalism does not reproduce the waged worker as a waged worker herself, but as a natural force of social labour.[22]

---

22   The original does not include a note, but these quotations can be found in Marx, *Grundrisse*, 474–89.

The liberty of the free worker to become a waged worker corresponds to that of the woman to become an indirectly waged houseworker and sex worker. What must be grasped is that it is precisely the diversity of the formal relations of production established by capital with the man and the woman that causes the profound inequality in the relationship they have with capital itself. This inequality translates into a *profound inequality between the man and the woman themselves* in their individual relationships. Such inequality is inevitable because *capital transforms the relationship between man and woman* from a relationship of exchange of labour in its immediately living form into a formal relation of production established between them.

This transformation affects many aspects of the gendered relationship. The man is formally given the right/duty to initiate relations of production with the woman. The relationship between them can now formally arise and exist as one of production only to the extent that the form of the exchange between man and woman is presented in terms of an *exchange of objectified work*, a relation between exchange value and *living labour*. The relationship between the man and woman is no longer an exchange relationship in the form of exchange of work with work in its immediately living form for the purpose of mutual consumption of the use values produced. It is no longer a *relationship based on mutual working cooperation*. It becomes a specific formal *relation of production* between the male worker and the woman in which the worker, in exchange for his wage, consumes the living labour that the woman provides. We specify this as a *formal* relation because the individual relationship between the man and the woman established as a relation of production between the two is the form of the real relations of production between capital and women. This relationship is one of indirectly waged labour. The capitalist transformation of the relationship between man and woman also implies a restructuring of the consumption involved. While, in the pre-capitalist modes of production, the relation between man and woman did not presuppose the separation of the working subject from the subject of consumption, because both men and women worked for each other and both consumed the product of their labour, capitalism presupposes such a separation because it is the man in this case who buys the labour power of the woman.

Capitalism also transforms the quality of the subject that expropriates the woman from the product of her reproductive labour. In pre-capitalist modes of production, the woman was expropriated, like the man, from the product of her labour of reproduction of individuals as exchange value. If she was a slave, this appropriation was performed by her master who possessed slaves as 'work machines'. If she was a serf, this appropriation was performed by the feudal lord because he possessed serfs as 'part of the feudal property . . . as accessory of the land, just like cattle for work'. Under capitalism, the woman is not formally expropriated from the product of her reproductive labour (individuals as labour power) by capital. Rather, she is expropriated by the product of her labour power itself – waged labour power – which must formally belong to itself as a presupposition and condition of existence of capitalism. While, in pre-capitalist modes of production, the relationship of exchange between man and woman was subordinate to the consent of the master in the case of enslavement and to that of the feudal lord under serfdom, with the advent of capitalism this relationship of exchange became *free*. Following the liberation of labour, the relationship of exchange between man and woman was configured as a free exchange: free in the twofold sense that man and woman become free both to exchange without having to depend on the consent of anyone (even the consent of parents is gradually diminishing), and to choose, within certain limits, with whom to exchange.

If these are the transformations that, under capitalism, have affected the relationship between men and women at a general level, what are the changes that have taken place in the relationship between men and prostitutes? Our argument is that the advent of the new mode of production, just as it radically transforms the relationship between man and woman at a general level, also radically changes the relationship between man and prostitute. The continuity that seems to bind pre-capitalist and capitalist forms of prostitution reveals all its inconsistency when subject to analysis.

In pre-capitalist modes of production, the exchange between man and woman takes the form of an exchange of labour with labour in its immediately living form. This is true with the exception of a particular type of exchange: that between the man and the prostitute. The objects of this exchange are in fact basically *money* and the *living labour of sexual reproduction of the individual*. In this case, money presents itself as money in the form of hoarded wealth. This exchange therefore implies a relationship held mainly by those men who own themselves and possess money, such as, for example, feudal lords or priests. This category does not totally exclude the serfs because, most likely, a certain amount of the payment of the prostitute was, on occasion, made in kind.

Under capitalism, this type of relationship between man and woman includes above all the waged male worker. The money that is exchanged is no longer hoarded wealth, but variable capital. Prostitution then transforms from a trade to become *labour that is indirectly waged*, even if it is paid monetarily. The fact that the prostitute now works for the waged male worker means that the development of the waged labour relationship is also linked to the development of this specific form of exchange between man and woman. Development of capital means development of prostitution.

4

Housewives, Prostitutes and Workers: Their Exchanges

As we have said, the man/woman relationship is not a relationship between individuals, even if it is represented as such. It is a relation of production between women and capital mediated by men. It is a complex relationship, played out through *duplicity*, and notable for the contrast between its representation on levels of the formal and the real. This complexity is obviously reflected in the *exchange* presupposed by this relationship.

The exchange implied in the man/woman relationship has a twofold nature: on the one hand, it is an exchange between variable capital and domestic labour; on the other it is an exchange between variable capital and prostitution. On the formal level, it represents itself as an exchange between the wage and domestic labour or prostitution labour and between male worker and housewife or prostitute. However, in reality it is an exchange between variable capital and the labour of domestic work or prostitution and between the houseworker or sex worker and capital, mediated by the male worker. In other words, the exchange of the wage for domestic work (or prostitution) between the male worker and housewife or prostitute is the *form of the real exchange* that takes place between the houseworker or sex worker and capital. The fact that the exchange between variable capital and reproductive work adopts a twofold character is a necessary condition for the exchange itself. Capital cannot exchange directly with the labour power of reproduction because it has established the capacity of reproduction as a natural force of social labour. Capital is thus forced to resort to the mediation of a third party in exchange with the woman: it must pass through the male worker who engages with the female houseworker and sex worker as a form *of capital*, which is the true subject of this exchange.

In relation to the male worker, capital imposes a representation of the labour power of reproduction as a form of personal service, domestic labour or prostitution. At the same time, it imposes a representation of the woman as housewife or prostitute, instead of representing her as a houseworker or sex worker, and a representation of the labour of production and reproduction of male labour power as personalised services, instead of indirectly waged work.

Compared to the exchange between the male worker and capital, the greater complexity of the exchange between the female houseworker and capital is immediately apparent. But this complexity is necessary for its capitalist functioning: it is precisely this complexity that implies that it is not only the form but also the very act of exchange (and the essential conditions required for it to occur) which are very different on the formal level from those necessary to the exchange between male workers and capital. More precisely, the exchange between the female houseworker and capital differs from that between male workers and capital more profoundly than the exchange between the female sex worker and capital mediated by male waged worker. The reason for this differentiation is that the labour of prostitution, unlike domestic labour, has a price, so that even if neither are waged, the latter assumes characteristics similar to the exchange between male workers and capital. Besides the differences these two forms of exchange assume with respect to that between workers and capital, the most relevant factor remains the dissimilarity of both from the exchange between male workers and capital.

In contrast to a popular view, our argument is that such dissimilarity does not mean that these exchanges are not organised in a capitalist manner. The dissimilarity must instead be considered as the prerequisite and condition for the ordinariness of the exchange between male workers and capital. Although these forms of exchange diverge formally, in reality they work in a related fashion in that, as we demonstrate below, the exchanges between houseworker or sex worker and capital are not exchanges of equivalents. As with the process of exchange between capital and waged labour, in which capital appropriates the male worker's labour time not through direct exchange but through the waged form or exchange, likewise in capital's exchange with the labour power of reproduction, capital appropriates the female houseworker's or sex worker's labour time not through the mediation of the wage but indirectly through the exchange with the male worker.

The fundamental relationship to reproduction no longer coincides strictly with the man/woman relationship, but is articulated through many other relationships: man/man, woman/woman, men/women and so on. Similarly, the fundamental exchange of reproduction is no longer merely that between woman and capital through the male worker, which is the one we are considering here, but it is articulated in many other forms. A major struggle against the macro-inequalities of exchanges, such as those between man and woman, has emerged on a mass level both through struggle within the exchange relationship itself, and through the refusal of the exchange altogether. Exchanges within communes, or homosexual and lesbian relationships, are behaviours with significant consequences. These exchanges are potentially less unequal than the heterosexual exchange. We say 'potentially' because, we repeat, the heterosexual model is so dominant as a power relation on a social level that it is hard to practise equality within such a structure. Reduced inequality in the exchange between subjects, however, does not necessarily mean less surplus value is appropriated by capital; it only means a more equal redistribution, on four shoulders instead of two, of the exploitation of labour power on the grounds of its own reproduction. Nonetheless, these upheavals can have devastating effects for capital on the overall functioning of reproduction. For example, they inhibit the kind of income redistribution within the proletariat which capital requires. If the male wage, which is typically higher than the female wage, is paired with another male wage, it ceases to subsidise the notoriously low female wage and ceases to command domestic work from women.

We consider here only the man/woman exchange, which is to say the one between the female houseworker and capital mediated by the male worker. We do so because, even if the reproductive exchange takes on other forms, the man/woman exchange is still the most common on the level of reproduction. A first difference stands out with respect to the exchange between male workers and capital. While the exchange between male workers and capital is formally an *exchange of equivalents*, the man/woman exchange is not, even formally, one of equivalents because the objects that capital and the female house-worker exchange through the male worker (variable capital and the labour power that produces and reproduces labour power) are not defined as exchange values. The labour power at issue is a non-value in terms of exchange – a mere use value. Does this mean that it has absolutely no exchange value? Not at all. The female houseworker can in fact establish her domestic labour as a unity of use value and exchange value only insofar as her labour power exists for capital as a natural force of social labour. She can do so only insofar as capital does not present itself as the owner of the objective conditions of repro-duction. The houseworker's labour power has an exchange value not as labour power, but as domestic labour, because the latter has use value for the waged male worker. In other words, the female houseworker can sell domestic labour to the male worker, because he needs it for his personal consumption and for his reproduction as labour power. The male worker appears to buy domestic labour while in reality he buys female labour power as the capacity of production and reproduction of labour power. The exchange value of female labour power cannot represent itself in formal, *monetary*, terms as exchange value. However, such value can still be defined through the quantity of labour objecti-fied in her labour power itself, which is to say through the quantity of labour expended to produce the female houseworker. If, on a formal level, female labour power represents itself as non-value, it is indeed exchange value on a real level though appearing under the guise of domestic duties of the housewife.

The primary object of exchange, variable capital, on the other hand, is represented as exchange value. It is, however, a particular kind of exchange value, because it does not appear as exchange value as such. As Marx says, variable capital – the object of exchange between the male worker and capital – poses itself as follows:

> The object of his exchange is a direct object of need, not exchange value as such. He does obtain money, it is true, but only in its role as coin; i.e. only as a self-suspending and vanishing mediation. What he obtains from the exchange is therefore not exchange value, not wealth, but a means of subsistence, objects for the preservation of his life, the satisfaction of his needs in general, physical, social etc. It is a specific

equivalent in means of subsistence, in objectified labour, measured by
the cost of production of his labour.[1]

But this is true for the male worker. For the female houseworker, variable
capital operates as capital. The exchange between the female houseworker and capital via the male worker does not formally involve
exchange value. On the one hand, there is an object of exchange value:
variable capital, which is not exchange value as such. On the other hand,
there is a non-exchange value: female labour power, which, for the
woman, can only become exchange value as domestic labour. The fact
that these two elements *do not represent themselves as exchange values*
does not mean that they are not such in reality. They do not represent
themselves as exchange value because this exchange must not appear as
capitalist, because it does not include capital on a formal level, as a
subject of exchange. They are both, however, in reality, forms of exchange
value. Although this exchange does not formally appear as one of
exchange values and thus not as an exchange of equivalents, it is still, in
reality, *an exchange of exchange values.* The very fact that these cannot
be represented as exchanges of equivalences, even on a formal level, is the
very condition of their existence as exchange values. In other words,
the fact that the exchange does not appear capitalist is the condition for
its capitalistic functioning.

   Assuming that, on the level of the real, this exchange involves
exchange values, we should ask ourselves if, on the same level of reality,
it is an exchange of equivalents. While the male worker exchanges a
portion of his wage which corresponds to the value of the housewife's
means of subsistence, the female houseworker exchanges her domestic
labour. The housewife receives money, or the means of subsistence,
directly, while the worker receives a commodity, which has a price that,
for him, is equal to the money, or to the means of subsistence, that he
paid for that commodity. Everyone here appears to receive an equivalent.
In reality, the male worker *does not receive an equivalent.* In this exchange,
what he acquires is domestic labour only on a formal level, while in
reality he acquires labour power as an equivalent in the exchange. With
this, the worker 'has acquired labour time – to the extent that it exceeds
the labour time contained in labour capacity – in exchange *without*

---

1   Marx, *Grundrisse*, 284.

equivalent; it has appropriated alien labour time *without exchange* by means of the *form* of exchange.[2] While the worker receives such added value, he does not take possession of it for himself. As the purpose of his exchange with capital is not exchange value as such, but the fulfilment of his needs, likewise his exchange with the housewife is not the appropriation of the value created by the living labour of the woman herself, but the fulfilment of his needs. He operates solely as a conductor of capital. Thus, when capital buys labour power through the wage, it appropriates the value created by women's labour power, which is incorporated in waged labour power as capacity of production. Such appropriation does not usually happen through a direct exchange with the houseworker but is mediated by her exchange with the worker. To conclude, we have proved that such exchange is not an exchange of equivalents, because the worker receives much more value than the value he gives to the woman, even if he does not appropriate such value for himself, but for capital.

The possession of a wage by a woman who is both a houseworker and a worker in the production process obviously affects the exchange between her and the male worker. She has, in fact, more contractual power in relation to him. In the last few decades, the possession of wages by women has become more common and sustained. This means that the terms of exchange between women and waged male workers have been considerably redefined. The supply of female domestic labour appreciably decreases, while the male supply increases. However, reduced inequality of the objects of exchange for the male worker and the houseworker does not automatically mean that capital appropriates less surplus labour from domestic reproduction. Rather capital appropriates surplus labour from two subjects, instead of one. However, it is an established fact that the increase in male workers' domestic labour does not compensate for the decline in female domestic labour due to the great momentum towards socialisation of such labour (we eat out more and more, we send our clothes to laundry services, etc.) and due to the increasingly persistent demand by women for either more money or more commodities from men for the labour they supply.

Just as the exchange between the worker and the housewife takes on particular significance, the way in which the two parties are positioned as individuals in the act of exchange takes on specific connotations.

---

2   Ibid., 674.

Because the female houseworker is established as non-value, as opposed to the free male worker, she cannot, with her domestic labour, buy money or receive a wage from the male worker. The legitimate holder of the wage is always the one who earned it, that is, the male worker. Variable capital remains always the product or outcome of the production process, and thus the male wage. Variable capital is never a formal object of exchange between the worker and the houseworker. Because 'money only gives the equivalent its specific expression, makes it into an equivalent in form, as well', the non-monetary nature of the exchange between domestic labour and wage has a precise consequence.[3] The worker, exchanging his labour power with money, which is to say with the general form of wealth, 'becomes co-participant in general wealth up to the limit of his equivalent – a quantitative limit which, of course, turns into a qualitative one, as in every exchange'.[4] The houseworker, whose labour power is domestic work performed for the male worker, cannot exchange her labour power for money, that is, for the general form of wealth. As opposed to the male worker, she cannot formally own that part of variable capital that corresponds to her own means of subsistence. If we consider that her equivalent (her labour power), does not have a limit, because it does not have a price, it is evident that the houseworker is not entitled to participate in the enjoyment of general wealth. She does not, through the exchange, have the right to the money that expresses the value of her labour power. She only has the right to consume that part of the wage that corresponds to the value of her means of subsistence.

The difference between the houseworker and the waged worker described above indicates that the houseworker is bound by a major constraint. While the male worker 'is neither bound to particular objects, nor to a particular manner of satisfaction', the houseworker *is always bound to the agreement of the male worker in terms of the details of her consumption.*[5] Because her relationship with money is not a relationship of ownership, but just the *use of someone else's ownership*, it is almost irrelevant for the houseworker whether the worker provides her with means of subsistence in their natural form, or as money. *Almost*

---

3 Ibid., 246.
4 Ibid., 283.
5 Ibid.

irrelevant because, in reality, money is less restrictive than means of subsistence. Moreover, the equivalent of what the houseworker gives to the waged worker within the exchange does not have a formal limit, because it does not have a price. This implies that:

1. The houseworker's consumption has a quantitative limit which always tends to be lower than that of the factory worker;
2. The sphere of her enjoyment is also *qualitatively limited*, and this is true in and of itself, while for the waged worker this is true as a reflection of the quantitative limits of his consumption.

It is important to note that, since the Second World War, women have initiated a cycle of intense struggles over the dynamics of consumption within the family. First, women started to demand that husbands deliver their pay checks to them, so that women could handle them themselves. It is in this period that the wage becomes a crucial site of struggle between workers and capital. The direct management of the male wage by women within the family is as strategic in the struggle between women and capital as it is between women and male workers. This crucial move has been passed off by many women simply as an ideology of rational management of consumption but, in reality, it is simply a different, clearly anti-capitalistic management of the male wage. In fact, the direct management of the male wage does not aim at guaranteeing the steady reproduction of the working class, but, on the contrary, at determining a reproduction of the class constantly opposed to capital. The criteria of consumption become both more unproductive for capital, and more disruptive for the hierarchy of family consumption. More generally, these criteria help to dismantle the stratification of power within the class. It is now the woman who determines the priority of needs and their satisfaction among the family members and decides the quality and quantity of consumption with respect to the wage. She is the one who, as a strategic workerist defence, refuses the pressure to scrimp and save every penny, and makes the total consumption of the wage a normal condition, and a factor in the continuation of struggle. It is, of course, always the worker who has the last word, because the one who earns the wage is always the one in power. But now his words carry a different weight, and many mediations occur between the possession of money and its transformation into something that can be used. It should be noted that women in the 1960s made use of the wage mostly for their children, and not for themselves. One of the few simple achievements made by women for themselves in these years in the realm of consumption was establishing a weekly appointment with the hairdresser.

But in the 1970s, family consumption shifted again in the sense that: 1) women began to consume for themselves as well; and 2) families came to consume more than they earned.[6] It was women's mass achievement of their own wage that contributed to the development of their new agency, with full rights over their own consumption and even more control over the management of family wages. With the 1960s, the policy of abstinence, sacrifice and saving as criteria to manage the family budget ended. The 1970s began with a new phase of management of the proletarian wage, based on mass indebtedness. Credit cards and loans became instruments for exceeding the wage on the level of circulation. To spend today what you can earn tomorrow is the new motto characterising the dynamics of consumerism, especially in the United States. Once again, women are the battering ram that creates these breakthroughs. If workers have always calculated that their wages will arrive after a month or a week of work, these new social behaviours and patterns of consumption by the working class now assume consumption before paying for it with labour.

The formal non-equivalence of the objects involved in this exchange relation between man and woman leads to specific formal consequences. These consequences are very different from those related to the exchange between worker and capital, in which labour power in its capacity of production is sold as a commodity by the worker as its free owner. When the worker encounters the owner of money on the market, they 'enter into relations with each other on a footing of equality as owners of commodities, with the sole difference that one is a buyer, the other a seller; both are therefore equal in the eyes of the law'.[7] On the contrary, the exchange between women and capital is mediated by the worker. Women's labour power, under the guise of domestic labour, is sold by the housewife to the waged worker as a commodity. However, domestic labour is not formally a commodity. When the free woman worker meets

---

6 These phenomena are especially observable in some countries, including the United States.

7 Marx, *Capital*, 271.

the owner of money (in the form of the wage) on the market, they enter into relations with each other, but not on a footing of equality as owners of commodities, and not as equals in the eyes of the law. It follows that the inequality in the relation between man and woman is neither a dysfunction in the capitalist mode of production nor a legacy of some pre-capitalist barbarity. It is, instead, inherent and ingrained in the functioning of the capitalist mode of production. Equality of exploitation between man and woman cannot exist in a capitalist society precisely because such exploitation is based on power differences that are present within the class itself. Either the struggle for *equal rights* becomes a struggle against the dominion of capital, or it becomes nothing but the impracticable programme of a reformist utopia.[8]

To the constitutive aspect of inequality, we must add that of non-freedom. The factory worker and the houseworker both identify one another 'reciprocally as proprietors, as persons whose will penetrates their commodities', and they both alienate their property of their own free will; however, while the housewife's freedom consists, on the formal level, in the free property of a non-value, the male worker's freedom consists in the free property of a value.[9] What defines the freedom of women and the freedom of men is thus profoundly different in content. If the freedom of men is, as Marx pointed out, only formal, the freedom of women, though also only formal in nature, is even less so than that of men.

The *essential conditions of exchange* between the female houseworker and capital – conditions mediated by the male factory worker – are also different from and sometimes in opposition to those which must be fulfilled so that capital encounters labour-power as capacity of production on the market. As we have seen, these differences do not contradict the argument that this exchange is organised in a capitalist fashion. These differences demonstrate the elasticity with which capital has shaped its own laws to apply them to reproduction. Capital found itself with a very particular commodity: labour power. The only way to organise its production on capital's terms has been to implement a particular organisation of its production process and of its relative exchanges.

The issue of time is central here. On the one hand, we consider the first essential condition for the continuation of the relationship between

---

8   This is in English in the original.
9   Marx, *Grundrisse*, 243.

free worker and the owner of money as capital, who enter relations with each other on a footing of equality as owners of commodities,

> with the sole difference that one is a buyer, the other a seller; both are therefore equal in the eyes of the law. For this relation to continue, the proprietor of labour-power must always sell it for a limited period only, for if he were to sell it in a lump, once and for all, he would be selling himself, converting himself from a free man into a slave, from an owner of a commodity into a commodity. He must constantly treat his labour-power as his own property, his own commodity, and he can do this only by placing it at the disposal of the buyer, i.e. handing it over to the buyer for him to consume, for a definite period of time, temporarily. In this way he manages both to alienate (*veräusser*) his labour-power and to avoid renouncing his rights of ownership over it.[10]

On the other hand, the continuation of the relationship between the female houseworker and capital, mediated by the waged male worker, does not require that she sell her labour power for a definite, clearly delimited period. This is true both formally and in practice. The sale formally appears to be a sale of domestic labour, that is, a personal service. But in reality the question is more complex. Her labour power – the real object of this exchange – is firmly established as non-value, whether the houseworker sells it for a definite or indefinite period of time. In fact, the choice of selling her own labour power either for a defined or indeterminate amount of time does not affect the possibility of owning her own labour power, because in either case her labour power is configured as a property of non-value. This means that the time period of the relationship between the houseworker and capital is established as radically different. In this configuration, the female houseworker must sell to the male worker her domestic labour, or rather her labour power, without any time limitation. She sells her labour power *for an amount of time that is indeterminate with respect to both the single working day and the entirety of her working days*, which may correspond with the entirety of her life. The relationship between the houseworker and capital require this arrangement because, for different reasons, both capital and the

---

10   Marx, *Capital*, 271.

worker need the woman to make her labour power constantly available. Both capital and the worker need the woman to sell her labour power for her entire life so that she can guarantee a continuum of labour reflecting only the natural limits of the single working day and her working life. Given the twofold nature of this specific form of labour power, capital requires it because the more the houseworker works, the more domestic labour is appropriated by capital. The more capital appropriates domestic labour, the greater the exploitation of what appears to be a natural force of social labour. The male worker, on the other hand, needs it because the reproduction of his labour power – a particular commodity insofar as it exists within the individual – requires a consumption of domestic labour marked exclusively by the temporal dimension of his own existence.

Because the purpose of capital is to appropriate the value created by the houseworker's living labour, it has no interest in placing time limits on this exchange, nor in determining a time frame for the worker to have such labour at his disposal. Moreover, the male worker himself needs to have uninterrupted domestic labour at his disposal because the purpose of his exchange with the houseworker is the satisfaction of his needs. As a result, the essential condition for the worker to exchange his wage with domestic labour is that domestic labour is sold to him by the houseworker for an undetermined period. This is exactly the opposite of what occurs in the production process. On the one hand, this means that the houseworker can formally own her labour power only when she chooses to break off her relationship with the free worker. On the other hand, if we compare the two situations, the male worker sells his labour power to capital, and he allows capital to make temporary use of his labour. After working hours, the worker returns to owning himself for a limited period, which is the time of consumption for his reproduction. The houseworker, on the contrary, sells to the factory worker her labour power as domestic labour, which allows him to have ownership of her labour without any temporal limitation. Therefore, she cannot freely regain possession of herself and consume as she likes, even for a limited time. The time of consumption that the houseworker uses to reproduce herself is basically inseparable, both spatially and temporally, from the labour time required for individual consumption of the male worker and of future workers. To conclude, it needs to be specified that, in production, the relationship between workers and capital is not as continuous as it once was because periods of work now alternate with periods of voluntary unemployment. Likewise in reproduction, man/woman relationships tend to be increasingly determined in time. Relationships tend to be constructed less in terms of lifelong commitments. Their duration tends to be shorter, both in terms of years and in terms of the amount of time spent together within a day; consider for example how many contemporary relationships do not involve the man and woman living together. The second essential condition of exchange between the female houseworker and capital is that the owner of money as a wage must encounter domestic labour on the market as commodity. This encounter arises in very different, even opposed conditions to those required by the exchange between the labour of production and capital. In the latter case, the condition

> which allows the owner of money to find labour-power in the market as a commodity is this, that the possessor of labour-power, instead of being able to sell commodities in which his labour has been objectified, must rather be compelled to offer for sale as a commodity that very labour-power which exists only in his living body.[11]

The question is, however, more complex in the exchange in which we are interested. The houseworker, as much as the male worker, is not able to sell commodities in which her labour has been objectified and is rather compelled to offer for sale as a commodity her very own labour power. But, for the woman, two possibilities present themselves here: to offer her labour power for sale to capital as a waged worker; and to offer herself for sale as a domestic worker or prostitute to the male worker. She is practically compelled by capital, however, to primarily offer her labour power in sale to the waged worker as the capacity to produce and reproduce labour power under the guise of domestic labour or sexual reproduction. Only secondarily can she offer her labour power to capital as the ability to produce commodities. On the mass level, the woman thus finds in the worker a secure buyer as he is compelled to buy domestic work in order to reproduce himself. In this exchange, she is more likely to find a buyer as a houseworker than as a prostitute. On the other hand, as a worker, she may find in capital a buyer of her labour power which subordinates this exchange to that between the woman and the waged male worker. It does

---

11   Ibid., 272.

so by restricting the number of jobs available to women according to the needs of the latter exchange, and by ensuring that the value of female labour power in production is such that the woman is compelled to offer her domestic labour to the worker regardless of her waged employment. Capital must compel the woman to present herself primarily as a house-worker because it is only in these terms that the exchange between domestic labour and variable capital and the exchange between capital and the labour of production become reciprocally essential. To conclude, I want to summarise the second essential condition which allows the worker to encounter domestic labour on the market as a commodity. First, capital must not be compelled to buy the capacity to produce and reproduce labour power as a commodity; and second, the sale of women's labour power as the capacity for production must occur within such limitations as to force women to sell their labour power as the capacity to produce and reproduce labour power to the worker.

Obviously, this entire discourse must be understood in the context of a specific tendency that capital has been developing in response to struggles over the working day that have been taken up by the industrial working class, initially in England. During the period of original accumulation, proletarian women often had roles other than wives and mothers, including prostitution. With industrialisation, women and children became the backbone of the working class. The factory also became a site of prostitution where women as waged workers were not taken seriously. In subsequent periods of its development too, capital was distinguished by its voracious and elastic exploitation of women. Whenever convenient, capital has not hesitated to exploit women simultaneously as workers, prostitutes and houseworkers; or, in other times and places, to exploit them primarily as prostitutes. What is clear is that capital has tried to ensure that, for women, the sale of their own labour power in commodity production would be not an alternative, but only complementary to, their own domestic labour.

This exchange has another peculiar characteristic with respect to the exchange between the labour of production and capital. Here 'the worker advances the use-value of his labour-power to the capitalist. He lets the buyer consume it before he receives payment of the price. Everywhere the worker allows credit to the capitalist.'[12] On the contrary, in the

---

12   Ibid., 278.

exchange between the female houseworker and capital, the houseworker as housewife does not advance to the worker the use value of domestic labour for two reasons. First because the woman sells her domestic labour to the worker – or in other words she sells her labour power to capital via the worker – for an indeterminate amount of time. This means that she cannot be paid, like the worker, 'until it has been exercised for the period fixed by the contract, for example, at the end of each week'.[13] Second, because, for the housewife/houseworker, the moment of consumption of her means of subsistence is not detachable in terms of time from the moment of the formal alienation of her domestic labour/labour power. The reconversion of variable capital into the means of subsistence for the entire working family, housewife included, is in fact part of domestic labour. The housewife/houseworker does not earn money, which would function as payment, in exchange for her labour. Therefore, the reconversion of part of variable capital into the means of subsistence is not detached – either spatially or temporally – from the reconversion of variable capital in its entirety into the means of subsistence for the entire working-class family.

Thus, it is to capital that the houseworker, like the waged worker though in a different fashion, provides in advance the use value of her labour power. She does so in a different way from the waged worker because, while the latter advances directly to capital the use value of his labour power, the houseworker does so indirectly. Let us take as an example a case in which the waged worker is paid on a weekly basis. The worker advances the use value of his labour power to the capitalist as the capacity of production. In other words, capital pays him with the wage when the work is done. For the houseworker, the advance of the use value of her labour power to the capitalist occurs via the worker, and specifically when the price of his labour power as capacity of production is established. Variable capital includes, in fact, the value of female labour power. When capital buys the worker's labour power, he – the worker – advances to capital both the use value of his own labour power and that of the houseworker. Thus, the waged worker serves as a liaison for the direct advance of the use value of the houseworker's labour power made by her to capital. This is the advance which, when the worker is paid his wage, will be paid indirectly to the houseworker.

---

13   Ibid.

The exchange between the houseworker and capital has yet another peculiarity with respect to the exchange between labour in production and capital. This peculiarity concerns not so much the possibility of choosing whom to sell to, but rather the possibility of changing the subject to whom to sell oneself. The free worker owns his capacity of production and 'within certain limitations he may choose to sell himself to whomever he wishes', because he 'must indeed sell himself to capital, but not to a particular capitalist'.[14] Similarly, the houseworker, as owner of her domestic labour/labour power, may, within certain limitations, choose to sell herself to whomever she wishes, because while she must indeed sell herself to variable capital, she is not bound to sell to a particular worker. The difference between the two consists in the fact that the worker has more freedom to change the capitalist he sells himself to than the houseworker has to change the worker. The free worker may choose to both sell himself, within certain limitations, to whomever he wishes, and change, within certain limitations, his boss. For women, such a possibility is much more limited. Because a woman must offer her domestic labour/labour power for sale for an indeterminate amount of time, her choice must be almost definitive. The relationship between the houseworker and the worker is much more binding than the relationship between the worker and the capitalist. In fact, it is significant that the right to divorce is still not formally recognised in many countries. Between the two, the houseworker and the male worker, it is the houseworker who has limited options for extra-domestic labour, generally earns lower wages and has less social power. Thus the relationship is, for her, far more binding.

Another peculiar characteristic of this exchange is the *specificity of labour itself*. What the worker sells to capital 'is the disposition over his labour, which is a specific one, specific skill etc.', so that the disposition of the capitalist over labour power is limited to a specific job or jobs.[15] On the contrary, what the houseworker sells to the worker is the disposition over a form of labour that is only *relatively specific*. If it is true that its specificity consists in the fact that it is domestic labour, we need to acknowledge that the peculiar nature of the commodity produced – labour power itself (since every human being is unique and

---

14   Ibid., 1033.
15   Marx, *Grundrisse*, 282.

unrepeatable) – requires the externalisation of domestic labour in forms that are unlimited from a quantitative point of view and also qualitatively unlimited in terms of difference.

'From whore to pope, there is a mass of such rabble . . .'[16]

Let us now consider the exchange between the labour of prostitution and the wage. Like the exchange between workers and capital, this exchange is also posited as an exchange of equivalents. The objects of exchange are the wage – that is, exchange value – and the labour of prostitution, which has a price and thus is formally a *commodity*, an exchange value. The worker exchanges some of his variable capital corresponding to the value of the labour of prostitution, while the woman exchanges her labour of prostitution, which is her labour power. The woman receives money, and the worker receives a commodity, which, for him, is equivalent to the price he paid for it. Thus everyone seems to receive an equivalent. But, because he received labour power – and not the work of prostitution – as equivalent in the exchange, the worker 'has acquired labour time – to the extent that it exceeds the labour time contained in labour capacity – in exchange without equivalent; it has appropriated alien labour time without exchange by means of the form of exchange'.[17]

In the second phase of exchange between the work of prostitution and the wage, the equivalent received by the worker turns out not to be an equivalent – but not for the worker. Just as the purpose of the worker's exchange with capital is not exchange value as such, but the satisfaction of his needs, likewise the purpose of the worker's exchange with the prostitute is not the appropriation of the value created by her living labour, but again, it is simply the satisfaction of his needs. It is capital, once again, that appropriates the value created by female labour power

---

16   Ibid., 272. Marx here shows a lack of understanding for the productive role of prostitutes and sex workers in capitalist society and indulges in completely inappropriate and offensive language.

17   Ibid., 674. 'Labour capacity' here refers to Marx's term *Arbeitsfähigkeit* used in the *Grundrisse*. The Italian edition (translated by Enzo Grillo) used by Fortunati renders the term as *forza-lavoro*, more commonly simply translated as 'labour power'. Fortunati consistently uses *capacità di riproduzione* (capacity of reproduction) relative to *capacità di produzione* to indicate distinct, though mutually dependent, aspects of labour power. See Translators' Note.

as the capacity of sexual reproduction of male labour power. Capital does this when it buys the worker's labour power within which such value is incorporated. It follows that this exchange is not really an exchange of equivalents. Once again, the worker receives much more value than he gives to the prostitute. He does not appropriate such value for himself, however, but for capital. Even though this is formally posited as an exchange of equivalents, the worker and the prostitute are neither equal nor equally free. In other words, this exchange in the relationship between men and women is a denial of freedom and equality even greater than that in the relation between workers and capital. While the worker's sale of his labour power is considered legitimate, given that he earns money with his labour, the sale by the sex worker of her labour power is, on the contrary, considered illegitimate and criminalised. She is, in fact, free to sell her work/labour power as a commodity, only insofar as such freedom would prevent her from being a free person. It is not an accident that the client – who pays for the work of prostitution – is rarely prosecuted, while she, who sells it, often is. The exchange between the work of prostitution and the wage thus not only lacks freedom, but also equality. The objects of such exchange, even if they are formally equivalent, are not equal: the money exchanged by the worker is juridically recognised as legitimate, while the work of prostitution exchanged by the prostitute is juridically illegitimate. It follows that man and woman, while they are in a reciprocal relationship as owners of commodities, do not have the same rights, and thus are not equal under the law. If the woman as housewife is not in an equal relationship with the worker, the prostitute is even less so, because she pays for the money she earns with her own criminalisation.

Let us now consider the essential conditions for exchange between the work of prostitution and the wage. These conditions are not so different from those at the basis of the exchange between the labour of production and capital. They are, on the contrary, very different from the conditions of the exchange between houseworker and capital mediated by the worker. In the exchange between the work of prostitution and the wage, the prostitute or sex worker is the free owner of her sex work, her labour power, as much as the free worker is the owner of his own labour. This is true even though she is bound in the sale of her commodity. The prostitute can always refer to her own labour power as her property, and thus as her own commodity, because she offers it for sale to the buyer only temporarily, for a defined period. As opposed to the exchange between domestic work and variable capital, the position of the worker engaged in prostitution is temporally specific. It is, moreover, limited to a specific form of work, which is highly regulated (intercourse with or without a condom, oral sex, BDSM and so on).

There is a second condition necessary for this exchange to take place. For the owner of money as a wage to find female labour power available on the market as a commodity, the woman must be prevented, once again, from selling any commodity other than her own labour power. She must offer her labour power for sale not as a factory worker or houseworker, but as a prostitute. The sale of the labour of prostitution formally excludes the possibility of sale of the other two forms of labour power (housework or waged work). On the one hand, a woman is formally prevented from selling herself simultaneously as housewife and prostitute because these two subjects, the one legal and the other criminalised cannot coexist formally within the same person. On the other hand, the sale by the prostitute of her labour power as a capacity of production is also incompatible on the formal level. In practice, however, the borders of the reproductive sphere have always been quite permeable in relation to the vicissitudes of the proletarian wage. Today, for example, because of the economic crisis, more and more full-time housewives are part-time prostitutes. Many students, factory workers, teachers and secretaries also work as prostitutes. The domestic labour-market has become less rigidly separated from that of prostitution. Women come and go more frequently within these two markets, but, above all, prostitution has grown far beyond what had been considered its optimal dimension. The increase of prostitution, together with women's absenteeism from domestic labour, has been dangerously changing the face of workers' consumption. Capital requires that the consumption of domestic labour should be the crucial moment of workers' consumption; complementary and not an alternative to that of prostitution. Capital's response has been to intensify control over the quantity of the 'free' exchanges between the labour of sexual reproduction of male labour power and variable capital. The intensification of the repression of prostitution is nothing less than an attempt to modify the exchange between prostitute and worker so that their exchange might, once again, be complementary and quantitatively secondary to the one between housewife and worker.

This exchange between the work of prostitution and waged labour presents another characteristic of the exchange between productive labour and capital. As much as the free worker advances the use value of his labour power to the capitalist by letting him consume it before he pays its price, the prostitute also advances the use value of her work/labour power to the worker. Like the worker who may choose, within certain limitations, to sell himself to whomever he wishes, the prostitute/sex worker can do the same. The restrictions she faces are, however, greater than those on the free worker, because she is denied as a 'free person'.

To conclude, the prostitute/sex worker may, like the waged worker, change within certain limits the subject to whom she sells her work in prostitution, which is to say her labour power, for a definite period.

5

In the Sphere of Circulation . . .

The question is: *Which form of circulation?*

Within which relationship of circulation should we place the exchange between factory worker and houseworker, and factory worker and prostitute? We argue, following the line of reasoning developed in the previous chapter, that such twofold exchange, like every other exchange of capital made for purposes of production, is a relationship of *complex circulation*. This is true even if, given its twofold nature, it appears formally as a relationship of simple circulation for purposes of consumption.

However, given that housework and prostitution are formally defined as personal services, arguing that these exchanges belong to complex circulation is to contradict Marx's discourse on the personal provision of work. While Marx does not exclude the existence of personal services bought for purposes of production, he places this possibility within a precise historical moment: that of the dissolution of pre-capitalist modes of production. It is not by chance that he examines personal services while analysing the 'various conditions . . . which have to have arisen, or been given historically, for money to become capital and labour to become capital-positing, capital-creating labour, wage labour'.[1] Marx affirms that these conditions 'reveal at first glance a two-sided character – on one side, dissolution of lower forms of living labour; on the other, dissolution of happier forms of the same'.[2]

---

1 Karl Marx, *Grundrisse: Foundations of the Critique of Political Economy*, trans. Martin Nicolaus (London: Penguin Books, 1993 [1973]), 463.

2 Ibid., 464.

For Marx, free workers' personal services may be bought for the purposes of consumption, and thus the exchange of objectified labour for living labour can either be included *within the relation of simple circulation,* or they may be bought for purposes of production. The latter occurs in the epoch of the dissolution of pre-capitalist relationships for production purposes, although in this case:

> firstly, even if on a large scale, for the production only of *direct use values*, not of *values*; and *secondly*, if a nobleman e.g. brings the free worker together with his serfs, even if he re-sells a part of the worker's product, and the free worker thus creates *value* for him, then this exchange takes place only for the superfluous [product] and only for the sake of superfluity, *for luxury consumption*; is thus at bottom only a veiled purchase of alien labour for immediate consumption or as use value. Incidentally, wherever these free workers increase in number, and where this relation grows, there the old mode of production – commune, patriarchal, feudal etc. – is in the process of dissolution, and the elements of real wage labour are in preparation. But these free servants [*Knechte*] can also emerge, as e.g. in Poland etc., and vanish again, without a change in the mode of production taking place.[3]

In this passage, Marx examines personal services in opposition to waged labour. He argues that, even when they are bought for the purposes of production, this turns out to be the production of direct use values and not of value. Outside this particular historical moment, Marx excludes the possibility that, in the capitalist mode of production, there could be personal services not bought primarily for the purposes of consumption and therefore not included in simple circulation.

In bourgeois society itself, all exchange of personal services for revenue – including labour for personal consumption, cooking, sewing etc., garden work etc., up to and including all of the unproductive classes, civil servants, physicians, lawyers, scholars etc. belongs under this rubric, within this category. All menial servants by means of their services – often coerced – from the least to the highest, obtain for themselves a share of the surplus product, of the capitalist's revenue.

---

3   Ibid., 469.

But it does not occur to anyone to think that by means of the exchange of his revenue for such services, i.e. through private consumption, the capitalist posits himself as capitalist. Rather, he thereby spends the fruits of his capital. It does not change the nature of the relation that the proportions in which revenue is exchanged for this kind of living labour are themselves determined by the general laws of production. As we have already mentioned in the section on money, it is here rather the performer of the service who actually posits value; who transposes a use value (a certain kind of labour, service etc.) into value, money. Hence in the Middle Ages, those who are oriented towards the production and accumulation of money proceed partly not from the side of the consuming landed nobility, but quite the opposite, from the side of living labour; they accumulate and thus become capitalists, δυνάμει, for a later period. The emancipated serf becomes, in part, the capitalist. It thus does not depend on the general relation, but rather on the natural, particular quality of the service performed, whether the recipient of payment receives it as day-wages, or as an honorarium, or as a sinecure – and whether they appear as superior or inferior in rank to the person paying for the service. However, with the presupposition of capital as the dominant power, all these relations become more or less dishonoured. But this does not belong here yet – this demystification [*Entgötterung*] of personal services, regardless of the lofty character with which tradition may have poetically endowed them.[4]

But what kind of jobs does Marx have in mind? He lists some that may be exchanged with 'the surplus product of the capitalist's revenue' and are thus 'unproductive'. It is clear that he is not at all thinking here of the exchange between objectified labour (as variable capital) and living labour, as with domestic work or prostitution, for the purposes of the worker's individual consumption. And yet reproductive labour is the most macroscopic example of the devaluation and desecration to the detriment of specific work to occur in the capitalist mode of production. It is not by chance that Marx does not consider reproductive labour at all. He is, in fact, ignoring the time frame and composition of working-class consumption itself. In other words, Marx does not acknowledge that the

---

4   Ibid., 468–9.

worker's individual consumption is not a direct consumption of his wage, and that the wage does not have a direct use value for the worker, which means that the consumption of its use value requires labour: primarily domestic work and prostitution.

The act of transforming the wage into a use value directly consumable by the worker involves multiple stages. Even after its initial transformation into a use value, the wage may not yet be directly and immediately consumable by the worker – additional labour remains necessary for the worker's reproduction. Transforming the use value of the wage into one that is directly and immediately available for consumption involves both initial labour and the subsequent production of those immaterial use values necessary for the workers' reproduction – a process which also involves labour. Finally, producing and reproducing new labour power is labour. Thus, possession of the wage by the worker does not automatically imply that he can exercise his ability to reproduce his own labour power. Nor does it imply any possibility that workers could produce labour power by having children, given that this ability is generally vested in women; nor does he have the ability to reproduce himself sexually, since this would require another person. Thus the worker, with his salary, must purchase labour power as the capacity to produce and reproduce labour power itself, and labour power as the capacity for sexual reproduction of male labour power. The worker buys both, under the guise of forms of work which appear as the performance of personal services – both domestic work and prostitution.

Marx sees an incomplete composition of the worker's individual consumption, which, he believes, is constituted by three elements: the wage; the wage's direct consumption; and the production and reproduction of labour power, which is realised by the worker in an immediate fashion. The worker's individual consumption and his reproduction seem to coincide as much as the subject of consumption and that of labour. Because Marx does not see the consumption of the working class in its reality, he does not see the exchange occurring between worker and houseworker, nor that between worker and prostitute.

Even when Marx examines the case of the worker buying labour, he examines it superficially, and concludes that such consumption of labour, even if it is provided by the workers for their individual consumption, is always a service and thus simply unproductive labour. For example:

The labourer himself can buy labour, that is, commodities, which are provided in the form of services; and the expenditure of his wages on such services is an expenditure which in no way differs from the expenditure of his wages on any other commodities. The service which he buys may be more or less necessary – for example, the service of a physician or of a priest, just as he may buy either bread or gin. As buyer – that is, as representative of money confronting commodity – the labourer is in absolutely the same category as the capitalist where the latter appears only as buyer, that is to say, where there is no more in the transaction than the conversion of money into the form of commodity.[5]

Marx is expressing here, without acknowledging it, the point of view of the worker, not of capital. His conclusion is not that this is consumption of unproductive labour, which is, however, unproductive for the worker, but rather the opposite: that this is consumption of labour that is unproductive for capital. It is crucial for us to understand why this exchange occurs. Clearly, neither the houseworker nor the sex worker are sharing the surplus product, nor are they sharing the capitalist's income, but they are sharing variable capital in its role as capital. Domestic work and that of prostitution therefore do not belong to the category defined by Marx as 'unproductive' labour which may be exchanged with the capitalist's income.

We are witnessing two peculiar exchanges, within two peculiar relationships of circulation, where the consumption of labour is, as we will discuss shortly, productive for the capitalist and thus unproductive for the worker. We believe that this consumption happens within the limits of what is absolutely necessary. Marx, however, considers the consumption of domestic work and that of prostitution 'a merely incidental part of the production process', in which the worker:

provides himself with means of subsistence in order to keep his labour-power in motion, just as coal and water are supplied to the steam-engine, and oil to the wheel. His means of consumption are

5   Karl Marx, *Theories of Surplus-Value*, Part I (Moscow: Progress Publishers, 1963), 404.

then merely the means of consumption of a means of production; his individual consumption is directly productive consumption.[6]

If we distinguish the two different forms of consumption, we can say that the consumption of domestic labour is within the limits of what is absolutely necessary mentioned above as regards the waged worker's individual consumption nexus. It is worth repeating that domestic consumption takes place within absolutely necessary limits for reproduction and is indispensable for the production of labour power. The consumption of the work of prostitution takes place within these same limits. This is not because the worker has greater sexual needs than the woman, but because he can achieve a greater satisfaction of his sexual needs than that allowed to women owing to his greater economic power.

If 'we contemplate not the single capitalist and the single worker, but the capitalist class and the working class, not an isolated process of production, but capitalist production in full swing, and on its actual social scale', it is clear that the consumption of domestic labour and prostitution is the condition for the conservation and continuous reproduction of the working class.[7] Now, because the reproduction of the working class remains 'a necessary condition for the reproduction of capital', it follows that such consumption 'is productive to the capitalist and to the state, since it is the production of a force which produces wealth for other people' and is unproductive for the worker 'for it simply reproduces the needy individual'.[8]

But how is such consumption a moment in the production and reproduction of capital? Is it productive for capital only because it reproduces the capitalist relationship, or does it also reproduce capital as value? Marx affirms that the worker's individual consumption is productive because it reproduces the capitalist relationship. He thus only sees the process of reproduction as one of productive consumption, and not as one of production (or of productive labour). Marx states this clearly:

---

6   Karl Marx, *Capital*, vol. 1, *A Critique of Political Economy*, trans. Ben Fowkes (London: Penguin, New Left Review: 1990 [1976]), 717.

7   Ibid., 717.

8   Ibid., 718–19.

Now, as regards the worker's consumption, this reproduces one thing – namely himself, as living labour capacity. Because this, his reproduction, is itself a condition for capital, therefore the worker's consumption also appears as the reproduction not of capital directly, but of the relations under which alone it is capital. Living labour capacity belongs just as much among capital's conditions of existence as do raw material and instrument. Thus it reproduces itself doubly, in its own form, [and] in the worker's consumption, but only to the extent that it reproduces him as living labour capacity. Capital therefore calls this consumption productive consumption – productive not in so far as it reproduces the individual, but rather individuals as labour capacities.[9]

Here too:

But in so far as capital is a relation, and, specifically, a relation to living labour capacity, [to that extent] the worker's consumption reproduces this relation; or, capital reproduces itself doubly, as value through purchase of labour – as a possibility of beginning the realisation process anew, of acting as capital anew – and as a relation through the worker's consumption, which reproduces him as labour capacity exchangeable for capital – wages as part of capital.[10]

In opposition to Marx, we argue that the worker's individual consumption is productive for capital precisely because it is also the consumption of domestic work and prostitution, and insofar as it *reproduces capital as value*. We repeat: when the worker satisfies his needs, it means that he is devaluing and depreciating his money. His destiny is of a tantalian nature: to reproduce himself only and always as mere labour power. But, as we have seen, it is in his own labour power that the time of domestic work and prostitution may be objectified. This is a value that does not interest the worker, because it does not increase the exchange value of his own labour power. It interests capital, however, because it does increase the use value of the waged worker's labour power, which in turn creates value for capital.

---

9   Marx, *Grundrisse*, 676.
10   Ibid., 676–7.

Our perspective is thus in contradiction with Marx when he argues that personal provisions of work performed by free workers are bought only for the purposes of consumption. We argue that Marx's perspective cannot be applied to the reproduction of domestic work and that of prostitution. While these are represented as personal services, they are, in reality, bought not only for purposes of production, but also for production in which consumption is doubly productive for capital. This means that the development of the capitalist mode of production tends to destroy personal services performed for the purposes of production by free workers, but it does so only in the context of commodity production. When we consider reproduction, on the other hand, the capitalist mode of production tends to develop such services in their capitalist form in which the relationship of domestic labour and prostitution is shaped as indirectly waged.

This double exchange falls, on the formal plane, within the relation of simple circulation, as the worker buys the woman's personal service for purposes of his own individual consumption. The worker and the woman are, in fact, reciprocally exchanging use values: he is exchanging his wage and means of subsistence; she is exchanging specific work (domestic work or that of prostitution) that the worker consumes directly. The difference between past labour objectified in the wage and that of its present living labour which exists as domestic work and prostitution presents itself here as a formal difference between past and present temporalities of labour. There is in fact only a formal difference, mediated by the division of labour and by exchange, in these two scenarios: the one in which it is the woman herself who produces her own means of subsistence; and the other where she receives her means of subsistence indirectly from the worker in return for the material and immaterial use values she produces for him.

As explained above, these use values require a certain amount of domestic work or prostitution, and thus they materialise not only as a use value but also as value. Such value does not exist for the worker, however, because he consumes the use values produced by the woman rather than trading them. Within the exchange, the worker does not receive domestic work and prostitution as work that can create value, but as creative activity that produces a use value that he consumes as such, without transforming it from an activity into a thing. In the case of domestic work, given that the woman does not receive money but only immediate use values, it seems that, in the exchange between the waged worker and the houseworker as much as in other simple relationships, the distinction between values and use values may be irrelevant. Even if the worker paid money for the domestic labour he received, this would not mean a transformation of his money into capital. Let us consider just one of the use values necessary for the worker to reproduce himself: food, for example – not in a general sense but prepared so that it can be immediately consumed. To the worker, it does not matter whether the food is prepared by the houseworker, by the waged domestic helper or by the waged worker (of whatever gender) at the deli around the corner. All that matters to him is that he eats. Generally speaking, he proceeds with the first option, the exchange with the houseworker, because this is the most efficient solution for him in all aspects. First, the food costs less; second, the houseworker prepares meals of whatever he wants, however he wants it prepared, at the time that he wants it (within certain limits which are becoming narrower by the day). She also guarantees him, in addition to food, the production of all material and immaterial use values that he needs to reproduce himself. It follows that, for the worker, it is advantageous overall to exchange with the houseworker.

In any of the cases mentioned above, the worker does not transform money, with which he buys ready-made food, into capital, but simply transforms money into food. He uses money merely as a means of circulation, without converting it into a specific use value. Even though, in the first and second options, he buys labour itself as a commodity, money does not function here for the worker as capital, but merely as money and, more precisely, as a means of circulation.

None of these people – the houseworker, the domestic assistant, the deli worker – are productive workers in the eyes of the factory worker. This is true even though each of them provides the worker, through their labour, with a product – ready-to-eat food – and he compensates them for the price of their labour with money or the direct means of subsistence. The factory worker is absolutely indifferent to the fact that these workers' labour might be greater than the money or the means of subsistence they receive from him. He cares only about the use value, ready-to-eat food. Naturally, whether he buys it in one way or the other, he has an interest in paying as little as possible, about paying only its normal price, because this is an expense for his consumption, a reduction, and not an increase in his money.

The same thing happens in the exchange between worker and prostitute. The work of prostitution is understood in this case not as a use value that produces value, but as work that only produces a specific use value. The exchange seems not to produce wealth, but to consume it. Following Marx, we reiterate that, for the worker, the problem is not that a certain amount of labour time and thus of value is objectified in the material and immaterial use values produced by the houseworker, but simply that they satisfy some of his needs. The money he exchanges with the houseworker or the prostitute is not money that, by buying domestic work or prostitution, can be conserved and valued.

In their exchange with the worker, domestic work and prostitution are accepted as specific use values in which the form of value is purely evanescent. The greater continuity there is within this exchange, the more impoverished the worker becomes. The exchange of money as wage with the living labour of domestic work or prostitution cannot establish money as capital for the worker. This means that this specific kind of labour cannot be established as waged labour in a purely economic sense, because the worker, while spending his wage, is obviously not producing money. Moreover, because it is money that mediates this exchange, the determination of its price will become important not just for the worker but also for the woman. That this price is determined economically, through the relationship of supply and demand or through the production costs required to produce the houseworker and the prostitute, does not modify the substance of the relationship because the determination of the price is still always a formal moment for the exchange of simple use values.

The discourse changes completely if we consider the same situation on the level of the real. Our double exchange is an exchange where women's personal services are bought for the purposes of production of a commodity: labour power. Here, the worker is a liaison for capital in the purchase of labour power, both as the capacity of production and reproduction of labour power, and as the sexual reproduction of male labour power. These exchanges thus belong without a doubt to the relationship of complex circulation. *The double exchange belongs indirectly to the relationship of complex circulation only insofar as it belongs directly to the relationship of simple circulation on a formal plane.* The result is that domestic work and the work of prostitution, which *appear* devalued by capital on the macro level (to the extent that they are posited as natural and unnatural social labour power respectively) and valued by the worker (because he is the one who exchanges with them), serve actually *to value capital and devalue the worker*.

On the other hand, there is an exchange that clearly belongs to simple circulation: that between prostitute and pimp. This exchange is born out of the need for protection, which derives from the kind of labour the prostitute performs. She cannot, in fact, demand that her civil rights be guaranteed during her duties by bourgeois law, because as a prostitute she is considered an illegal (even criminal) worker. When she resorts to the pimp, however, she is buying protective labour and that means she must pay him for her status as an illegal or criminal worker, because she cannot expect that even he will guarantee her civil rights. This is one of the reasons why the costs – in terms of income consumption and violence – that women must pay in this relationship have always been high.

The need for protection is not the only aspect of this relationship. There is also the prostitute's reproductive sphere, which is even more problematic than that of the housewife. As opposed to the latter, the prostitute does not need to find a husband for whom to work and with whom to reproduce within marriage. She is in fact already working, and often with better pay. What she needs is someone with whom she can exchange for the reproduction of both parties. This person – someone who would be available to reproduce her sexually, emotionally, affectively – cannot be, generally speaking, a factory worker. This is true both because he needs a *wife*, a woman who will be a housewife and attend to all aspects of his reproduction or at least the greater part, and because he is a legal worker who lives in a different environment, with different reproductive habits.

The man who can reproduce a prostitute, and reproduce himself in the relationship with her, must protect her and must be someone who does not work, so he is professionally criminal or at least prepared to act illegally. He must be a man who belongs to her environment and is thus not in need of a wife. In exchange for what he gives her, he demands an extremely high price. This is both because the kind of commodity he offers has a very restricted market, and because, if he does so, the social relationship between him and the prostitute – and its related exchange – is configured in a similar way to that between the worker and the houseworker; though in this case it is the woman who pays the man – and thus the relation is not humiliating for him.

The possibilities of reproduction, which are freed for the prostitute by having plenty of money, as opposed to other women, and thus by not having to perform domestic labour for men, are however paralysed by capital which surrounds her on the level of her own reproduction. The sex worker is forced to compensate so much for the fact of having money that, even when it is she who is paying a man, the relationship between the two cannot be represented as such. In this exchange, even though she is the source, the owner of the money, it is the pimp who is the master. This is because the bribe he asks is so high that he acts as if he were the master controlling her labour and granting her some money that is, at this point, much closer to that of the average female income. In other words, the exchange can exist without becoming too threatening only if the work of the pimp has a price so high that it seems that the prostitute is – and ultimately she really is – the one working for him, and not the other way around. Only in this way, with the relationship presenting itself as a reversal of its real arrangement, can it be more readily assimilated to the general relationship between men and women.

The history of the prostitute's reproduction has obviously been much more complex, as it has often developed within the social fabric of the working class. Many wives and mothers of the working class have been prostitutes. There is no doubt that a great part of the income of proletarian families has always come, and still does come, from prostitution. At the same time, many working husbands have pretended not to know how their wives rounded up the family's wages to make it to the end of the month. There has also been a large segment of prostitutes who were able to escape the exchange with the pimp, with all its restraints and bribes: so-called clandestine prostitution. This has been particularly relevant during the organised struggles of sex workers as the role of the pimp has increasingly declined. This mass rejection of the pimp by prostitutes is related to many factors, both objective and subjective. Among them we can mention:

1. the much less rigid separation between prostitution and the marriage market resulting from the cycle of struggle during the 1970s (a woman who works as a prostitute or has done such work has a lot less difficulty in finding a husband who may reproduce her even outside a criminal environment);

2. the large diffusion of lesbianism everywhere, including among sex workers (as a consequence, the prostitute is less affectively, sentimentally and sexually blackmailed by males and, at the same time, can reproduce without having to pay exorbitant economic costs);
3. the greater mobility acquired by female labour power generally speaking (so that a woman today can move more easily not only from one city to another, but also from one productive sector to another);
4. the enormous growth of part-time work in prostitution; and
5. the greater organising power and solidarity gained in these years of struggle, both among prostitutes and with women who do not work in the sector.

Through these years, it has emerged that the pimp and the client are just the initial object of struggle. The final objective is the state. The state is the great, true pimp that tries to impose price controls on prostitutes' incomes relative to those of other women, bleeding prostitutes dry through fines, multiple financial penalties, incarcerations and so on. The state is the true exploiter not just of houseworkers, but also of sex workers. It is against the same objective, the state, that the struggle of the former must connect to the struggle of the latter, by immediately assuming the objective of international feminist strategy: say no to the criminalisation of prostitution.

The Market of Female Labour

Let us linger another moment within the sphere of circulation to examine the question from another perspective. The exchanges we are interested in belong to the sphere of circulation of capital, which means they operate for purposes of production. Living labour – as domestic work and that of prostitution – thus fully belongs to that particular section of commodity circulation constituted by the labour-market. To claim this is to say that the labour-market is, in reality, very different than it appears: that it has a hidden life which twists, turns and unwinds unexpectedly for those who remain focused on surface appearances. This hidden life has somewhat come to light following the recent debate on the magnitude of illicit work and the black market. Previously however, the feminist movement had already revealed how its structure was much more complex, because it included sectors such as domestic work and prostitution that, although subterranean, were nonetheless fundamental.

This statement is in sharp contrast with the argument made by Marx, who excludes prostitution from even the relative surplus population to place it, together with 'vagabonds [and] criminals', within the lumpenproletariat.[11]

In other words, it is sufficient to recognise the morbid sensitivity and obsessive interest of capital in the sexual, racial and generational composition of labour power to understand why the real labour-market does not correspond with the waged labour-market, as is generally assumed, but includes the market of indirectly waged labour, of reproduction and prostitution. The functioning of the labour-market is thus rather complex: first, because it works on multiple levels – an official level of waged labour; an unofficial level of domestic labour; an illegal level of the labour of prostitution; and an 'underground' level of black-market labour. Second, because the labour-market includes sectors that are governed by laws that are very different from each other, separated from each other rigidly, and organised within a precise hierarchy, this reflects the stratification of power that exists within the class.

What we are interested in here is examining the circulation of female labour power. With this term we do not mean exclusively the waged market of female labour, but also, and primarily, the market of reproductive labour. This area of the market is that most overlooked by economists, but it is, I argue, one of the foundational pillars of the labour-market. These two arenas, constituted by reproductive labour and waged labour (acknowledged and accounted for or not), are the two major pillars of the labour-market. Separated from the latter through the line of sex, reproductive labour is generally positioned as a female labour-market, while waged labour must position itself primarily as a male labour-market. This separation functions within certain limits, because, although the market is fundamentally rigid, it must be flexible enough to allow the use of female labour power in production – both as a secondary workforce and, whenever the need arises, even as a massive influx. In fact, such a separation has not been able to confront the influx of women into the waged labour-market (mainly the black market), an influx that was massive in the 1970s.

---

11   Marx, *Capital*, 797.

However, this influx has been conveyed in the section of the female waged labour-market that is most separated from, and subordinate to, that of male waged labour, a sector dependent on domestic labour, as we will see below. The dimension of this influx is indeed considerable. In the United States, for example, more than 50 per cent of female labour power is now active in the production process. Whatever the dimension, it has not modified the status of this sector within the hierarchical structure of the labour-market. Female waged labour remains subaltern to male waged labour, both in terms of the salary and quality of such labour. It also remains corollary and dependent on domestic labour. This remains true despite the fact that waged labour has been used by women as crucial leverage in their struggles against domestic labour, to reject it and dump it first on the husband/partner, and subsequently on the state.

The market of reproductive labour is divided into two sections – domestic labour and that of prostitution – of which the first is fundamental and the second corollary. These two sectors are also internally differentiated, but, in this case, they are separated from one another through the line of legality that differentiates licit and illicit trades. As we already know, even though it was induced by capital, this separation has become very flexible, especially over the past century as a consequence of women's pressure to modify the structure of the labour-market to meet their new needs. For example, the entry and exit of female labour power from the two markets has become much more frequent and casual, and the labour-market of prostitution has grown beyond any limit of functionality and safety for the capitalist organisation of society.

These two important separations – male waged labour/reproductive labour and reproductive labour/prostitution – underlie the labour-market, dividing it through the lines of gender and legality. The first separation entails the interdependence of the two sectors considered, and the second separation their complementarity, but both are necessary to guarantee the conservation and reproduction of the working class. This guarantee is established through different strategies. On the one hand, it is achieved by commanding workers and housewives to *marry the wage with the non-wage* for the construction of the working-class family. On the other hand, it is done by commanding workers and prostitutes to exchange the wage with the work of prostitution for the very preservation of the working-class family. When we say command, we mean capitalist command. Marx affirms that 'the capitalist may safely leave [the maintenance and reproduction of the working class] to the worker's drives for self-preservation and propagation', and he is correct insofar as we specify that the mode of capitalist production had, since its birth, to organise the transformation of this drive into a capitalist relationship.[12]

In this context, the first sector to investigate by revisiting all the elements of its functioning is obviously that of domestic labour.

Let us first consider the family, which assumes a precise function both as a centre for the formation of domestic labour power and as its arena of permanence, of its exit and entrance into the labour-market.

The law governing this section is as follows. In the waged labour-market, the active industrial army is accompanied by a reserve industrial army; in the market of domestic labour there is no such reserve at all. The law is reversed. In the first case, the relative surplus population is both the result of the development of labour productivity and 'condition for the existence of the capitalist mode of production'. In the second case, full employment is the necessary product of capitalist accumulation and acts as a leverage for accumulation, if not as one of the very conditions of existence for the capitalist mode of production.

Faced with domestic labour framed as a natural force of social labour, capital has every interest in ensuring that all women, in their totality, are houseworkers. Full employment in domestic work can be established because it is a hidden form of employment. Starting from the premise that the labour-market coincides with waged labour, and that the only commodity circulating in it is labour power as a capacity to engage in production, economists have thus far framed housewives in the category of the inactive population – or, if considering them at all, have regarded them as a reserve industrial army. Moreover, economists have defined the female labour-market by assuming it as synonymous with waged female labour. Because we start from the opposite premise, we must reformulate such definitions by turning them upside down.

We begin to redefine the female labour-market starting from a critical analysis of marriage which arises as the work contract (and relationship) between a non-waged houseworker and a waged factory worker. As such, it is, in reality, the fundamental *work contract* for female labour power, even if it is not represented as such to the contracting parties.

12   Ibid., 718.

Quite to the contrary, it can only exist as a domestic work contract insofar as it does not appear as such. This explains the gap that exists between the wage contract and the marriage contract. From early on, the waged labour-market has not had two defined protagonists – two owners of different commodities, isolated on the market as separate individuals. Rather, it has had two major social classes, both with their respective institutionalised organisations for collective bargaining. On the contrary, in the market of domestic labour, the exchange of labour power continued to have the subjects of the exchange as protagonists, isolated on the market as two separate individuals. In other words, marriage is a work relation which is not formally subject to collective bargaining between two major social aggregates, otherwise it could not exist as a relationship of indirectly waged domestic labour. This has consequences, of course, based on the kind of work relation that exists. First, let us consider competition. While competition soon more or less ceased to exist between factory workers, it persists to a greater extent between houseworkers. While the market of waged labour is free only on a formal level, the market of domestic labour is *freer* in this regard – not always on a formal level but also in reality, although within certain limits.

The question of competition is much more complex than this. If it is true that competition exists between workers in the waged labour-market, it is also true that it exists between the active industrial army and the industrial reserve army. The latter, 'during the periods of stagnation and average prosperity, weighs down the active army of workers; during the periods of over-production and feverish activity, it puts a curb on their pretensions'.[13] This pushes the supply and demand law to move in the context of the relative surplus population. By contrast, within the market of domestic labour, the competition between individual house-workers is counterbalanced by the fact that there is no domestic reserve army. The law of supply and demand thus works in the context of a tendency towards full employment, which mitigates and balances out competition derived from the non-existence of a collective bargaining of domestic labour.

What we are interested in here is not so much whether there is more competition within the male or female working class, but to highlight

---

13   Ibid., 792.

that, behind every proletarian man and woman, there are different histories of organisation required to break their shackles, and different paths of struggle to negotiate, either collectively or individually, based on their respective needs.

Another consequence of the true nature of marriage is that, while it is not subject to collective bargaining, it cannot be a *private contract*, because the production of surplus value depends on it. Capital has the inescapable need to guarantee for itself the regulation of such a contract, and it does so in the only way it can: by intervening through the state whose authority establishes the content of the marriage contract. Today, while the intervention of the state is still functioning for the most part, several elements of its operations have been jeopardised. First, the official content of the marriage contract has been changing because of the ways in which it is regulated through individual, bottom-up practices (by means of private legal agreements, for example). Second, the rejection of marriage itself, seen as an intervention by the state on the regulation of personal relationships, has been more and more frequent and it has also revealed the more clandestine development of an alternative form of relationship between men and women. Third, many couples now do not intend to have children or they do not have the necessary resources (time and money) to take care of children. Fourth, the marriage contract is now entered into independently between women: there are an increasing number of lesbians who decide to marry without having children or who raise children they have adopted (or brought from previous marriages). This arrangement would not change anything at a productive level except that this tendency throws into crisis the state's control of the human body and sexual identity of the population, which is so intimately connected to the structuring of social roles. This profoundly affects the capital and state control of social organisation and discipline, as well as the gendered division of labour and how the whole society is designed. Obviously, if marriage is the fundamental contractual relationship of female labour power, divorce represents its rupture, and this is why divorce corresponds, within the process of production and reproduction, to dismissal and resignation within the process of production.

We also redefine the female labour-market through a critique of the concepts of female employment rate and labour mobility. While economists argue that the female employment rate is expressed by the ratio between the number of women who are of working age and women who are obviously employed in the production process, we argue that such a rate is expressed by the relationship between the number of women who are of marriageable age and that of married women. In this context, the minimum age at which a woman can marry must be understood as the age from which a woman can be employed. At the same time, the minimum age at which a woman is married must be understood as the average age of her entrance in the female labour army. It follows that women's occupational mobility rate is, in our perspective, given by the relation between the number of divorced women and the number of remarried women.

Labour mobility is increasingly an emerging character of domestic labour power, and it has some contradictory aspects. On the one hand, divorce overturns one of the fundamental conditions of the exchange between variable capital and domestic labour: that of the indeterminacy of the duration of the exchange. In other words, divorce challenges the assumption that domestic labour power cannot be mobile, and that it can only be an uninterrupted working continuum. In overturning the exchange and the relationship between the factory worker and the houseworker, divorce functions as a negative element for capital. Its negativity is accentuated by the fact that the rupture of one domestic labour contract to start another causes a major decrease in terms of absolute productivity for the entire family unit.

On the other hand, divorce also has a certain positive impact for capital. When the relations of production between a man and a woman no longer function, and there is a lowering of productivity which is destined to linger forever, divorce opens up new possibilities for the two parties (and for capital). They can remarry, and thus the productivity of the houseworker and of the entire household can increase. Until the 1960s in the United States, and the 1970s in Italy, divorce was often the prelude to another marriage, often a more successful marriage because it was undertaken with greater maturity and experience.

For capital, however, the negative aspects of divorce have been preponderant in the last decade. We have seen, in fact, a more workerist than capitalist use of divorce – especially by women. In recent times, divorce has functioned more as a destruction of the marriage institution than an attempt to repair it. It often ends the marriage career, as more and more women, once divorced, do not remarry. Today, the mobility of houseworkers' labour power often precedes divorce or is separated from divorce because increasing numbers of women do not marry at all and have relationships that start and finish outside any statistical registration or state control.

'Underemployment' and 'unemployment' must also be redefined in the context of a different understanding of the female labour-market. A woman of a certain age who does not position herself as a wife or mother, and thus does not belong, for any given reason, to the domestic labour force, is to be considered underemployed. This means that this woman performs domestic labour in a limited way with respect to her potential work capacity. The following women are thus underemployed: a single mother, insofar as she does not reproduce a husband; a childless married woman, insofar as she does not reproduce her children's labour power in addition to that of her husband; a widow; and a divorced or separated woman who does not remarry, insofar as she does not reproduce a husband. A woman who, within specific age limits, remains unmarried, and thus does not reproduce a husband or a wife and does not produce and reproduce children, is to be considered *not employed*. We do not use the term 'unemployed' here, because a woman who does not live off private income in the capitalist world always necessarily reproduces labour power: first and foremost, her own.

A redefinition of the current meaning and terminology of the female labour-market is necessary to express the precise consequences derived from the laws of full employment, which, as we have seen, regulate the domestic labour-market. The consequences are:

1. The female employment rate must be as high as possible. This means that the number of women who comprise the recorded female population of marriageable age must tend to coincide, broadly speaking, with the number of married women.
2. Likewise, the mobility level of female labour must also be as high as possible. As much as the capitalist mode of production demands and entails that all women of marriageable age be married, it also demands and entails that they remarry in cases where they divorce. In sum, the capitalist mode of production demands that every woman always and everywhere has a man and some children for whom to work. This is the motto of capital.

3. The number of underemployed and non-employed women must be minimal. This is because the houseworker's underemployment and non-employment do not perform any productive function with respect to the process of capitalist accumulation. They are, instead, an obstacle. This explains capitalist society's condemnation of underemployed and non-employed women (for example, the social contempt expressed for 'spinsters'). This might appear a moral and ideological condemnation; it is, in fact, a condemnation of their low level of production in domestic labour.

4. The period of time for which houseworkers are employed must be full time. The only limits to this period of time should be the birth and death of the woman herself.

Given the specific character of the exchange between factory worker and houseworker, once she is employed, a woman can never retire: not only because she must continue to reproduce the worker once they are retired, but also because she must continue to be a mother forever. Not only must she be the mother of his own children, but, if they produce their respective families, she must be a mother for their grandchildren as well.

Full employment also means that a period dedicated to apprenticeship must be concluded before the employment relationship starts, and that this period must be as full of work as subsequent domestic labour itself. For the future houseworker, the period preceding employment must be a full-time apprenticeship. A woman must learn from infancy how to perform domestic work from her mother but only partially what such work entails. We say *partially* here because, as opposed to the apprenticeship in waged labour, that of domestic labour between mother and daughter is really a partial education and a partial training. This is true both quantitatively and with respect to the content of the domestic labour that the houseworker will have to supply as a mother and wife. The new labour power will be educated and trained only for the domestic labour she must be able to supply. On anything else, she will be given only highly ideological and very limited information. This is necessary because the division of domestic labour must guarantee at all costs not only the privatisation and individualisation of knowledge regarding sexuality and maternity, but also a lack of knowledge about the real magnitude of the workload that marriage entails for a woman.

The working continuity described above means that, within the family, women perform, at the mass level, both child labour and labour into old age. In fact, these two kinds of labour are the conditions for the existence of the domestic labour-market. This is not the case in the waged labour-market, where neither child labour (although it persists in spite of juridical regulation) nor the labour of the older adults constitute necessary conditions of existence.

It is evident from what we have said so far of the female labour-market that any struggle over marriage, divorce, sexual identity, illegitimate children and refusal of maternity must be reinterpreted as struggles that undermine the mechanism of capitalist accumulation itself. This must be emphasised, as it is of utmost importance. Those who continue to speak of the 'transformation of customs', as if nothing had happened, do not grasp the true character of these behaviours. Women's struggles must be interpreted within the process of class struggle as directly affecting the production of surplus value.

As for the market for the labour of prostitution, let us start by acknowledging that there are too few direct testimonies, voices beyond the official declarations, which as we know are unreliable. As a result, what can be said about prostitution is very limited.

Without going into details, we can say that, within the prostitution market, both the active army of prostitutes and the reserve army that accompanies it are illegal, and thus *sui generis*:

1. they do not reveal themselves as such;
2. the full dimension of such work cannot be greatly known or controlled by the state since the demand from which it originates, with all its modifications and contractions, cannot be regulated.

Given these particular characteristics, any attempt to apply the laws of the labour-market in this sector is quite problematic. Today this is truer than ever, because of the higher number of women who work in the black market of prostitution – that is, the market that evades the control of the pimp (whether he is entrepreneur or exploiter), and thus the control of the state. However, this illegal engagement in the work of prostitution has consequences for the organisation of this work that reach far beyond the state's lack of control over the mass of women employed in this sector alone. The first effect has been on the sex worker's income, which grows as it is increasingly freed from the payment of bribes to the pimp or to the state. Another concerns sex workers' employment, which has become more and more part time, following the well-known adage that the better work is paid, the less one is forced to work.

Another effect of women's increasingly workerist use of prostitution concerns the sphere of reproduction. The prostitute's reproduction functions less and less through the mediation of a pimp: a relationship which implies paying a man handsomely both to be reproduced by him and for the work of reproducing him. Yet another effect concerns the conditions of the work of prostitution. When a prostitute is released from the protection of the pimp, her conditions of work become, to a greater degree, self-managed and more and more favourable for entering and exiting from the market of prostitution at will. If the full-time entrance into this market was, in the past, relatively coerced, because, among other things, it was a mandatory transition for the woman who transgressed the rules of the marriage market, this is no longer true today for a large segment of women. Many women enter prostitution because they *choose* to – as much as one can choose in a capitalist society within specific limits – and they also make this choice because this is a better-paid sector of the female labour-market, and its level of danger has been consistently diminishing.

The same argument is valid for the conditions of *exit* from the market. If, in the past, these conditions restricted women's freedom and once a woman entered the market it was very difficult to leave, today they are much more liberalised. The struggles of the 1970s in particular have managed to sweep away some of the slave-like character that marked this specific sector, although this character remains common for immigrant women or victims of human trafficking.

However, the fact remains that, in the market of prostitution, as with that of domestic labour, labour power continues to have only its own parties of exchange as protagonists – that is, it is still not characterised by collective bargaining.

Although one might think that competition would be at a maximum in this sector, given that the existence of individual bargaining is coupled with the pressure of the reserve army, competition is rather limited by the fact that supply rarely exceeds demand. After the most recent cycle of organised struggle in 1975, led by prostitutes in Lyon, sex workers have been vocal in their demands on the state, about matters including retirement, fines, child custody and criminalisation.[14] In doing so, they have been raising once again the question of collective bargaining. These struggles have often been wrongly labelled as trade unionism by those who either think that the labour of prostitution must be destroyed or consider its conditions unsuitable for collective bargaining. In reality, the struggle in Lyon has shown quite lucidly that bringing these problems to the table opens up so many contradictions for the state that collective bargaining for prostitution cannot be framed in terms compatible with capitalism because it would greatly disrupt the structure of the state itself, its assets and institutions.

As for the conditions of permanence within the market, it must be clarified that, as opposed to the market of domestic labour, that of prostitution is not subordinate to the laws of marriage; rather, it is both complementary and at the same time opposed to the institution. In prostitution, a woman ceases to be primarily a housewife. She is a prostitute first – she is a sex worker, and, as such, she is not allowed to be wife and mother at the same time. Her status as prostitute jeopardises her role as a housewife, not the other way round (as would otherwise be the case), where her role as housewife would *directly determine* the conditions of being a prostitute, as with any other form of waged female labour.

We emphasise the direct nature of this determination because, at its root, it is always a woman's existence as a housewife on the social level that determines the conditions of prostitution itself. For any other waged labour, it is the cycle of domestic labour that structures the conditions of entry, duration and exit from this market. For labour as prostitution, this dynamic is reversed: it is the labour of prostitution that prevents the unfolding of such a cycle, and the birth and growth of children. In fact, the capitalist division of sexual work does not mean only a division between prostitute and housewife, but also the impossibility of the prostitute being at the same time wife and mother. It is not a coincidence that child custody for sex workers has been one of the most important points of 1970s struggles.

---

14   Fortunati refers here to the famous ten-day occupation by French sex workers of the church of Saint-Nizier in Lyon, starting on 2 June 1975. The event incited a series of solidarity actions at other French churches and was galvanising for a range of feminist movements, Lotta Femminista and the Wages for Housework campaigns in particular.

Obviously, the cycle of struggles of the 1970s have also precipitated huge transformations in the conditions of permanence for women in the prostitution market. On the one hand, many prostitutes today are also housewives, and vice versa, in such entanglement that the existing separation between housewife and prostitute, between the market of domestic labour and that of prostitution, between the one productive sector and the other, have become extremely flexible. This is also a consequence of a more ambitious bargaining with men over money – more so than over other commodities – and of the end of the obligation to save sex (always previously a sacrifice on the part of the woman). On the other hand, the aspect of prostitution present in marriage, and in every other relationship with men, emerges from the abyss of ideology in a self-evident fashion. It emerges in the acquisition of the consciousness that we are all prostitutes, the discovery that prostitution, a monster with many heads, with many nuances and variations, is recomposing itself and is taking shape throughout the entire social body.

As has been said, there is a separation, within the market of waged labour, between female and male labour. Such separation is caused by the fact that the former is subordinate to the domestic labour-market, such that it develops different, if not opposed, characteristics from the latter. For a woman, the conditions of entry, duration and exit from the extra-domestic labour-market are different from those of male workers. Let us examine the time periods of entry into waged labour by female labour power within the duration of her working life. We immediately see that the curve of her activity rises precisely at the moment in which her domestic workload is not so great as to be incompatible with extra-domestic labour, for example when she does not have children to tend to. The curve then falls in the period of maximum productivity of domestic labour, in relation to the care of young children, and then, in some countries, rises again when children are older and require less labour. At least this was the case before the last decade, when a new tendency in the dynamic of female extra-domestic employment emerged. The cycle of domestic labour does not have enough weight and strength to bend the curve of the female extra-domestic employment rate up or down. Today, women tend to start wage labour again immediately after their children are born.

In Italy, where capital managed to command a domestic working day of exceptional length and intensity, marriage and children meant

a definitive exit from, rather than an interruption of, women's participation in extra-domestic labour, or at least from the official waged
labour-market. It is evident from the rises and falls in the rate of extra-
domestic female labour that it is the cycle of domestic labour that
drives it. Extra-domestic female labour is established as temporary
employment to functionalise and augment, when and insofar as possible and convenient, women's permanent employment: domestic labour
within marriage. The entry of female labour power into the waged
labour-market before marriage is motivated either by the need to
supplement the budget of the family of origin (as in many working-
class families) or for women to maintain themselves. But these
conditions are also an attempt to escape domestic work as far as possible, transferring it on to the mother or other caregivers. It is not only
when, but also *for how long* women remain in extra-domestic labour
that is determined by the overall female production cycle, which is
primarily a domestic one.

The conditions in which female labour power exits from the extra-
domestic labour-market are also very specific. While, for male workers,
these conditions are either retirement or layoff, the most common form
of interruption to a waged labour relationship for women is voluntary
resignation. This moment usually coincides with the woman's entry, as
houseworker, into the most productive cycle of domestic labour and thus
into a period incompatible with extra-domestic labour. Not all employed
women exit from waged labour because they have reached retirement
age. Even in those cases, not all women who retire have undertaken the
maximum length of waged working life.

Understanding the specificities that mark the conditions of entry into,
duration and exit from the waged labour-market of female labour power,
and the specific causes behind these conditions, requires us to offer yet
another political interpretation of the vicissitudes of female labour
power that is different from the one through which economists have
been working to address the problems of the labour-market.

For example, if we want to examine the struggles against layoffs
within a female waged labour-market, we must remember that the real
problem is not the *exit* from such a market, which has its origins in the
cycle of domestic labour, but it is the question of who *decides* the details
of any specific exit. In other words, the problem is not the layoff itself,
but determining whether the woman voluntarily resigned or if she was

fired by her employer. We also must bear in mind that women have rarely had the time and space for struggles against layoffs from their extra-domestic employment, precisely because the question here is one of time and space.

When a woman is fired, she does not become unemployed, but generally returns to full-time domestic labour. For women, being fired does not mean being jobless. On the contrary, it means having to do a full-time job, one that, when she was employed in extra-domestic work, she would perform 'before going to work' and on 'return from work', and then on Sundays, Saturdays and during all vacations and holidays. It means that the home, her primary workplace, now becomes the workplace to which she is perpetually chained. Domestic labour and the home thus become formidable instruments in the division between women who have been fired, impeding their possibility of struggle in extra-domestic labour. Moreover, the question is one of the importance of specific struggles for women. Given that a layoff is, for women, merely an anticipation of the eventual exit from extra-domestic labour at the optimal moment for marriage, women often respond to a layoff by quickly marrying – that is, entering the market that is fundamental for their labour. In such circumstances, struggle against layoffs could not be advantageous for women, because it would have meant starting from the tail end, and not the head, of her exploitation, and in all probability, it would have been a losing struggle.

Today, women's position regarding layoffs is rapidly changing. Capital forces women into an increasingly stable relationship with waged labour, even when there are young children to tend to. This radically redefines women's interest in defending their workplace and income. Women started to determine through absenteeism the conditions of their permanence in the waged labour-market, so that they were able to define not just their working hours but the wage of their entire working day. In fact, the rate of women's absenteeism is much higher than that of men. What has absenteeism been for women if not *a specific and macroscopic form of struggle for the appropriation of a wage for domestic labour*, and for the reduction of the overall working hours?

The female sector of the waged labour-market develops the mobility of its labour power in a particular fashion owing to the discontinuity of women's extra-domestic work life. There are a very high number of female job candidates circulating through extra-domestic workplaces.

Rather than coming from other sectors of extra-domestic work, these candidates come from women's primary productive sector – the home. Moreover, this number is destined to grow because of the increasing number of women working in the black market. For the bosses, the turnover of female workers has had many advantages: first, the factories are guaranteed a continuous fresh supply of working energy; further, they can continuously disrupt the organising efforts of a female workforce by breaking their organising ranks whenever such develop; and, in the process, they introduce future working-class housewives into the domestic labour-market who have been disciplined for the family by working in the factory.[15]

The third element developing very differently in the two sectors we are considering here is that constituted by the relative wages of men and women. For equal rank and performing the same tasks, women make much less than men. Endless discussions have been had, and national and international data have been analysed on the so-called *gender pay gap* that affects women in the extra-domestic labour-market. No one, however, has ever enquired seriously into the different conditions of female and male labour power as they present themselves on the waged labour-market. While we are not taking up this task here, it is important to say that, while the male worker is a free worker, the female worker is a less-free worker, given that she is selling waged labour power which is subordinate to her ability to produce and reproduce labour power. The latter is her primary trade, though it is not represented as a trade of commodities. It is clear that these different starting points imply different abilities to bargain for a wage, which explains women's apparent willingness to accept extra-domestic employment at wages far below those of men.

---

15 In English in the original.

6

The Hidden Abode: On the Domestic Working Process as a Process of Valorisation

We enter now, finally, together with the factory worker – the holder of the wage – and the houseworker – the owner of domestic labour power – into the secret laboratory where labour power is produced.[1] Here, we do not examine the working process of reproduction in its entirety, but only in its fundamental sector, constituted by the cycle of production and reproduction of labour power – a cycle always present in any process of production. We choose to visit only this wing of the laboratory, both to make the discussion more agile and simple, and because this analysis, being the most crucial, constitutes a solid point of departure for that of the other working processes that give life to the general process of reproduction.

What is the image that the process of production and reproduction of labour power returns to us? We have already said as much but will

---

1   The opening passages of this chapter play on the famous concluding passages of Chapter 6 of Marx's *Capital*, which describe the descent into 'the hidden abode of production' in the company of the two subjects of production: 'the owner of money and the owner of labour-power'. Karl Marx, *Capital*, vol. 1, *A Critique of Political Economy*, trans. Ben Fowkes (London: Penguin, New Left Review: 1990 [1976]), 279. Cantimori's Italian translation of the 'hidden abode' rendered Marx's 'die verborgene Stätte der Produktion' as the 'segreto laboratorio della produzione' – literally, 'the secret laboratory of production'. We maintain the literal translation of 'laboratory' here because, at times, Fortunati plays on the idea of the laboratory of reproduction as a building with multiple wings or research branches.

repeat it here: reproduction presents itself as the mirror image, the photographic negative of the production process. In reproduction, labour power as capacity of production is produced. In production, this labour power is consumed. In production, the worker is a means to labour, while in reproduction the worker is the object of labour, and his means of subsistence are instruments of labour for the woman. These two processes of production oppose one another. In production, the exchange value of labour power as a capacity of production is produced, and its use value is consumed. In reproduction, the use value of labour power is produced, and exchange value consumed. The laboratory of the process of production and reproduction of labour power is not simply the site of production of labour power, but it is simultaneously the site where the process of the worker's individual consumption takes place. In the production process, the worker's labour power is consumed. Here, it is reproduced through the consumption performed by the worker. In the domestic working process, the labour power consumed is that of the houseworker, so that a double consumption of labour power occurs.

When Marx affirms that 'the process of the consumption of labour power is, at the same time, the production process of commodities and of surplus-value', he is clearly talking about the productive consumption of labour power that takes place in the arena of production, and not addressing the double consumption that takes places in the sphere of reproduction.[2]

We argue that the process of consumption of labour power produces commodities and surplus value not only when it takes place in the arena of production, but also when it takes place in that of reproduction. This means that the dual consumption occurring in reproduction is doubly productive. On the one hand, it is productive as the worker's individual consumption produces and reproduces the individual as a commodity. On the other hand, it is productive because the process of consumption of domestic labour power is simultaneously the production process of a commodity and of surplus value.

Three points need to be mentioned in the context of this process. First, there is no direct consumption of the means of subsistence on the part of the worker; rather, domestic labour is positioned between the

---

2   Marx, *Capital*, vol. 1, 279.

worker and his individual consumption. Consequently, variable capital represents the sum total of the values of the means of subsistence of labour power understood as both the capacity of commodity production and the production and reproduction of labour power. The only direct individual consumption that does not simultaneously presuppose the consumption of one's own means of subsistence as the means of subsistence of someone else's labour is the domestic worker's consumption. Second, domestic work, as an activity in accordance with its purpose, is the labour of production and reproduction of labour power. This means that the purpose and the product of domestic labour is labour power. Third, domestic labour, as is the case with any other labour, 'uses up its material elements, its objects and its instruments. It consumes them and is therefore a process of consumption.'[3]

As stated above, the worker's individual consumption presupposes the productive consumption of reproduction and simultaneously differs from it. The productive consumption of the worker in reproduction consumes products as a means of subsistence; in other words, it is the actualisation of the houseworker's labour power. The product of the worker's individual consumption – which is the same consumer – is different from the result of the productive consumption. This product is the labour power of the worker and future workers as commodities; in other words, this is the commodity produced in this working process. Now, entering this production process, we see not only how the worker 'produces by consuming', but also how the worker is produced and thus the secret (l'arcano) of profit making must be laid bare.[4]

The unfolding of this working process is marked by specific phenomena distinct from and opposed to those constituting the production process. The phenomena at the basis of the production process are described by Marx as follows. First, 'the worker works under the control of the capitalist', and, second, 'the product is the property of the

---

3   Ibid., 290.

4   Here, Fortunati is again playing on the passage mentioned above concluding Chapter 6 of *Capital*, vol. 1, where the English rendering of Marx's 'Das Geheimnis der Plusmacherei muss sich endlich enthüllen' is 'The secret of profit making must at last be laid bare' (ibid., 280). Cantimori renders the line as 'Finalmente ci si dovrà svelare l'arcano della fattura del plusvalore', or literally 'Finally we must reveal the mystery of the invoice of surplus value'.

capitalist and not that of the worker, its immediate producer'.[5] In the process we examine here, neither does the houseworker work under the direct control of the capitalist, nor is the product of this working process the property of the capitalist. The diverse nature of these phenomena does not however deny the capitalist character of the production process in question but speaks to its peculiarity.

As to the first phenomenon of this working process, capitalists cannot force the houseworker to work under their direct control but require the worker to act as a mediator of such control. This is the only way in which capital can establish domestic labour as a natural force of social labour.

As for the second phenomenon, here too the capitalist cannot be the owner of the product of labour (the worker's, houseworker's and future workers' labour power). Nor can the houseworker be the owner of the product of this labour, even though she is its immediate producer. She can, however, be the owner of that part of the product that is inherent within herself, which is to say her own labour power. Nor can the worker pose himself as the mediator of the relation of production between women and capital because – we repeat – the presupposition and condition of existence of capital is that the *free worker*, understood in general terms, must be positioned as the direct owner of its own labour power. This means that even though the reproduction occurs between things (housework and commodities) that belong to him because as he has bought them in a certain sense, he can only be owner of his own labour power.

We want to clarify now how this process unfolds. One of the causes of the political confusion that looms over domestic labour and the condition of women in general is the confused analysis of this process as it generally unfolds. As with any other production process, a portion of the initial money (variable capital) is converted into the means of production (raw material, instruments of labour and auxiliary material) and another portion is converted into labour power, in this case that of the houseworker. Here we distinguish for clarity's sake the production of labour power from reproduction. This distinction is not arbitrary, because these are two distinct processes, even though the former cannot exist if untied from the latter.

---

5 Ibid., 291–2.

Let us start from the production of new labour power. The production of this labour power consists in two distinct moments: procreation and gestation. Procreation cannot occur if the woman does not perform sexual labour, which is reproductive labour. This is true in the majority of cases, even though the creation of sperm banks allows limited cases of the insemination of women without direct sexual contact with men. In the moment of procreation, the raw materials are the sperm of the man and the body of the woman in its entirety. This latter body also functions at the same time as an instrument of labour. All the means of subsistence and service labour consumed by women during gestation are auxiliary material in the production process of labour power, and simultaneously represent a portion of the means of subsistence of the woman herself.

The consequences presented by these means of production are as follows. First, where they coincide, they are consumed by the woman both as productive consumption and as individual consumption. Second, a portion of the objective factors, which is to say of the means of production, are inherent in the body of the woman herself, within which is inherent the personal element of labour power.

Gestation is the consumption of the means of production performed by the houseworker. This process, whose last moment is that of childbirth, is extinguished by the product – new labour power: 'Labour has been objectified, the object has been worked on.'[6] Labour power is therefore always raw material because, even at the moment of birth, the individuals have incorporated nine months of labour performed by the mother. They are not exclusively an *object of labour*, in the sense implied by Marx when he defines labour power as 'above all else, the material of nature transposed into a human organism'.[7]

It is clear that capital has not developed the production of individuals by introducing new instruments of labour, as it has in other forms of production. It has transformed the way in which such labour is performed, however, including by transforming the relationship between women and their bodies (which are the means of production in this process). Capital expropriated women not so much of their

---

6   Ibid., 287.
7   Ibid., 323.

bodies, but rather of the possibility of controlling their bodies – in particular, the control over their own uterus – through interventions of various sorts, not least of which has been the bloody legislation on abortion and birth control more generally.[8] At first as a prerequisite and then as a condition of its existence, capital has transformed women's bodies, with their inherent capacity of producing the individual, into a machine for the production of new workers, of new labour power.

This machinisation of women's bodies is the greatest technological invention introduced by capital into this production process. It is no longer the woman who uses her body, but it is her body as an instrument of labour that uses her. Her body becomes not only alien to her, as it is subject to the command of others, but it also becomes her enemy, consuming her as ferment necessary for its vital process.[9]

Passing to the reproduction of labour power, two points need clarification. First, the production of commodities does not occur directly, and this working process is composed of two distinct phases, separated by the moment of consumption. Second, the process involves production of both material and immaterial use values.

Let us analyse the first point. Between production and its product – labour power – another moment is presupposed: the consumption performed by the individual of the use values produced for him by reproductive labour. Such consumption is a necessity owing to the basic characteristics of the labour power commodity: first, the fact that labour power is not a thing, an object, but a capacity, or more precisely, the capacity to work; second, that this capacity does not exist apart from the individual in whom it persists.

---

8   For an overview of feminist movement struggles and state policy on abortion in the Italian context, see Maud Anne Bracke, *Women and the Reinvention of the Political: Feminism in Italy, 1968–1983* (London: Routledge, 2014).

9   '. . . ma diventa anche il suo nemico, in quanto la consuma come fermento del suo processo vitale': here, Fortunati paraphrases the passage from Chapter 11 of *Capital* describing the transformation of the means of production in the creation of absolute surplus value. Fowkes's English translation renders the passage as follows: 'The means of production are at once changed into means for the absorption of the labour of others. It is no longer the worker who employs the means of production, but the means of production which employ the worker. Instead of being consumed by him as material elements of his productive activity, they consume him as the ferment necessary to their own life-process' (Marx, *Capital*, vol. 1, 425).

These characteristics have a precise consequence: that both the consumption and the production of labour power take place only indirectly. In the case of consumption, the capitalist, after purchasing the capacity of labour power, does not consume it directly in the process of production, but requires that the waged worker consumes his labour power by himself. Work is precisely the mediating activity performed by workers by consuming their own capacity to work. The consumption of labour power by the capitalist cannot be direct, like the consumption of raw materials, auxiliary materials and of instruments of labour by the worker. It is, in fact, the worker himself who needs to consume his labour power by working. When Marx describes the production process, he speaks of the consumption of labour power *tout court*, because within this discourse a description of how this consumption occurs would have been useless. The result of the process of production – the consumption of labour power obtained by the capitalist – is self-evident. We need to examine it, however, because the dynamic that concurrently takes place in the process of domestic labour does not reveal plainly where the product (labour power) comes from – indeed, it confuses any analysis of the process.

In the reproduction process, the houseworker cannot directly reproduce the worker's labour power, because labour power is not a thing, but a capacity inherent in the worker himself. The worker consumes labour power during the production process, and it is he who must perform the action of consuming the use values produced by the houseworker that are necessary for his reproduction. Between the houseworker who extracts her own labour power and the product of her labour, which is the worker's, future workers' and her own labour power, the individual consumption of each of these subjects must act as mediation. This means that the houseworker cannot produce labour power directly. This is true except for the case in which the producing subject coincides with the consumer, which means that the houseworker works and produces her own labour power in a finite fashion and without resolution or continuity. In all the other cases, the process requires that the worker, while consuming the product of domestic labour, produces his labour power.

The failure to specify this crucial dynamic has been the cause of many misunderstandings and errors by those who have attempted to analyse the process of domestic labour. One of the most common conclusions of such analyses is the claim that this process is not a direct production of commodities, but only a production of use values. In this case, the moment of consumption is not understood as a moment within the process, but as a moment subsequent to it. As a consequence, labour power (as a use value for value) is seen not as a result of the process of domestic labour, but as the product of the worker's individual consumption *tout court*, and thus this working process came to be seen as pre-capitalist.

Another conclusion is that reproduction is a process that has such different characteristics with respect to production that it does not belong to the capitalist mode of production. In this case, reproduction is classified as existing outside of the capitalist mode of production, not because it belongs to a pre-capitalist mode of production, but because it is understood as belonging to a different mode of production altogether.

The inconsistency of these conclusions is clear: if in consuming his labour power in the production process, the worker creates value and transfers this value into the product, then he consumes the use values produced by the houseworker in the process of reproduction. Similarly, when he consumes the use values produced by the houseworker in the process of reproduction, he transfers the value created into the product of domestic labour – his own labour power.

But what does it mean to define the consumption of the worker as a *moment* in the process of domestic labour? As we have seen, the commodities into which variable capital can be transformed do not have direct use value for the production of labour power, because they are not directly consumable: 'Use-values are only realised [*verwirklicht*] in use or in consumption.'[10] These commodities do not have direct use value for the worker. This means that a part of variable capital can be converted into exchange values only because another part is converted into a specific kind of exchange value (the houseworker's labour power) that is able to transform these commodities into real, directly consumable use values. This is why the conversion of a part of variable capital into an exchange value that does not have direct use value for reproduction is plausible. In this context, their real use value is revealed. Before becoming a direct use value for the worker, these use values have a direct use value as the means of production of domestic labour. By acknowledging that the reproduction of labour power occurs indirectly, we can see how this process of production develops in two phases. First, the means of

---

10   Ibid., 126.

production of domestic labour are transformed into directly consumable use values for the worker. Second, these use values are transformed into labour power.

The second point to clarify in the analysis of the reproduction of labour power is the existence of an immaterial production within the process of domestic labour. It has been said previously that domestic labour is not only the making of beds, washing and ironing of clothes, house cleaning and so on. Domestic labour is not only labour that satisfies, within given limits, the material needs of the individual's belly, but is also labour that responds to immaterial needs. The needs that the male worker expresses as an individual who inherently owns labour power are both material and immaterial, and domestic production is also organised around the immaterial pole.

But what does it mean to speak of immaterial use values? The immaterial use values most relevant here are, first and foremost, those goods produced and consumed within the process of domestic labour that do not have a clear material substratum. They are emotions, affects and sexuality: products of domestic labour that satisfy the immaterial needs of the individual. These needs are as important as a well-cooked steak and a clean shirt, if not more so, for the reproduction of his labour power. They are not commodities (true exchange values), as they are not sold on a free market. As intermediary moments of the process of commodity production (of labour power) they are *use values for value*.

Previous discussions of immaterial use values have grasped only those aspects that are detached from the direct process of commodity production. In other words, immaterial use values have been conceived idealistically as objects of mutual exchange between male workers and women as houseworkers for the mutual satisfaction of their respective needs. The differences in the use of immaterial use values, which is to say in their consumption by individuals, have been acknowledged. These differences have largely been understood as stratifications on the basis of age, race and sex that are a result of past sedimentations, of historical determinations affecting the whole of society. For example, the idea that men are more selfish in love has been accepted as a given fact. The explanation for this kind of behaviour was found in an outdated mindset or, in more thoughtful analysis in the relative power differentials between men and women that are reflected in love.

Contrary to these explanations, the differences in the consumption of immaterial use values between men and women are implemented in a much more material fashion. In the couple, the adult man can consume while the woman must primarily work. The man is selfish because he consumes love, while the woman is generous because she produces love. But how does she produce love? She does not do so freely, outside of a working process, but within the process of domestic labour to produce a commodity: labour power. Although it may seem strange at first glance, things such as sentiments and sex are not necessarily natural, nor are they mechanically and automatically altered with the transformation of the productive relations of the entire society. Any sentiment we work on (if we are women) or consume (if we are men) is fabricated, both formally and in its substance as a commodity

Since the advent of capitalism, immaterial use values have been fully and directly subject to the laws of the production of value. Only if we are conscious of their tendential aspect as commodities can we understand how strategic this realm is to the command of capital. Permanent reproduction of the working class – its working discipline and productivity, as well as its adaptation to the overall conditions of life – are all crucially dependent on the command of capital in the realm of immaterial use values. There are now oceans of literature on how children who do not feel loved in the family (especially by the mother) become outcasts and misfits, rebelling against their environment as rebels-in-miniature against the established order. Similarly, there is a substantial debate on the existing relationship between factory and domestic productivity and the sexual and sentimental reproduction of workers. But this literature generally treats the problem in a moralistic fashion. The tendency is to blame the mother or wife for the fact that the child is maladjusted or that the husband does not want to work. She is reproached because she does not perform her duty within the family – because she does not succumb to her moral imperative. In other words, women's struggle against domestic labour is totally misrecognised, and their productivity is mystified in moralistic terms.

The real problem, however, is that immaterial reproduction is perhaps the section of proletarian reproduction most in crisis today, because it is so difficult to command and control. The refusal of domestic labour by women causes a dissatisfaction and frustration of immaterial needs so pervasive and profound that it constitutes a deterioration of proletarian living conditions more severe than those brought about by the crisis of prices for food and clothing. The depth of this crisis can only be understood if we consider that, within the process of domestic labour, the realm of immaterial needs is growing exponentially, especially compared to the realm of material needs. At the same time, the impact is particularly strong because of the aggravating contradictions on this matter: above all the fact that in this realm the woman is established as a working subject, and the man as a subject of consumption. This is a terrain where the possibilities of struggle and subversion are, and have always been, great – especially for women as working subjects – due to the extreme difficulties in controlling the extent and intensity of immaterial domestic labour. These difficulties are encountered not only by capital, but by the male worker as mediator of the relationship of production between women and capital.

It has always been easier, and it is now more so than ever, for capital to command women in the material chores of domestic labour than to force them to love, to function sexually or to give affection when they do not want to do so. There has been an evident fall of productivity over the last century in the realm of sexuality, sentiments and affects. Its effects are even more totalising than the current ones, because more and more male/female relationships concern only the realm of sexuality. Increasingly, women refuse to live with men whom they are in a relationship (or even in love) with. This refusal removes from the relationship most of the issues related to the division of labour and the quality and quantity of the consumption of what is materially produced in the domestic production process. What remains on the table is the issue of the division of labour and the consumption of what each party is willing to produce at the level of immaterial labour. Accordingly, enhancing this struggle and its organisation would be strategically valuable, especially for women.

The cycle of struggles of the 1970s, however, has already fully demonstrated the profound crisis into which state policies established in the realm of immaterial reproduction have been thrown. Today, the issue can no longer be addressed by the state simply in terms of 'repression' or 'permissiveness' – or, in other words, with interventions for the containment or expansion of the forms assumed by adult, female immaterial domestic labour and of the consumption by men and children of its related products. The issue must be addressed relative to the decline of the productive substance currently existing in that process, which is to say of the great refusal of labour that is here expressed, first and foremost by women. This is an issue that the state is addressing, and that we must address as well in terms of organisation. When this archipelago of gestures, words and gazes goes adrift (when the woman negates herself as a subject of labour, refuses the denial of her needs and proposes herself as subject of consumption), then new possibilities open for the unbinding of this terrain from the iron laws of surplus value, and from its related work of discipline and domestic confinement.

What kind of production is the production of immaterial use values? According to Marx, immaterial production is of two kinds. The first 'results in commodities, use-values, which have a form different from and independent of producers and consumers'.[11] The second is the one in which 'the production cannot be separated from the act of producing, as is the case with all performing artists, orators, actors, teachers, physicians, priests, etc.'[12] 'Here too,' Marx affirms, 'the capitalist mode of production is met with only to a small extent, and from the nature of the case can only be applied in a few spheres.'[13] Marx concludes by arguing that 'all these manifestations of capitalist production in this sphere are so insignificant compared with the totality of production that they can be left entirely out of account'.

It is clear that immaterial production performed within the process of reproduction belongs to the second form of immaterial production, which alone would be enough to refute Marx's claims. In other words, the development of domestic production and, within it, the further development of its immaterial part would suffice to prove how much this second form of immaterial production has been developed. But the history of the capitalist mode of production has proved Marx wrong in other ways too. In contrast with Marx's claim, the immaterial production that is inseparable from the act of production has expanded hugely, both within the process of reproduction and that of production. With respect to the latter, suffice it to mention the production of information or service work, and in the process of reproduction about that of prostitution, which was already widespread in Marx's time.

---

11   Karl Marx, *Theories of Surplus-Value*, Part I (Moscow: Progress Publishers, 1963), 410.
12   Ibid., 410.
13   Ibid., 410–11.

What are the means of production in this domestic working process, relative to the reproduction of labour power? First, we need to distinguish the production of material use values from that of immaterial use values. In the former, raw materials include food, clothing, furniture and housing, while the instruments of labour include the washing machine, refrigerator, dishwasher and so on. The auxiliary materials include electricity, water and gas. The woman uses the instruments of labour as conductors of her own activities over food, clothing and so on. In the second case, the production of immaterial use values, the raw materials and instruments of labour include the houseworker in the entirety of her person or, to use a common binary, in both her body and soul. This means that her immaterial needs should not and cannot exist unless they are such as to satisfy the immaterial needs of the male worker or of her children. This also means that she is at the same time labour power and the self-perpetuating machinery of immaterial production. The houseworker is, in this sense, the greatest technological invention made by capital in the process of reproduction.[14]

With this in mind, we can see how make-up, for example, is part of the 'auxiliary materials' in the process of immaterial production, because it is added to the 'raw material' (the woman's body) to effect a material change. Similarly, women's clothes function as auxiliary materials, because they too assume the function of helping her do her housework. In the first phase of the working process, the houseworker transforms these means of production of domestic labour into both material and immaterial use values that have a direct use value consumable by the worker, by the future workers and by herself. But, while the consumption of the former material use value is separated from the moment of their production, the latter consumption of immaterial use value is not. This means that their production and consumption must occur simultaneously. The former aspect of the working process (that concerned with immaterial production) manifests in a way that the

---

14   Here Fortunati develops a critical variation on the opening passage of Part III of *Capital*, vol. 1. In Marx's account, the term rendered here as 'auxiliary materials' (*materiale ausiliario* in Italian, rendered by Fowkes as 'an accessory') is differentiated from 'raw material' (*materia prima*) in that it 'may be consumed by the instruments of labour' (*mezzi di lavoro*) before it reaches a state in which it is directly consumable (Marx, *Capital*, vol. 1, 288–9).

individual consumption of the waged worker is not an isolated moment within the working process.

Now we must consider how these use values are positioned within the process of domestic labour. In this context, they must be considered as an intermediate and not as a final product; those who have defined domestic labour as exclusively the production of use values have failed to understand this. As an intermediate product, they are the result of the first phase and the starting point of the second. In this second phase, these use values assume the function of raw materials, and, at the same time, of auxiliary materials.[15] Paradoxically, the instrument of labour is simultaneously the worker, future workers and the houseworker: they are the machinery through which the houseworker produces labour power. This is the second great technological invention introduced in our production process, and it explains why raw materials and auxiliary materials here coincide. Individuals, whose reproductive capacity inheres in them as labour power, are the machinery of this production process. This is why it is meaningless to distinguish between raw materials and auxiliary materials: they are both consumed by the individual, as coal is consumed by the steam engine, and as both simultaneously constitute the primary substance of the product – its labour power.

As opposed to other machines, however, the individual generally consumes raw and auxiliary materials directly. Except in specific cases, this consumption does not presuppose further labour from the houseworker. These specific cases are ones in which she has to reproduce the labour power of an individual who is not yet or no longer self-sufficient in their consumption. In other words, she must also do the work of providing this individual with the use values she produces and ensuring that they are consumed regularly. The feeding of children is exemplary in this regard: the mother or caregiver prepares food and feeds the children, checking on them to confirm that they eat regularly without tantrums. Parenthetically, this is also an example of a struggle that is

---

15   Here, Fortunati again uses the terms '*materie prime*', the general Italian translation of 'raw materials', or in Marx's original German *Das Rohmaterial*, relative to *der Hilfsstoff* or 'auxiliary materials' (*materiale ausiliario* in Cantimori's translation). In this case, however, Fortunati charts an alternative course for the auxiliary and raw materials of reproduction as occurring simultaneously in the process of reproduction (ibid., 287–9).

generally unrecognised as such: one performed by children, who throw tantrums and refuse to eat when, what and how others demand.

But, excepting such cases, it is through the direct consumption by the waged worker himself of use values produced by the domestic worker (in his role as instrument of domestic labour) that his labour power is produced. Thus, his labour power is the final product of the domestic working process. But, apart from those cases in which the individual is not self-sufficient in their own consumption, it is through the worker's own direct consumption (in his role as the auxiliary means of domestic work) of the use values produced by the houseworker that produces the latter's own labour power – the final product of this labour process. However, such a claim entails that, first, the male worker's individual consumption emerges through the indirect con-sumption by the houseworker of the worker himself as the indispensable means of domestic work. Therefore, individual con-sumption is entirely encompassed within the process of reproduction. Second, this means that labour power itself is the direct result of the workers' individual consumption; however, this consumption is both a moment of the process of reproduction, as well as the final product of this process.

The domestic working process is not a process of production of use values, because, as we have seen, these are merely the product of its first phase. Rather, it is a process of commodity production – of the commod-ity labour power, as use value for value. As a process of commodity production, it does not represent a distinct mode of production, but as shown below it is the capitalist mode of production of individuals, who cannot be reproduced except as labour power.

In analysing the domestic labour process, we have established that it is a process of commodity production: the production of labour power to be precise. As commodity production, this process will necessarily also be a process of value creation. To define this as a capitalist produc-tion process, however, it is not enough to say simply that it is a process of commodity production, because the commodity in question is that of labour power. Labour power is, in fact, a special type of commodity because, while like any other commodity is both use value and value, the use value of labour power is produced and consumed separately from its exchange value. More precisely, its use value is produced in the process of reproduction and consumed in the process of production and vice versa: its exchange value is produced in the latter and consumed in the former. Even though labour power is celebrated as the queen of commodities in the production process, in the process of its reproduction it is denied as a commodity in its aspect and substance. Consequently, this process is very specific, because, while it does indeed include commodity production (that of labour power), such is produced here only in its use value and not its exchange value. This would seem to make it a natural production process rather than a capitalist one. In fact, the value of a use value cannot be expressed and cannot be measured. In other words, such a process of production does not seem to be a process of valorisation. As we will demonstrate, however, even though such a contradiction exists, it is only apparent: the process of production of labour power, like that of other commodities, is both a working process and process of value formation.

But is it true that the use value of labour power is produced in the process of reproduction? Is the use value the only thing produced? It appears so, and it seems that there is also an internal logic within the overall cycle of capital. In fact, while all the other use values are generally 'produced by capitalists only because and insofar as they form the material substratum of exchange-value, are the bearers of exchange value', labour power is a use value produced only because and insofar as it is the bearer of its own use value.[16] This is what interests capital, because it is the use (or the consumption of labour power) on which the creation of value in the production process depends. As Marx says, 'a thing can be a use-value without being a value', and 'a thing can be useful, and a product of human labour, without being a commodity'.[17]

There are, however, two contradictions at play here. First, labour power is not only useful, and a product of human labour, but also a thing that has a use value for others (capital), a social use value. While the domestic labour incorporated in it is established as a natural force of social labour, it cannot be considered as simple human labour. Rather, domestic labour must be considered as abstract labour, otherwise we would find ourselves in an absurd situation. We would have a use value, a product of domestic labour, that, in the process of reproduction, was not a commodity but, as soon as it crossed the threshold into this

---

16   Ibid., 293.
17   Ibid., 131.

process, became one, and thus an exchange value. We would have a use value that does not have value in the process of reproduction, but that has exchange value in the process of production.

Second, if, in the process of reproduction, the value of labour power must be measured in terms of use value and not in terms of exchange value, as is the case with any other commodity, this means that this value of labour power could not be expressed. It could neither be expressed in another commodity (since use value cannot constitute a measure of value) nor, vice versa, relative to another labour power commodity (because the value of labour power cannot be expressed in labour power itself). Labour power's equivalence with labour power is not an expression of value because such an equation would claim that labour power is nothing but a determined quantity of a useful object. The simplest expression of value for a commodity is constituted by the 'value-relation . . . of one commodity to another commodity of a different kind (it does not matter which one)'.[18]

But is it really possible that a commodity like labour power that is so precious for capital would be produced in such a way that its value (on which the value produced in the production process depends) could not be measured, could not be determined and controlled? No. As we will demonstrate, in the reproduction process, labour power is produced as a commodity, as a unit of use value and of value. We will also demonstrate that what is produced here is not only its use value but also its value, a concept that is different from use value and from exchange value: 'A use-value, or useful article . . . has value only because abstract human labour is objectified (*vergegenständlicht*) or materialised in it'.[19] It is once again Marx who specifies:

When, at the beginning of this chapter, we said in the customary manner that a commodity is both a use-value and an exchange-value, this was, strictly speaking, wrong. A commodity is a use-value or object of utility, and a 'value'. It appears as the twofold thing it really is as soon as its value possesses its own particular form of manifestation, which is distinct from its natural form. This form of manifestation is exchange-value, and the commodity never has this form when looked at in

18   Ibid., 139.
19   Ibid., 129.

isolation, but only when it is in a value-relation or an exchange relation with a second commodity of a different kind. Once we know this, our manner of speaking does no harm; it serves, rather, as an abbreviation.[20]

It is only by starting with the clarification that value and exchange value are not the same concept (but on the contrary that their confusion can generate great misunderstandings) that we can arrive at an understanding of the value of labour power. In examining the relative form of value, Marx lashed out against Samuel Bailey, and against all the other economists who had expressed interest in the issue, precisely because they had confused the value form with value. Marx's propensity for abbreviation was risky as well, however. If it is not possible to make a distinction between the concept of value and that of exchange value, there is no way to reach a correct definition of the value of labour power. Our resort to the concept of value to express the value of labour power is further supported by Marx's remarks: 'The form of value, that is, the expression of the value of a commodity, arises from the nature of commodity-value, as opposed to value and its magnitude arising from their mode of expression as exchange-value.'[21] And again: 'It is not the exchange of commodities which regulates the magnitude of their values, but rather the reverse, the magnitude of the value of commodities which regulates the proportion in which they exchange.'[22]

It is worth pointing out that the Marxian discourse on value reveals that value and exchange value are not simply two different concepts, but that it is the exchange value to arise from the nature of the value of commodities, and not vice versa. It is the magnitude of the value of commodities that regulates the relations of exchange of the commodity, and not the reverse. It remains to be clarified, however: What exactly is understood by the value of labour power? This value is posited as use value, because, once again, capital is not interested in the exchange value of labour power, but in its use value. It is interested only in the extent and intensity of the consumption of labour power itself, because it is upon this consumption that the creation of value in the production process depends. Because the measure of this consumption depends upon the magnitude

---

20   Ibid., 152.
21   Ibid.
22   Ibid., 156.

of this consumption of labour power (produced in the reproduction process), the magnitude of the value created by labour power depends upon the magnitude of the use value of labour power.

In other words, while the use value of other commodities cannot constitute the measure of their value (it is, in fact, the labour time required to constitute their exchange value that makes it possible to calculate such use values), in the case of labour power it is precisely its use value that constitutes the measure of its value.

The value of labour power, like that of any other commodity, relates to the fact that abstract human labour is objectified within it. The value of labour power consists of the materialisation of the objectified, abstract human labour it incorporates through the process of reproduction, which creates the material body of the commodity labour power. From here, it is possible to compare labour power to any other commodity, even though the former is produced for its use value while all the other commodities are produced for their exchange value; and through such comparisons it is possible to establish the value of labour power.

How, then, is the magnitude of this value to be measured? This question is necessary and pertinent here, given that every commodity that must be expressed as value is an object of utility of a given quantity, and it contains a given quantity of human labour. This means that 'the form of value must not only express value in general, but also quantitatively determined value, i.e. the magnitude of value.'[23] The value of labour power is qualitatively expressed through its exchangeability with any other commodity. This value is quantitatively expressed through the exchangeability between a determined quantity of a commodity and a determined quantity of labour power. The magnitude of its value, like that of any other commodity, is measured 'by means of the quantity of the "value-forming substance", the labour, contained in the article. This quantity is measured by its duration.'[24] Marx continues by saying that 'the labour that forms the substance of value is equal human labour, the expenditure of identical human labour-power', and that

the total labour-power of society . . . [is] composed of innumerable individual units of labour-power. Each of these units is the same as any

---

23 Ibid., 144.
24 Ibid., 129.

other, to the extent that it has the character of a socially average unit of labour-power . . . What exclusively determines the magnitude of the value of any article is therefore the amount of labour socially necessary, or the labour-time socially necessary for its production.

This magnitude corresponds to the magnitude of the (use) value of labour power, within which is included its exchange value. The exchange value corresponds to the amount of labour necessary to the worker for the production of his means of subsistence in the production process. At the same time, the exchange value also functions as means of production in the reproduction process and is thus incorporated into the final product of this working process, which is labour power. The magnitude of the (use) value of labour power itself is therefore determined by the value produced by the houseworker, who adds value to the exchange value of labour power in the process of reproduction.

In monetary terms, labour power represents only exchange value, and not use value. This is because the process of production and that of reproduction are respectively self-contained and inescapably connected. These two processes – production and reproduction – are separated by the line of value and constitute two distinct moments in the extraction of surplus value. Exchange value and the (use) value of labour power are produced respectively in the commodity production process and in the process that produces and reproduces labour power. However, both exchange value and the use value of labour power also function in the other process where they are established as prerequisites and conditions of existence. This allows capital to save great amounts of money and to plunder significant surplus value throughout its accumulation cycle. The separation between the two sides of the process of valorisation leads to a double *salto mortale* (death-defying leap) of the product of one process into the other, and the reverse. This is disadvantageous for both the worker and the houseworker. Besides representing what the workers have earned, variable capital also performs the function of capital in the sphere of reproduction. This means that capital disburses only once in the reproduction process. This disbursement happens in the process of production, when capital gives the worker a salary.

At the same time, labour power represents what the houseworkers have produced, and it is consumed in the production process. This means that capital exploits the houseworker while also taking advantage of the worker. The double *salto mortale* mentioned above is made possible by the fact that capital establishes the process of reproduction as a natural process of social labour with respect to the production cycle. At the same time, capital organises reproduction as a process of valorisation.

Defined as a natural force of social labour, domestic labour seems, in its entirety, to be unpaid work, and, as such, it could be considered pure surplus labour, extra labour that capital manages to extort beyond paid necessary labour in the production process. Because domestic labour is commanded by variable capital in its function as capital, however, it gives life to a self-contained process of valorisation in which the fact that variable capital comes from the production process is irrelevant. This is why, like labour in the production process, domestic labour is divided into necessary labour and surplus labour. Therefore, the magnitude of the value of labour power is measurable through the amount of domestic labour socially necessary to produce and reproduce such labour power.

The magnitude of the value of labour power is not represented entirely in its exchange value. This should not surprise us, because: 'The value of a commodity is independently expressed through its presentation (*Darstellung*) as "exchange-value".'[25] Moreover: 'The form of direct and universal exchangeability, in other words the universal equivalent form, has now by social custom finally become entwined with the specific natural form of the commodity gold.'[26] This means that: 'The general form of value comes to be transformed into the money form.'[27] This is why we should not be surprised by the fact that this magnitude of value cannot be completely expressed in its monetary representation. In other words, we should not be surprised by 'the possibility of a quantitative incongruity between magnitude of value and price, i.e. between the magnitude of value and its own expression in money'.[28]

> With the transformation of the magnitude of value into the price this necessary relation appears as the exchange-ratio between a single commodity and the money commodity which exists outside it. This

---

25   Ibid., 152.
26   Ibid., 162.
27   Ibid., 163.
28   Ibid., 197.

relation, however, may express both the magnitude of value of the commodity and the greater or lesser quantity of money for which it can be sold under the given circumstances. The possibility, therefore, of a quantitative incongruity between price and magnitude of value, i.e. the possibility that the price may diverge from the magnitude of value, is inherent in the price-form itself. This is not a defect, but, on the contrary, it makes this form the adequate one for a mode of production whose laws can only assert themselves as blindly operating averages between constant irregularities.[29]

Later, Marx adds: 'Hard cash lurks within the ideal measure of value.'[30] And, again, he states, that the 'leap taken by value from the body of the commodity into the body of the gold is the commodity's *salto mortale*, as I have called it elsewhere. If the leap falls short, it is not the commodity which is defrauded but rather its owner.'[31] For the wage, that is, the monetary representation of the value of labour power, this triple *salto mortale* has always been to the disadvantage of the owner of labour power for two reasons. First, such a disadvantage is always inherent in the price of labour power, which hides the quantitative inconsistency between exchange value and the value of labour power. Second, the separation, through the line separating value from non-value, between the process of reproduction and that of production means that the reproduction of labour power happens through one wage that pays two different workers. Thus, it is doubly appropriate to conclude with the expression used by Marx, that 'tout est pour le mieux dans le meilleur des mondes possibles'.[32]

It has been useful, indeed indispensable, to clarify what valence of labour power is produced in the process of reproduction. By demonstrating that this is the value of labour power, we demonstrated how the process of reproduction is a full-fledged process of commodity production in its own right. It is now important to examine how this value is produced.

In the domestic labour process, the capitalist wants to obtain two things. First, that workers reproduce themselves as labour power: that is,

---

29   Ibid., 196.
30   Ibid., 198.
31   Ibid., 200–1.
32   Ibid., 302.

that a use value is produced with an exchange value, a commodity (labour power) that the worker can sell. Second, the capitalist requires that the production of this commodity occurs such that the magnitude of its value is greater than the 'sum of the value of the commodities necessary for its reproduction' (that is, its exchange value). To achieve this, capital forces the worker to exchange a portion of variable capital with the woman to obtain from her the use value of her labour power as the capacity of production and reproduction of labour power. But the costs for the maintenance of the houseworker and the expenditure of her labour power are two entirely distinct magnitudes. The value of the commodities necessary for the reproduction of the houseworker (value contained in the exchange value of labour power as a capacity of production) is less than the value produced by the houseworker. The first magnitude is expressed in its exchange value, the second in its (use) value. This means that the exchange value of labour power as capacity of production and its valorisation in the process of reproduction are two entirely distinct quantities. It is precisely this difference of value that the capitalist relies upon. At the end of the domestic labour process, the product (labour power) has a much greater value than its exchange value. This difference of value is accentuated in those cases where the woman produces new labour power.

Because the worker is not interested in the use value of his labour power but only in its exchange value, when he is on the labour-market to sell his commodity, he bargains for the exchange value with the capitalist who buys his commodity in exchange for its (use) value. This latter value is much greater than its exchange value, however, because within it is objectified both the socially necessary labour provided by the worker himself in the production process and the socially necessary domestic labour required to reproduce labour power. The transformation of money into capital occurs here because the capitalist buys at below cost. After buying the worker's labour power, the capitalist consumes it in the production process to extract surplus value. Here, the transformation of money into capital occurs because capital earns more than it spends.

In both cases, the transformation of money into capital occurs both within and outside the sphere of circulation. It occurs, in Marx's account, through the mediation of circulation, with the precondition of the purchase of the houseworker's labour power performed by the worker. In this case, the transformation does not take place wholly within the sphere of circulation, because this sphere starts from the end of the process of valorisation occurring in the sphere of reproduction. Thus, the sphere of circulation of that particular commodity that is labour power is present both before and after the process of valorisation. Through its mediation the transformation of the capitalist's money into capital takes place. This transformation has two conditions. First, that the purchase of the houseworker's labour power is performed by the worker. Second, that the purchase of the worker's labour power is performed by the capitalist himself. This means that the formation of capital needs to be explained through a difference of value production, and with an understanding of the production of surplus value occurring in both production processes.

The same dynamic is present in the domestic process – only the lead actors, the extras and scenery change. The *capital* from which the process starts is variable capital: it is money that does not *appear* as real capital. In reality, while, for the worker, money is a means of circulation, it actually functions, as we have seen, as a means of production, and more precisely as a value for capital initially advanced in the production process. In this case, however, it is the worker, and not capital, who advances it. This is, in fact, the same money used to pay him, now used to pay the houseworker. As we have said, this can happen because the two production processes are self-enclosed. The disadvantage resulting from this enclosure is only for the waged worker and houseworker, because capital, with respect to the overall production cycle, saves a great deal of money.

In the process of reproduction, variable capital, like capital in the production process, is transformed into various forms. A part of it is transformed into the means of production, including raw materials, auxiliary materials and instruments of labour, and another part is transformed into labour power as the capacity of production and reproduction of labour power. Here too, the means of production and labour power perform different functions in relation to the formation of the value of the product – labour power. Here, the means of production cannot add any additional value to labour power greater than what they already possess, regardless of the domestic working process. On the contrary, the houseworker's labour power conserves value while adding value. This surplus value constitutes an excess of the value of the houseworker's labour power.

That part of variable capital which transforms into means of production without changing the magnitude of its value can be called the 'constant part of variable capital'. The part of variable capital transformed into the houseworker's labour power can be called the 'variable part of variable capital', given that it changes its value by producing surplus value. Therefore, the same constitutive parts of variable capital that, from the point of view of the labour process, can be distinguished as subjective and objective factors – means of production and labour power, from the point of view of the valorisation process – can be distinguished as the constant part of variable capital and the variable part of variable capital.

The variable part of variable capital is clearly the one that corresponds to the value of the houseworker's means of subsistence, whose labour power is consumed in the process of production and reproduction of labour power. If we want to distinguish the constant part of variable capital, however, we need to return to the distinction between the production and reproduction of labour power we made in our analysis of the domestic labour process.

Relative to reproduction, we distinguish the constant part of variable capital in its two phases. In the realm of the production of material use values, the first phase corresponds to the value of raw materials, the instruments of labour and the auxiliary materials necessary to the production of use values for the entire working-class family, except the houseworker. In the realm of the production of immaterial use values, a specific part of constant variable capital cannot be isolated because the value of auxiliary materials – such as make-up – belongs to the value of the houseworker's means of subsistence, and raw materials and instruments of labour coincide with the houseworker herself, who, however, has no value. Such is a prerequisite, a condition of existence for capital. If we examine the second phase, we see that there is no specific constant part of variable capital, because raw materials and auxiliary materials are the result of the first phase, and the instrument of labour is the worker himself, who, however, has no value. This again is a prerequisite, a condition of existence for capital.

Having defined the constant and variable part of variable capital, we can understand how, in reproduction as in production, the value of the product is not equal to, but greater than the value advanced by capital. Such excess in the value of the product, which is to say the excess of the value of the worker's labour power with respect to the value of the products consumed (means of production and the houseworker's labour power) constitutes the hidden surplus value produced here. We speak of hidden surplus value in this case because, in effect, neither the worker nor capital have ever had an interest in its discovery. The worker never had an interest because this surplus value does not concern him, given that he is interested in the exchange value of his labour power and not its use value. Indeed, the only thing that he notices is that his wage, at the end of this process, has been used up. The capitalist, aiming precisely for this surplus value, has obviously never been interested in the situation appearing as it is.

And yet, this surplus value nonetheless exists because the value advanced (variable capital) valorises and generates surplus value. In what sense does this occur? Here, the image of the photographic negative reappears. In fact, the production of surplus value in the reproduction process cannot but occur as an inversion of what occurs in production. Here, money does not transform directly into capital; it does not transform into a greater quantity of exchange value which would be advantageous for the worker, and not for the capitalist. Rather, money transforms into a greater quantity of value as use value for value. At the end of this production process, the value of the commodity produced (labour power) coincides, in terms of exchange value, with the total value of the elements of its production. But the magnitude of this value changes because it becomes greater than the sum of its elements. In other words, it becomes greater than the value advanced by capital, which is the exchange value of labour power itself.

To conclude, the reproduction process, as much as the production process, is a unity of its working processes and the process of value creation, and thus it is a process of commodity production. It is also, insofar as it is a unity of working process and valorisation process, a capitalist process of production – the capitalist form of the reproduction of individuals.

7

Revising Marx's Chapter on Surplus Value: Correcting the Map of Exploitation

Assuming that the production and reproduction of labour power is a process of value creation, and that the valorisation process proceeds on two tracks that are closely connected if distinct, it is now necessary to develop some observations on the concept of necessary labour. The topic of necessary labour is inexorably linked in Marx to that of wages and the value of labour power. In Marx, these themes coincide, particularly in the first volume of *Capital*, to such an extent that he places the wage and the value of labour power within an equation of value, in which the value of labour power coincides with its exchange value.

In the last few pages, we have demonstrated how such an equation cannot exist. Though the wage does indeed correspond to the exchange value of labour power, the value of the latter is much greater in terms of its use value. This means that the overall necessary time frame of the labour required for the reproduction of labour power is much greater than such an equation assumes. Moreover, this necessary labour is not linked only to a single working subject (the waged worker) as Marx suggests, but it is linked to two separate working subjects (the waged worker and the house-worker) who operate within two distinct production processes and within two distinct processes of value formation. The *overall necessary time frame* mentioned above includes the necessary labour performed in both the process of production and that of reproduction. This time frame is, however, fragmented, because these two sectors need to be combined in order to be sufficient for the reproduction of labour power.

Marx does not understand the scale or scope of the necessary labour time frame, and thus he does not understand the scale of capitalist exploitation. He is also uncertain in defining the relation between necessary labour and the reproduction of labour power relative to the different historical phases of capital. This chapter examines the period that Marx dwells on the most, that of modern industry; this is the period of development of the true capitalist mode of production.

There are moments in which Marx seems to identify clearly the passage from a relation between necessary labour and the reproduction of the working-class family, to a relation between necessary labour and the reproduction of individual labour power. For example, when he talks about the consequences of the introduction of machinery in the capitalist mode of production, Marx argues that the advent of modern industry causes a distortion of the pre-existing relation between necessary labour, wage and, on the one hand, labour power value, and on the other hand, labour power. During the period of manufacture, this relation is clearly operating on the level of the entire working-class family and not on the level of the individual labour power. With large-scale industry, this changes radically. The destruction of working-class families founded on a single wage, or, better, on a single relation of waged labour, tends to tie necessary labour, wage and value of the labour power to a single individual's labour power. The worker turns from waged head of the family to slave dealer:

> The value of labour-power was determined, not only by the labour-time necessary to maintain the individual adult worker, but also by that necessary to maintain his family. Machinery, by throwing every member of that family onto the labour-market, spreads the value of the man's labour-power over his whole family. It thus depreciates it.[1]

And again:

> Machinery also revolutionises, and quite fundamentally, the agency through which the capital-relation is formally mediated, i.e. the contract between the worker and the capitalist. Taking the exchange of

---

1   Karl Marx, *Capital*, vol. 1, *A Critique of Political Economy*, trans. Ben Fowkes (London: Penguin, New Left Review, 1990 [1976]), 518.

commodities as our basis, our first assumption was that the capitalist
and the worker confronted each other *as free persons*, as independent
owners of commodities, the one possessing money and the means of
production, the other labour-power. But now the capitalist buys children and *young persons* [our emphasis: young persons are women!].
Previously the worker sold his own labour-power, which he disposed
of as a free agent, formally speaking. Now he sells wife and child. He
has become *a slave-dealer*.[2]

Somewhere else, always within the analysis of the passage to large-
scale industry, Marx oscillates between connecting these concepts to
the individual's labour power and connecting them to the working-
class family. He affirms: 'The sum of means of subsistence necessary for
the production of labour-power must include the means necessary for the
worker's replacements, i.e. his children, in order that this race of peculiar
commodity-owners may perpetuate its presence on the market.'[3] On the
one hand, this uncertainty in Marx's treatment reflects the lack of a
systematic and organic approach to the definition of the conditions and
mechanisms of labour power as the reproduction of the working class.
It is not by chance that the working-class family is barely mentioned by
Marx, and then only as a backdrop for the wage, a place where the
commodity of labour power is reinvigorated. Therefore, the topic of
reproduction is addressed only in terms of the 'maintenance' of the
family by the worker. This means that the necessary labour time is calculated based only on the worker's workday. On the other hand, Marx's
uncertainty in addressing the topic of necessary labour time responds to
objective difficulties in the analysis caused by the complexity of the
relation between necessary labour, the wage and the value of labour
power on the one hand, and, on the other hand, the individual labour
power or working-class family. Even though all family members, including women and children, are involved in the relation of waged labour as
they each provide the factory with the necessary labour for the reproduction of labour power, domestic labour is still to be accounted for.
Domestic labour is, in fact, socially necessary for the production and the
formation of future workers, and it is provided for by all the members of

2   Ibid., 519.
3   Ibid., 275.

the working-class family. In Marx's definition, necessary labour, the wage and the value of labour power express the average necessary social labour for the mere reproduction of the individual as labour power, but they are not enough for the conservation and reproduction of the working class. The real existing relation in this phase between necessary labour, wage and the value of labour power, on the one hand, and labour power itself on the other hand, is defined as tending to coincide with the individual labour power.

Marx's treatment of this topic falls short of conceptual certainties. He also seems to have been unaware of the new, incipient phase of the capitalist mode of production that was already emergent in the second half of the seventeenth century. He did not grasp the profound crisis in the capital of large-scale industry, the bottleneck caused by the destruction of the working-class family and the resulting emergence of a cycle of workers' struggles (involving women, children and men) that was about to affect the reproduction of labour power itself, throughout the entire working class.

The cycle of workers' struggles occurring between the end of the eighteenth and the first decades of the nineteenth century completely overthrew the relation between necessary labour, the wage and value of labour power and the single individual. Generally speaking, the value of labour power returns to representing once again the value of the entire working-class family, and not the value of the single labour power. The necessary labour time provided by the worker in the production process tends to represent once more the value of the means of subsistence of the entire working-class family. This time, in addition to being necessary for the worker, and thus for capital, becomes necessary for the houseworker because it is the foundation of her existence. This means that the worker's necessary labour is nevertheless insufficient for the production and reproduction of labour power. This insufficiency constitutes a problem for capital, which is interested in its use value and not in its exchange value, and consequently in the fact that labour power is produced and reproduced at a greater (use) value than its exchange value.

The modern working-class family is the result of this overthrow of family relations. The adult male worker is progressively transformed once again from slave dealer to waged head of the family, reaffirming the relation between necessary labour, wages, the value of labour power and the working-class family. This transformation does not mean a reversion to a previous stage or that capital is retreating. In this context, *the wage takes on a new function of mediating the relation of production between those who are not directly waged – most importantly, women – and capital.* The worker becomes the tool through which capital takes possession of domestic labour, through exchange between capital and labour power in production, but without any exchange between capital and the labour power of reproduction. The wage is no longer exclusively an expression of the coercive power that ties capital to the waged working class, rather, *it becomes also an expression of the capitalist command and discipline of labour that is not directly waged* – first and foremost, of domestic labour. The wage thus becomes a cover for the exploitation of the houseworker.

The development of reproduction that took off during this phase, including the emergence of female labour power (not directly waged) as a working class of the house, radically challenged the equation between the wage and the value of labour power. These two elements also redefined the relation between necessary labour and the reproduction of the working class with respect to the overall cycle of capital. It is true that, nowadays, a single working day spent in the factory is enough for the worker to produce the value of the means of subsistence of the entire working-class family. Nonetheless, it is also true that another working day spent in the house is necessary for the houseworker to transform those means of subsistence into the labour power of the entire working-class family.

This workday can be divided into two segments: necessary labour time and surplus labour time. *Necessary domestic labour time* is that part of the houseworker's workday during which the reintegration of the value advanced to variable capital occurs; *necessary domestic labour* is the labour spent during this part of the workday. *Surplus domestic labour time* is that part of the workday during which the houseworker produces surplus value; *domestic surplus labour* is the labour spent during this part of the workday. Determining these two segments of time is not as easy for the houseworker as it is for the factory worker. For the houseworker, the domestic workday tends to coincide with the duration of the entire day itself, and it includes the houseworker's own time of consumption. This time of consumption is not easily distinguishable from the time during which she works to reproduce the entire working-class family. It is, nonetheless, possible to recognise and separate these two segments of time, and thus it is possible to determine the duration of surplus labour time that capital steals from the houseworker during the valorisation process described above.

The time of necessary labour provided by the worker is now insufficient to maintain and reproduce the working class. Its insufficiency cannot be resolved through the lengthening of their working day at the factory because this would mean an increase of the exchange value of their labour power. Similarly, incorporating in the exchange value of labour power the value of those means of subsistence that can be directly consumed cannot be the solution. In this case, the exchange value would become much greater, and thus it would be inconvenient for capital. Capital needs to engage necessary labour from another source that would make necessary labour sufficient for the factory worker, without increasing the exchange value of labour power. This other necessary labour time is precisely that provided by the houseworker, who transforms exchange value into use value that can be directly consumed.

Fully understanding the emergence of a working class of the house, and calculating the total necessary labour time performed in the overall cycle of capitalist production, requires that this necessary labour time be tied to the *real* value of the labour power of the entire working-class family. This value is not only a product of the necessary labour performed by the worker, but it is also a product of the necessary labour primarily performed by the houseworker. One could ask if this would mean counting it twice. The answer is no. As we have seen, the process of production and reproduction are distinct and appear as self-sufficient sides of the valorisation process. Therefore, the fact that the necessary labour time performed by the worker also includes the necessary labour time to produce the means of subsistence for the houseworker does not count within the process of reproduction. In the process of reproduction, the houseworker must re-earn with her labour that part of variable capital corresponding to the value of her means of subsistence.

Compared with the overall cycle of capital, the domestic workday is, in its entirety, unpaid labour time. On the contrary, for the factory worker the domestic working day is simply a lengthening of the necessary labour time he provides in the production process. For the factory worker, the domestic workday is necessary labour, required for him, and for his survival. This is true even though this necessary labour time goes beyond the necessary labour time (necessary because independent from the social form of his labour) the houseworker needs to reintegrate the variable value of advanced variable capital (the workers' wage). But we need to remind ourselves that, for the worker the need for surplus domestic labour derives from the very needs of his own existence. On the contrary, capital, which uses domestic labour as use value for value, yearns for surplus labour, including domestic surplus labour as the very basis of its existence.

We have also established that the domestic workday is composed of necessary labour time and surplus labour time. Now we ask: To what degree does capital exploit the houseworker's labour power? What is the rate of surplus value production? Drawing on Marx's formula, first, we notice that the proportional magnitude of surplus value, that is the proportion through which the variable part of variable capital (the worker's salary) is valued, is determined in this process, as it is in production, by the ratio between surplus value (s') and the variable part of variable capital (v').[4] This can be expressed as the formula:

$$sv' = \frac{s'}{v'}$$

We call the rate of surplus value sv' – this relative valorisation of the variable part of variable capital. Given that the value of the variable part of variable capital is equal to the exchange value of the houseworker's labour power that has been bought by variable capital, and given that this also determines the necessary part of the domestic workday, it follows that surplus value is to the variable part of variable capital what domestic surplus labour is to necessary domestic labour. The rate of surplus value in this production process is:

$$sv' = \frac{domestic\ surplus\ labour}{necessary\ domestic\ labour}$$

The specific production of surplus value in this process involves a specific form of exploitation of the houseworker by capital. The rate of surplus value described above represents the expression of her degree of exploitation. In the process of reproduction, the woman is not only

---

4   Ibid., 668–72.

oppressed, but also clearly exploited by capital. Nor is the worker inno-
cent. He also exploits, but he does so for his own needs, and not to
extract value. His exploitation is only the form through which capitalist
exploitation is made explicit. It is thus evident how variable capital
tends to correspond to the value of the means of subsistence of the
entire working-class family, but in a situation in which all the members
of the family, starting from the houseworker, are exploited. In this situation, everyone's exploitation, except for that of the worker, is hidden in
the shadow of the single wage, given to the worker in exchange for his
labour of production.

The fact that there is only one wage has meant, for the left, the
legitimation of the claim that exploitation has a single subject –
the worker; for capital the opportunity to allocate responsibility for
the control and discipline of those who are indirectly waged (women
and children) to a waged male workforce. All of this has meant great
savings on variable capital and a reduced potential for class struggle.
The working class has long risked being disarmed by this blindness in
the struggle against the entire process of the surplus labour, which is
to say, exploitation.

We should pause for a moment and consider the grave political consequences of the confusion of the wage with the relations of waged
labour in the strategy of the male left. It has been assumed that capitalist
exploitation does not exist where a wage is not present, and thus that
the exploitation of the unwaged does not exist. The fact that domestic
labour is not waged meant that it has never been considered labour. This
was true until the emergence of the feminist movement, and of a cycle
of struggles through which women have made domestic work visible and
revealed the correspondent exploitation of women. Under the pressure
of these struggles, and of the increasingly effective struggles of other
unwaged and indirectly waged groups, some sections of the male left
began to acknowledge not only that domestic labour exists, but also that
the potential for a struggle against it is at least as relevant as that taken
up by the waged working class.

The assumption of this perspective has remained superficial in many
cases as the mystification of the wage is still so great that we often hesitate
to understand or acknowledge surplus labour inside the relation of
indirectly waged labour. Today, it is well known that the relation of waged
labour includes the relation between the wage and non-wage, between

waged and indirectly waged workers – and also that the wage mystifies the relation of exploitation between waged labour power and capital by concealing the exploitation of indirectly waged labour power.

The feminist movement has brought this debate out into the open, and significant organisation around these topics marked a turning point in the struggle against surplus labour. In particular, a feminist movement emerged that organised for the reduction of the workday for women, starting from the domestic workday (in anticipation of its definitive destruction), and demanded money from the state as a means of opening up a direct struggle against capital. This movement marked a turning point, a strategic leap in the struggle against women's exploitation and against the surplus labour delivered inside the home.

Within this picture of the process of reproduction as a site of capitalist exploitation, the duration and the intensity of domestic labour are crucial. These two elements not only relate to the worker's need to extract useful products from the houseworker for his reproduction. They are also crucial in relation to the production of surplus value. The surplus value produced here is incorporated into the worker's labour power, valorising it in terms of (use) value. While the surplus value produced in the process of production is used (re-transformed) as capital, the surplus value produced in reproduction cannot be changed directly into capital, nor can it give rise to the accumulation of capital. This surplus value can only be used to create surplus value in the process of production. In other words, it is transmitted in the process of production, where it is re-transformed in surplus value. The production of surplus value in the process of production and reproduction of labour power is established as a precondition for the production of surplus value in commodity production.

The reason behind our characterisation of surplus value s' as *hidden* surplus value is that domestic surplus value hides behind the appearance of exchange value. The fact that this surplus value is hidden is an absolute necessity for capital. While the surplus value of the production process is incorporated in the overall mass of the exchange values produced, and as such it is included by capital, domestic surplus value is produced to be consumed by the capitalist without being bought in terms of exchange value. This role reversal enacted by the capitalist (the fact that he behaves as buyer instead of seller) also implies a reversal in terms of the valorisation of the commodity produced (labour power). This reversal is necessary because, otherwise, the capitalist as buyer would pay labour power at a greater exchange value, and with an arrangement that is disadvantageous for capital and advantageous for the worker.

To conclude, the surplus value sv' does not only represent the valorisation of the value of the houseworker's labour power v', but also expresses the value of the worker's labour power v. If we call v'' the overall value of the worker's labour power at the end of the process of reproduction, when he sells it to the capitalist, we have $v'' = v + v'$.

Because this valorisation occurs in the shadow of exchange value, when capital buys labour power from the worker it has a double advantage. Because capital buys labour power at its exchange value, capital gains the availability of both the worker's and the houseworker's labour power. Capital benefits from this availability in two different ways. The worker's labour power has a direct use value for capital, while the houseworker's labour power has an indirect use value. In the first case, capital benefits from a use value of living labour, while in the second case it benefits from the use value of dead labour. It is precisely the fact that capital benefits from the houseworker's labour power indirectly that allows it to take possession of the maximum amount of surplus labour. Capital appropriates surplus labour when it buys the worker's labour power at its exchange value for much less than its real value. This means that, through this one exchange between capital and worker, capital appropriates surplus value of both the worker and the houseworker.

This is a two-way profit. In the purchase of the worker's labour power, the surplus value produced in the process of reproduction goes to the capitalist and leaves no visible trace. By exchanging the wage with the use value of the worker's labour power, the capitalist can take everything as if it were free and providential fruit. The development of the process of reproduction not only represents the development of a new side of the valorisation process: by separating the value of variable capital from that of labour power, it challenges the equation of value that is the expression of the rate of surplus value, and thus the degree of exploitation of labour power in the production process:[5]

$$\frac{s}{v} = \frac{surplus\ labour}{necessary\ labour}$$

---

5   Ibid., p. 326.

The process of reproduction challenges this equation, not only within the process of production but in relation to the overall cycle of capital.

Everything stays the same for the worker: the surplus value he produces seems to be in the same relation with variable capital, just as the relation of his surplus labour with his necessary labour. But the capitalist is no longer satisfied with that necessary labour, because it is insufficient to make the worker carry out surplus labour; the capitalist needs domestic labour too. In other words, to have the worker produce surplus value, capital requires the surplus value produced by the houseworker as well.

If one wanted to calculate the rate of surplus value for the system in its entirety, this would be the average of the rates of the different sectors of production and of the sector of reproduction. To highlight the sector of reproduction in relation to a particular cycle of production (a cycle of reproduction being always present within any cycle of production), one would need to calculate the average.

If one wanted to calculate the mass of surplus value produced for the system in its entirety, this would correspond to the sum of the masses of surplus value produced in each sector, including that of the production and reproduction of labour power. This means that the mass of surplus value produced for the system is equal to the amount of variable capital advanced, multiplied by the average of the rates of surplus value in each sector. In other words, it is determined by the total number of individuals whose labour power is simultaneously exploited both directly and indirectly by capital, and the average of the different degrees of exploitation of individual labour power, calculated in all the sectors.

PART II

8

The Labour of Reproduction Is Productive

The initial consequence of the preceding analysis, demonstrating that the process of reproduction is one of value formation, is that domestic labour is productive labour.[1] This is not the place to deal with the general issue of productive vs unproductive labour, an issue which has now become extremely problematic and complex. The argument here will be limited to the process of determining whether this analysis can also be applied to the sexual reproduction of masculine labour power: in other words – is the labour of prostitution productive? Our answer is yes, because these two processes, despite their different characteristics, function with a shared logic. This argument may be heresy in the context of a Marxist tradition which has always maintained an attitude that prostitutes need redeeming, and a position that excludes prostitutes from class composition.[2] From

---

1   The arguments of this chapter draw extensively from Marx's draft manuscript 'Theorien über den Mehrwert' (Theories of Surplus Value) from his works of 1862 and 1863, which, in the mid-1970s, when Fortunati was working from the text, were presented as the prospective fourth volume of *Capital*. The initial translation that Fortunati worked from was published in 1974 by the Rome-based publisher Newton Compton Editori, with an introduction by Lucio Colletti, as *Storia delle teorie economiche*. This Italian edition roughly followed Kautsky's original three-volume edition (1905–10) that significantly edited and rearranged the text. The references here are to page numbers in the English edition released in 1963 by the collaboration between Progress Publishers in Moscow and the London publisher Lawrence & Wishart; it was also largely based on the Kautsky edition. Below, we have added explanatory notes when the English version deviates significantly from the Italian.

2   The concept of class composition, so central to *operaismo*, had precedence in radical post-war Italian sociology and is often traced to the journal *Quaderni Rossi*,

our perspective, this attitude towards not only prostitutes but women in general is disgraceful insofar as it has proven to be blind, manipulative and violent, not to mention politically unproductive.

If we return to the origin, what is Marx's point of view on this issue? Marx touches upon it more than once in *Theories of Surplus-Value*, and once more demonstrates great conceptual uncertainty. The first of these moments is when Marx examines Adam Smith's second formulation of productive labour:[3]

> The largest part of society, that is to say the working class, must incidentally perform this kind of labour for itself; but it is only able to perform it when it has laboured 'productively'. It can only cook meat for itself when it has produced a wage with which to pay for the meat; and it can only keep its furniture and dwellings clean, it can only polish its boots, when it has produced the value of furniture, house rent and boots. To this class of productive labourers itself, therefore, the labour which they perform for themselves appears as 'unproductive labour'. This unproductive labour never enables them to repeat the same unproductive labour a second time unless they have previously laboured productively.[4]

Here, Marx characterises domestic labour as unproductive. He is referring to a mythical working class that is simultaneously labour power as capacity of production and as capacity of reproduction, engaged in labour that is alternatively productive (in the factory) and unproductive (at home). If, instead of envisioning a working class that goes from the hearth

---

particularly Romano Alquati's early studies on the factories of Fiat and Olivetti, though Alquati does not yet deploy the term. Romano Alquati, *Sulla FIAT e altri scritti* (Milan: Feltrinelli, 1975). Steve Wright elaborates the genesis and debates around the concept in his classic study. Steve Wright, *Storming Heaven: Class Composition and Struggle in Italian Autonomist Marxism* (London: Pluto Press, 2002). The exclusion of domestic workers and sex workers from the concept of 'class composition' within the groups of *operaismo*, *autonomia* and the left more broadly was a major theme for Lotta Femminista.

3   In this chapter, Fortunati refers primarily to 'Theories of Productive and Unproductive Labour', ch. 4 in Karl Marx, *Theories of Surplus-Value*, Part I (Moscow: Progress Publishers, 1963), 152–304. The Italian translation referenced in the original was this one: Karl Marx, *Il Capitale Libro Terzo*, trans. Maria Luisa Boggeri (Rome: Riuniti, 1968). For the sake of fidelity to Fortunati's text, we have used quotations from the Progress edition.

4   Marx, *Theories of Surplus-Value*, 166.

to the factory, from the factory to house cleaning, from labour that is productive for capital to labour that is unproductive, he had attended to the shift, already beginning in his lifetime, to a working class divided into two sections (males at the factory, females in the scullery), he would have had to address the kernel of the problem, instead of ignoring it.

The second of these moments is in the discussion of this problem where Marx cites (and agrees with) Smith:

> It remains true, however, that the commodity appears as past, objec-tivised labour, and that therefore, if it does not appear in the form of a thing, it can only appear in the form of labour power itself; but never directly as living labour itself (except only in a roundabout way which in practice seems the same, but whose significance lies in the determi-nation of different rates of wages). Productive labour would therefore be such labour as produces commodities or directly produces, trains, develops, maintains, or reproduces labour-power itself. Adam Smith excludes the latter from his category of productive labour; arbitrarily, but with a certain correct instinct – that if he included it, this would open the floodgates for false pretensions to the title of productive labour. In so far therefore as we leave labour-power itself out of account, productive labour is labour which produces commodities, material products, whose production has cost a definite quantity of labour or labour-time.[5]

Here, Marx is lucid enough to notice that Smith's exclusion of the whole of reproductive labour from the rubric of productive labours is totally arbitrary. He nonetheless sustains such a distinction because he fears that a possible inclusion of such labour could create false pretences by which some of these labourers could claim their labour as 'productive'. The fear of possible confusion is perhaps the sign of a real confusion in Marx: a confusion between domestic labour (housework) and the labour of house servants (menial servants' work).[6]

A third move occurs a few pages later, when Marx affirms that John Stuart Mill, in his book *Essays on Some Unsettled Questions of Political*

---

5   Ibid., 172.
6   The terms 'housework' and 'menial servants' work' in parentheses appear in English in the original.

Economy, added nothing to Smith's (second) definition except to say that 'labours which produce labour-power itself are also productive'.[7] Here, the problem is revisited, but, once more, it is not confronted. Marx's arguments to demonstrate that the labour of reproduction is unproductive remain inconsistent.

As concerns our argument, there is one issue that needs to be resolved. Does *this* labour – domestic labour and prostitution – share any characteristics that, according to Marx, would define any kind of labour as productive? Marx affirms: 'The only worker who is productive is one who produces surplus-value for the capitalist, or in other words contributes towards the self-valorisation of capital'.[8] In *Theories of Surplus-Value*, he clarifies this claim, saying that only 'labour that is directly transformed into surplus value is productive', and he further specifies that surplus value production must occur directly in order to qualify labour as productive. In addition, because he sees the production of surplus value as anchored only to the relation of waged labour – which is to say to 'specifically social relations of production, of historical origin, that mark the worker as a direct means of valorising capital' – he affirms that, for labour to be productive, it must be waged.

> Productive labour, as understood in the context of capitalist production, is wage-labour which, exchanged against the variable part of capital (the part of the capital that is spent on wages), reproduces not only this part of the capital (or the value of its own labour-power), but in addition produces surplus-value for the capitalist. It is only thereby that commodity or money is transformed into capital, is produced as capital.[9]

A secondary determination of productive labour, on the basis of which Marx formulates a supplementary definition of productive labour, is that 'a characteristic of productive labourers, that is, labourers producing capital', is 'that their labour realises itself in commodities, in material wealth'.[10]

---

7   Marx, *Theories of Surplus-Value*, 182.

8   Karl Marx, *Capital*, vol. 1, *A Critique of Political Economy*, trans. Ben Fowkes (London: Penguin, New Left Review: 1990 [1976]), 644.

9   Marx, *Theories of Surplus-Value*, 152.

10   Ibid., 410.

If we compare such characteristics with those of reproductive labour, we can see how their implications seem different – at least on a formal level. Formally, reproductive labour seems neither to produce surplus value nor to be waged, nor to produce commodities. In reality, however, its characteristics are similar:

1. It produces surplus value, even though it does not do so in terms of exchange values.
2. It is indirectly waged labour, though it is framed by capital as a natural force of social labour.
3. It produces a commodity (labour power) regardless of the fact that this commodity is saleable neither by capital nor by the house-worker (its producer), but only by the factory worker. Thus reproductive labour only assumes this secondary aspect of productive labour under its own special circumstances.

Does this specificity preclude reproductive labour from being productive? It does not. Its specificity must be understood in terms of its twofold character. This specificity does not undermine those elements that qualify it as productive labour; on the contrary, it acts as a mirror image of the characteristics that normally qualify productive labour in the production process. The labour of reproduction that is not directly waged is a prerequisite and a condition for the existence of waged productive labour. Similarly, the surplus value produced in the process of reproduction is a necessary condition for the surplus value generated in the process of production. Likewise for the labour that produces commodities, its direct transformation into capital is a necessary condition for its productivity, while for the labour of reproduction, the necessary condition for its productivity is its *indirect* transformation into capital. Finally, the labour of reproduction is productive, but it has a form of productivity with its own specific features, because it is a prerequisite and condition for the existence of the productive labour occurring in the production process.

At this point, there are still two issues to resolve. First of all, arguing that the transformation of this labour into capital is indirect means that this labour nonetheless produces surplus value. This is the only condition that allows capital to determine if it will transform such surplus value into capital, to determine when and how to make use of the labour power produced. If, hypothetically, the labour of reproduction were productive only in those cases in which it produced and reproduced the waged worker, it would mean that the production of surplus value in the process of reproduction was simply a consequence of the labour employed in production. In this hypothetical, reproduction would be positioned as a necessary condition for the direct creation of surplus value by the waged worker and subsequently transformed into capital.

In reality, however, housework must be perpetually productive. This consistent productivity is the necessary condition for capital to be able to subsequently determine how many workers to employ in waged work and how many to consign to the status of relative overpopulation. Capital *must* control such categories given the specific character of the surplus value generated by the houseworker, where the difference is not that between productive and unproductive labour, but between labour that is subsequently transformed into capital and labour that is transformed only into the worker's consumption. The only case in which the difference between the labour that transforms itself directly into capital and the labour that does so indirectly has to be related not to the production of commodities but to worker's consumption. It is only by such an arrangement that housework is transformed into capital – only if the labour power in which domestic surplus labour is incorporated is productively consumed within the production process – because, in this case, the surplus value incorporated in the worker is converted into exchange value, and subsequently capital. In any other case, the opposite occurs. In this regard, Marx is correct when he argues with economists who maintain that the productivity of any labour depends on the productive consumption of what it produces – as he points out: 'The producer of tobacco is productive, although the consumption of tobacco is unproductive. Production for unproductive consumption is quite as productive as that for productive consumption; always assuming that it produces or reproduces capital.'[11]

The second problem is to show how it is possible that the labour of reproduction appears to capital as productive labour, even if, at the same time, it is also naturalised (or considered *unnatural*) as a force of social labour. The contradiction is evident here. The same productive force is presented as productive for both labour and capital and apparently

---

11   Karl Marx, *Grundrisse: Foundations of the Critique of Political Economy*, trans. Martin Nicolaus (London: Penguin Books, 1993), 306.

counted twice. This contradiction is only an apparent one, however. Because reproductive labour, like all other productive forces, is concerned only with the working process where it is utilised – in reproduction – and only as use value, it is presented as capital's own inherent property – as a thing, as a use value – with no bearing on the exchange value of labour power. Regardless of whether the houseworker or the sex worker works, and whether she works more or less, the exchange value of what she produces (labour power) remains constant, because it is determined by necessary labour time as it is calculated in the production process. What changes is only its use value. With regard to labour power as the capacity of production, capital is only interested in *its use value* – not in its exchange value. As a consequence, because it is only use value that is affected by the different forms of productivity of reproductive labour, this productive force is not counted twice. For capital, reproductive labour is a productive force of labour, but one that is productive only based on the difference between its value and its valorisation.

9
The *Doppelcharakter* of Reproductive Labour

If the work of reproduction – understood as housework and prostitution, broadly speaking – is productive, then it goes without saying that, like any labour productive of value, it too takes on a double character. It is not only concrete, individually necessary and complex labour, but also abstractly human labour that is both socially necessary and simple. As with work that produces commodities, it too has passed through the historical transformation from work that produces primarily use values to work producing exchange value. This transformation of reproductive labour follows specifically from the labour of reproduction of individuals (posited as a natural condition of human existence and organic interchange between the individual and nature) to domestic labour and prostitution as the two specifically social forms of work required for the reproduction of labour power. It is in this passage, from pre-capitalist forms of labour to capitalist forms, that labour reveals its effective duplicity: the *Doppelcharakter* of labour that was recognised for the first time by Marx.[1] Although this passage has established the predominance

---

1 Fortunati's original text retains Marx's original German term in its title and deploys it at numerous points below in conjunction with the common Italian translation of the term as *duplice carattere*, as in 'Duplice carattere del lavoro rappresentato nelle merci', giving the title of the second section of the first chapter in the Cantimori translation of vol. 1 used by Fortunati. The same title would be rendered by Fowkes as 'The Dual Character of the Labour Embodied in Commodities'. See Karl Marx, *Il Capitale*, vol. 1 (Rome: Editori Riuniti, 1968), 73.

of exchange value over use value, of labour productive of exchange value over labour productive of use value, this transition maintains that value-producing labour has the same determinations as labour productive of use value.

This statement holds true both for the work of production and for that of reproduction. Productive labour is demanded in the process of production as it is in the process of reproduction. If labour in the sphere of production is abstract, social and simple, in the process of reproduction it must have the same characteristics. There can be no form of reproductive labour whose product (labour power) is expressed as abstract, social and simple labour, which does not possess these same qualities itself.

In the realm of production, capital needs to free itself from the concrete materiality, the particular qualities and infinite varieties of labour involved in the commodity's production in the determination of its exchange value. The same holds true in the realm of reproduction.

However, the labour of reproduction assumes the characteristics of value-producing labour in its own particular way. Reproduction is also abstract human labour, but – unlike the labour that produces commodities – it is not abstracted from the use value of its product (labour power), but from its exchange value. As with labour-producing commodities, reproductive work is social, but it is such because of its social characteristics. These characteristics are dual. The first is its universal character, because, while reproductive labour is performed by the individual houseworker or sex worker, it is undifferentiated from the labour of any other houseworker or sex worker. The second is its character of equality, because the labour of a houseworker or sex worker is equal to the labour of another houseworker or sex worker. Therefore, although reproductive labour is individually specific, it is labour in directly social form, like labour that produces commodities. It is a form of simple labour as well, but, as opposed to commodity-producing labour, it is simple despite the fact that the value of its product (labour power) is far greater than its exchange value.

That reproductive labour takes on the *Doppelcharakter* of productive work in its own particular fashion should not surprise us at this point. On the contrary, such doubling should by now be familiar, given that the commodity reproductive labour produces is unique, shaped in a peculiar fashion by those features that constitute it as value-producing.

As for the first characteristic, that of being abstractly human labour, reproductive labour is such regardless of the exchange value of the labour power it produces given that its product (labour power) is of interest to capital only as a use value. As a use value, labour power is of interest not from a qualitative point of view, but from a quantitative one – that is to say only as abstracted from the diverse aspects and bodily forms that constitute it as a use value. It does not matter that labour power belongs to a specific person: any labour power will do, as long as it has the capacity to produce abstract human labour. All its material qualities can be erased, except that which makes it productive of value.

Because the instrumental character of labour power as use value is not erased, the instrumental character of the labour represented in it also remains. What disappears are the different concrete material forms of such labour. Domestic labour, for example, is not distinguished from the labour of prostitution: both are reduced to abstract human labour, though they remain distinct because of their unique characteristics as reproductive labour.

This limitation on the abstraction of the reproductive work contained in the commodity of labour power also affects the abstraction of the work objectified in all other commodities because reproductive labour is an expenditure of human labour power distinguished not only by the fact that it is labour power but that it is a specific form of labour power as a capacity of production. Only if, beginning from here, a further abstraction is made considering the commodity itself, beyond the fact that it is an object or individual – that is, considering the overall cycle of capital – only then does labour itself appear as truly abstract human labour unlimited by its concrete materiality.

With respect to the second characteristic, the labour of reproduction is socially determined not because it is performed in a social context, but because any individual has value in the process only because they embody the abstract human labour of reproduction. It is only the quantity of such abstract human labour socially necessary for its repro-duction that determines the magnitude of its value as labour power available to capital. In the production process, capital requires an average social labour power, and requires the same in the arena of reproduction. These quantities must correspond to the necessary average, which is to say their socially necessary quantity; in other words, labour power must be de-individualised. To achieve this, capital needs to de-individualise the woman, to strip her delivery of labour power of its unique character and render her an average individual. This flattening is required because the socially necessary work of reproduction, expressed as labour time, can only be posed as a necessary average labour time, the time socially necessary to reproduction.

Finally, with regard to the status of reproductive labour as *simple labour*, this is the case despite the fact that the value of its product (the labour power utilised in production) is greater than its own exchange value. Reproductive labour is simple because it is the expression of a form of labour power whose product requires much more labour time than is apparent – although such additional labour time does not increase pre-production costs for capital. In the accumulation process, the most radical and at the same time the easiest way to simplify not only commodity-producing labour but also reproductive labour in general, is to position the latter as a natural force of social labour. In this context, the labour of reproduction is, a priori, rendered simpler than that of commodity production, since it is considered an extrinsic labour power, a natural power of social labour. Capital presupposes lower maintenance costs and lower value than the labour power of the waged worker.

As a job that is simpler on average than those in the factory, it is unskilled labour *par excellence*. It is labour that can be reduced to simple labour, the basic labour power that any average woman possesses in her physical person, without requiring any particular training. It is undifferentiated labour, uniform, always qualitatively homogenised: labour that can be different only in quantity.

Commodity-producing labour has therefore been simplified not only because it has been rendered undifferentiated, uniform and qualitatively consistent, and not only because the value of the labour power involved has been progressively reduced, but also because the use value of this labour power has always been greater than its exchange value. In other words, its cost of production has been reduced not only because the necessary labour time (the value of its means of subsistence) has been drastically reduced (today practically to zero) but also because the labour power of the houseworker has been presented as valueless.

In reality, the development of simple labour is much less extreme than it seems. All labour is made to appear simpler than it is, since the production of labour power generally requires much more labour time than appears reflected in exchange. This is particularly true of the labour power of reproduction however which manifests itself in labour whose quality is far higher than it appears and therefore constitutes a far greater value than is reflected indirectly in the exchange value of its product (the labour power of the production process). Thus, the average social labour in both production processes (production and reproduction) – regardless of the differences described above – is always more complex than it appears.

This produces no contradiction: the greater complexity costs capital nothing, even though, in the production process, it generates greater value. Similarly, it is not a contradiction that reproductive labour is simple work despite the fact that it produces a form of labour power more complex than it appears because it is subjected to one of the primary strategies used to simplify labour power: reducing its exchange value. In turn, capitalism must determine the magnitude of the value of labour power by reducing it to simple labour, purging it of the qualitative meaning and content contributed by the houseworker's labour power so that the latter may be reduced to an expenditure of simple labour power.

There is another point to clarify, however. While in reality, reproductive labour shares the characteristics of all labour that produces value, formally housework assumes these characteristics in a different fashion from the labour of prostitution.

The reason for this difference is clear. The commodity aspect of the prostitute's labour power is more evident as it is directly expressed monetarily. Consequently, the relative work is also represented, as we will see shortly, in a more explicit fashion as abstract, social and simple work. The labour power of the housewife, on the other hand, takes on the appearance of a commodity in a minor key, which allows capital greater latitude not only of ideological mystification but of formal representation.

How is this difference expressed on a formal level? While the labour of prostitution assumes the above-mentioned characteristics in a fashion closer to commodity-producing labour, domestic labour does so differently. Domestic labour displays only the characteristics of the labour of producing use values.

The more commodity-producing labour develops the characteristics of exchange value-producing labour, the more domestic labour must develop those of labour producing use value. The more the factory becomes the site where workers are posited as abstract, socially necessary and simple labour power, the more the house must be posited as the site where they exist as concrete, individually necessary and complex individuals. Housework can be mobilised by capital as abstractly human, socially necessary and simple labour only to the extent that this labour represents itself as the opposite.

Capital must establish such contradictory movements to confront the fundamental contradiction of its mode of production: to face the fact that the individual qua labour power is posited as a commodity, although individuals should be the negation of what a commodity is. Because of this contradiction, a large virtual space of refusal and struggle against capital is opened. To contain this space, it was necessary for capital to construct a representation of the home as the non-factory; a release valve for the worker. In relation to the factory that produces commodities, the factory that produces labour power cannot represent itself as such. The worker must maintain the illusion, assured by a specific organisation of domestic labour, that the ringing of the factory bell will put an end to his confinement in the factory – at least for that day.

From his earliest works, Marx had wondered: 'What is the meaning, in the development of mankind, of this reduction of the greater part of mankind to abstract labour?' He asked this question even though he was primarily focused on the production of commodities.[2] Now it is possible to answer this question not only by describing the overall repercussions of the process of abstraction, socialisation and simplification for the individual/labour power in reproductive labour, but also by describing, in parallel, the same processes as they apply to the organisation of housework on a formal level. Only in drawing out this parallel can we attempt to describe the progress of the abstraction, socialisation and simplification of labour in the overall cycle of capitalist accumulation with the differences and contradictions it sets in motion.

The expenditure of abstract human labour in the production process negates the concrete individual, as Mr So-and-so. It assumes individuals as indistinguishable and interchangeable, distinct from other commodities (as objects) only because the commodity these individuals possess can create value. In other words, the labour power commodity abstracts them by expropriating them of their specific qualities. But,

---

2   Karl Marx, *Early Writings*, trans. Rodney Livingstone and Gregor Benton (London: Penguin, 1992), 289.

since individuals are individuals only insofar as they are concrete and particular this abstraction is, in effect, dehumanisation.

The expenditure of abstract and social human labour implies that, in the process of production, the individual as labour power (who is required to produce a determined use value, a quantity of socially necessary labour) must disregard its own individual characteristics – the particularities with which it could potentially manifest labour power. In other words, the requirement to provide social labour translates into the forced adaptation of the individual as labour power to the average in which labour power is socially exerted. It translates in a necessary uniformity, undifferentiation and de-individualisation.

In the process of production, the worker is confronted with a general sociality of labour resulting from the average characteristics of social labour. The individual as labour power confronts other individuals not as distinct individuals bearing their own labour power in relation to a multiplicity of other singular individuals, but as an individual confronted with a mass average – a socialised dimension of labour within which they must include themselves. But as mentioned before, each individual is characterised by a particular set of attitudes and material and immaterial characteristics that defines them against the standardised, homogenised, mass individual. Even such socialisation and massification is therefore, in reality, a dehumanisation.

The expenditure of abstract, social and simple labour power implies that the individual as labour power is simplified and denied in his potential and actual complexity. The individual is therefore abstracted, de-individualised and depersonalised. The individual as labour power who is forced to expend simple labour is rendered indistinct with respect to other individuals as labour power, rendered uniform and homogeneous. But, since individuality expresses itself in complexity, this simplification also entails its dehumanisation.

If the abstraction, socialisation and simplification of labour has such consequences in the production process, it cannot simply be repeated in equivalent and parallel terms in the process of reproduction. This is not to say that the labour of reproduction is not in fact abstract, social and simple – rather, that the development of these characteristics must not preclude the representation of this work, on a formal level, as exclusively concrete, individually specific and complex. In other words, it must not conflict with its representation as a labour of production of use values, and therefore of individuals rather than abstract labour power.

As mentioned above, this is an obligatory passage for capital that must try to contain the space of potential struggle and sabotage allowed by its mode of production in which the individuality of labour power is also its own negation.

This is why domestic labour seems on the one hand to be the negation of productive labour as abstract, social and simple labour, because it is represented only as concrete, individually specific and complex. On the other hand, it appears:

1. as the most concrete form of labour, capable of splitting itself into infinite ways of working and of being implemented in a limitless variety of use values – as infinite as the variety of the specific needs of individuals themselves;
2. both as the most private and the most isolated form of labour, and as the most uniquely individual, able to be implemented in multiple ways, as diverse as the specificities of individuals/labour power to be articulated and tailored to the single individual whose labour power is produced and reproduced;
3. as the most complex form of labour, able to differentiate itself in infinite ways, in infinite different operations and to be qualitatively unique and unrepeatable compared to the work provided by other houseworkers.

The *Doppelcharakter* of domestic labour is in place because the more the work of production becomes abstract, socialised and simplified, dehumanising the worker, the more domestic labour must appear to humanise him. It appears to humanise him by giving him the illusion of being an individual in addition to his labour power, or better by giving him the illusion of *going back* to being an individual outside of the factory – to being himself, with his materiality, specificity and complexity, an individual with all his particularities and characteristics, starting from his personality.

This concreteness, with its non-social character and complexity, also affects the houseworker, who must be, for the worker, his opposite: an individual, not labour power. What is more, the houseworker must be a specific individual, a specific woman distinct from other women – an individual who enters a private relationship with him, and finally an individual in all her complexity. In the process of production of commodities, production is independent of the individuality of the individual/ labour power that produces it. This production demands from labour power its socialisation, indifference, standardisation and simplification. The more this process is put in place, the process of reproduction and production of labour power must be represented in such a way as to depend strictly on the individuality of the houseworker and to be founded, on the one hand, on her isolation and distinction from other houseworkers and, on the other, on her individual characteristics.

Even more, the individuality, the non-sociability and complexity of the houseworker must be made manifest to the greatest degree possible. The individual as labour power cannot represent themselves as reproduced by an indistinct, average and simplified individual, because this acknowledgement would pose the very negation of their individuality. Additionally, they must believe that their own reproduction as labour power requires a specific woman, one who is unique and unrepeatable in her complex individuality. Reproduction must be undertaken exclusively by that individual and only by that individual in a privatised and wholly unique fashion. This clarifies how the capitalist sentiment of love and falling in love is linked to the organisation of domestic labour – to this particular movement of its abstraction/materiality, sociability/ non-sociability and simplicity/complexity.

This contradictory movement is also reflected in the basic aporia that characterises the bourgeois social sciences. While these sciences assume the individual as the subject of social action and object, therefore, of scientific research, they are destined only to produce knowledge of the subject as an average individual, that is, as similar to other average individuals and not as a unique and unrepeatable human being. For vulgar political economy this so-called individual, who yet remains the subject of the discourse, is investigated as labour – that is, as one force indistinguishable from the others (land, capital). Here, the epitome of humanity (the individual) is overturned and transformed into a commodity among commodities.

The process of the sexual reproduction of male labour power, on the other hand, proceeds in a nearly inverse fashion. Here, it is evident, even at the level of formal representation, how the labour of prostitution has as its object not a concrete individual but *any* individual. The client can be anyone. The labour of prostitution appears not to satisfy the sexual needs of that individual – neither in terms of their specificity and materiality, nor in their complexity. The labour of the prostitute is also manifestly aimed at the satisfaction of the general sexual and social needs of the individual male as simplified, de-individualised and depersonalised. This does not mean that there is not a division in the labour of prostitution designed to satisfy various types of sexual needs, including so-called perversions. Even the latter are conceived as general types, however. It is not surprising therefore, that the worker as a client (or *John*) in this context perceives himself as a commodity and his sexual reproduction as a reproduction of a commodity – specifically of his labour power. In this context he suffers a blow to his individuality very similar to those caused by factory work that produces commodities: in a few words, his de-individualisation, standardisation and lack of differentiation.

Capital has managed to set in motion, govern and transform the constitutive characteristics of both productive and reproductive labour only to the extent that, in the process of producing and reproducing labour power, in addition to having set in motion and governed them together, it has simultaneously managed to pull them in opposite directions.

But what are the effects suffered by humanity from the reduction of the labour time of reproduction to abstract, social and simple labour? Unlike workers – who, the more abstract, socialised and simplified they are in the process of production, the more they are positioned as concrete, individualised and complex individuals in the realm of reproduction – the houseworker is subject to a further movement. In the moment of production, in addition to the progress on the real level of the abstraction, socialisation and simplification of her labour, she is also subject to the representation of her labour progressing in the opposite direction. She is subject to the representation of her labour as concrete, individualised and complex, or better as the *most* concrete, individualised and complex labour of all. For the houseworker, it is precisely her being subject to this further movement of representation in the production process that mitigates the contradiction of being reproduced '*meno e peggio*' than the worker.[3]

---

3   In the original this phrase is included in quotation marks meaning literally 'less and worse'. The houseworker generally incorporates less reproductive labour than the other members of the family (the male worker in particular) and she generally has fewer commodities at her disposal for consumption.

10

This Strange Form of Absolute Surplus Value

Having demonstrated that the labour of reproduction is productive, the question then becomes how such productivity is developed.

First, we must distinguish the process of production and reproduction of labour power from the process of sexual reproduction of male labour power, because their trajectories are different in this respect.

Our thesis is that the production and reproduction of labour power proceeds as an exact inversion of development in the production process. If, in the production process, the increase of productivity is historically pursued through the development of cooperation and division of labour and through the increased use of machinery, in the process that interests us here it is pursued by an *underdevelopment* in terms of both cooperation and division of labour, and only a limited use of machinery. The two production processes face completely different fates in the methods used to increase their productivity.

In the first place, it is clear that the productivity of domestic labour cannot be determined by the development of its productive force, since it is posited as a natural force of social labour. Due to the specificity of the commodity produced and the contradictions it poses, there is neither a development of cooperation nor division of labour.

To begin with, capital cannot accumulate houseworkers in the same place, during the same time and under the command of the same capitalist, as it does for the waged worker.

The conditions for achieving such accumulation are all in place. The number of women who work in this process is very high (including almost all women at some point in their lifetime). The working time is the same – limited by the hours spent in the production process on the one hand and on the other by the natural limits of the hours in the day. Although the place is not the same, the field of action is consistent. Production is the production of the same kind of commodity: labour power.

But there are differences. First of all, there is the fact that, in this process of reproduction, the wages of a worker can only buy the labour power of one individual woman. The waged worker generally possesses the means of subsistence both for himself and for his family. Consequently, since the individual worker can only control a single domestic labour process, each process must take place in an individual space, separated from the others.

As a consequence, the production process of reproduction turns out to be composed of discrete micro-production processes. Reproduction takes on this form because, to be established on a real global level by capital, it must be represented, on the formal plane, as a process of the worker's individual consumption governed solely by the individual wage. A factory-like structuring of reproduction that revealed itself as such would undermine its own functioning. It would imply such a direct takeover of the life of the proletariat by capital and the state that it has never been permissible, nor would it be now given the existing balance of power between the classes.

There is, moreover, another subjective condition which hinders the spatial accumulation of houseworkers. It is politically necessary for capital to divide, at least in the domain of reproduction, the workers, who have collaborated for many hours in the process of production, so that their potential path of organising is a more gruelling one.

A panoramic view of production displays an inversion of the process of reproduction. In production, capital accumulates workers and makes them cooperate. In reproduction, it disperses houseworkers, atomising them in a thousand different spaces: a thousand houses under the command of as many workers. Historically and conceptually, the starting point of capitalist production differs in each process. In production, it is the workshop through the entire period of manufacturing, and subsequently the factory, starting from the advent of large-scale industry.[1] In reproduction, it is the house, the atomised factory *par excellence*, which, despite being the factory specific to the domestic working process, appears as a non-factory. Its door presents itself as the place where the capitalist relationship ceases: the worker is no longer a worker, the woman is only a woman, work is not work. Indeed, capital can build the factory in the production process only to the extent that it builds the apparent non-factory of reproduction.

After all, the dispersal of houseworkers in the process of domestic labour does not inhibit the establishment of a socially necessary average of domestic work. The domestic labour objectified in the use value of labour power is, as we have seen, labour of an average social quality and the expenditure of a social average of labour power, since it is commanded and controlled by capital in its entirety. This makes it possible to speak of the domestic working day and consequently of the average magnitude of this working day. This is why the dispersal of female domestic workers does not invalidate the average socially necessary domestic labour, given that the different individual quantities of labour provided in different individual households by women cancel one another out and allow such an average to emerge.

This dispersal corresponds to the impossibility both of a common consumption of a part of the means of production and a corresponding impossibility of the development of cooperation. In the context of the household, given that the means of production are included in the means of subsistence of the individual worker, they are posited as means of production related to a single labour process, and thus only consumable by the individual houseworker. There is no accumulation of the means of production in the same space and, consequently, no common consumption. Instead, atomisation, dispersal and individual consumption are necessary for two reasons:

---

1   Here and throughout this chapter Fortunati critically adapts the historical periodisation found in the first volume of *Capital*, Chapter 14, 'Division of Labour and Manufacture', in which the period of manufacture generally refers to the mid-sixteenth through the late eighteenth century characterised by increased division and specialisation of labour but not yet the consistent use of heavy machinery that characterised large-scale industrial capitalism in the nineteenth century. Karl Marx, *Capital*, vol. 1, *A Critique of Political Economy*, trans. Ben Fowkes (London: Penguin, New Left Review, 1990 [1976]), 455–91.

1. There can be no joint possession by the collective of workers (not to mention a broader community) of their means of subsistence, and there are two explanations for this. First, the individual worker is the sole owner of the means of production of a specific house-worker's domestic labour, since they are part of the means of subsistence of his family. Second, the means of production of domestic labour although not fully owned by the individual worker, cannot, particularly since the advent of the Industrial Revolution be consumed in common. These resources are water, electricity, gas – in a word, energy – which capital has progressively transformed from a free natural resource into exchange value. Although energy is consumed by many houseworkers at the same time, suggesting *collective* consumption, this does not take the form of *common* consumption: that is, it does not assume a form of consumption that would involve the development of cooperation in domestic labour.

2. There can be no common consumption of the means of production of domestic labour, because there cannot be a large enough concentration of means of production of such labour in the hands of individual capitalists. Capitalists do not have an interest in concentrating such labour on a mass level since, to make women work side by side in the same work process, they would have to guarantee them a salary. It is much more productive for capital to posit domestic labour as a natural force of social labour. This is how it exploits two workers with a single wage.

Although no capitalist has an interest in organising such labour, the state, in its role as collective capitalist, is obliged to do so and to pose as the owner of an extensive means of reproduction. Though individual reproduction remains fundamental to the overall process of reproduction, it must be integrated through adequate levels of social reproduction of labour power. The social reproduction of labour power is, however, positioned as complementary to its domestic reproduction.

On the one hand, social reproduction is complementary because it can fulfil only some aspects of the domestic labour process, with respect to which it is a partial and incomplete process. Social reproduction can only undertake the reproduction, and not the production, of labour power. It is no coincidence that it provides only immaterial production of certain specific use values, such as information or sex, and not others, such as, for example, affection, love or care. Thus, social reproduction is a complementary and limited extension of the domestic labour process. This limit is determined by the fact that, although in social reproduction there are real and proper means of production (and they present themselves as such) and involve a common consumption of these means by many workers, this labour is necessarily waged labour. This is a disadvantage for capital, and nullifies any advantages, such that the family system remains the most economical.

The common consumption of the means of production of domestic labour is objectively prevented in the capitalist mode of production by the fact that one of the fundamental means of production of domestic labour is the body of the houseworker. This means that no individual besides herself and, to a lesser extent, the wage labourer who has purchased her labour power, can make use of the houseworker's body for their own reproduction. The same is true, albeit to a lesser extent, for the consumption of the male worker's body by the houseworker. Their bodies are the only means of production that presuppose a common consumption performed by both. But this is not exactly the *common consumption* alluded to above, because it is not a form of consumption shared between all houseworkers, but only between a single houseworker and a single waged worker in his role as a secondary subject of reproductive labour. In any case, such common consumption does not transmit any value to labour power, since bodies have no intrinsic value in and of themselves, because their existence is presupposed as natural.

The general lack of understanding about how reproductive labour is organised in a capitalist way and how it functions has led to many theories and exhortations that the working class collectivise its means of subsistence or push for their collectivisation by capital. Such exhortations can only distract from the emancipation from domestic slavery. Whether the proposal is to develop an organisation of domestic labour that will increase cooperation and productivity (a proposal directed to capital itself) or one that claims to create an alternative organisation of domestic labour opposed to that of capitalism, or to organise reproduction as a prefiguration of a future communist society, all these proposals have failed. Their failure is the clearest demonstration that there are specific laws that regulate reproduction. The only way to change them is by struggling against capital on the very terrain of reproduction.

The dispersal of female houseworkers fully corresponds to the unco-operative form assumed by their labour. In domestic labour, every single production process is isolated from the others; every female worker is isolated from the others. This lack of cooperation between female houseworkers is the prerequisite for the cooperation of male waged workers.

The fact that some simple cooperation does exist, and especially between women from the same family does not change this argument. This is not the formal cooperation that presents itself as a historical phenomenon peculiar to the capitalist production process.

The analogy of the photographic negative mentioned above appears once more. In the process of production, capital proceeds with the accumulation of workers in one place, sets average social labour into motion, causes a portion of the means of production to be consumed in common in the labour process and develops cooperation. In the process of reproduction, capital, proceeds with the dispersal of female houseworkers, atomises the sites and means of production and undermines cooperation, even as it sets in motion a domestic social average of labour. Within the reproduction process, the cooperation and the common consumption of the means of production would have no benefit for capital because they would not increase its productivity.

Any increase in collective consumption in the realm of reproduction would cause the value of its product (labour power itself) to fall. Capital desires that the value produced in reproduction be as great as possible, however, and it is precisely the individual consumption of the means of production that raises the productivity of domestic labour: the fact that this value does not decrease leads to a greater possibility for the subse-quent valorisation of capital.

As for cooperation, its development in the realm of reproduction would presuppose the accumulation of houseworkers in a shared space. The inconvenience of such an arrangement for capital testifies to the history of the division of labour developed as a productive force of social labour. In the process of production and reproduction of labour power, there is no division of labour among women as houseworkers within a single working process. There is, instead, a division of each working process from the others because, unlike all other commodities, labour power does not appear as the common product of many houseworkers, but as the individual product of a single houseworker. The woman here is not a partial worker within the division of labour but an overall one. She can produce the individual's labour power in its entirety, at least in relation to the process of reproduction. Of course, in this, she is assisted by the other members of her family and community, other partial and secondary workers in the house. However, the cooperation existing between her and the other members is, as we have seen, a simple one that has little relevance in the context of this argument.

What matters most is that there exists, to play on words, a certain *cooperazione* in consumption between the waged worker and the woman – in the sense that, since the means of production are also means of subsistence, even if they are not consumed in common by more women in the domestic labour process, they are consumed in common by family members.[2] This implies that, although in the domestic labour process there is no economy of the means of production, there is nevertheless an economy of the use of the means of subsistence. This economy has already been calculated in the workers' wages – that is, in the monetary representation of the value of the labour power of the entire working family.

The underdevelopment of cooperation in domestic work is accomplished in part, as we have seen, by its division. Here, again, we see an inversion of the production process. While, in the latter, cooperation rests on the division of labour, here it is the underdevelopment of the division in domestic labour, which, in turn, leads to a lack of cooperation. It is the separation, induced by capital, of the production process from that of reproduction which entails a rupture in the latter of the pre-existing cooperation of men with men, of women with women and of men with women, and, with this, the underdevelopment in the division of labour that takes place in reproduction. This is clear from a simple comparison between the development of reproduction in pre-capitalist societies and that in the capitalist mode of production. In the pre-capitalist societies, each individual is constituted as a partial reproductive worker. Consequently, the individual's reproduction is a

---

2 Fortunati plays on the homonymy between *cooperazione* meaning 'cooperation' and *operaio/operaia* meaning 'labourer'.

common product; the result of the work of many. But, at the same time, everyone is a partial worker with respect to the reproduction of many individuals. Everyone, therefore, is a partial worker of many related products. The partial nature of labour is determined not only by the sexual and generational division of labour, but also by the further division of labour existing in these categories, based on the fact that there was cooperation in reproductive labour, between man and man, between woman and woman and between woman and man.

In these societies, many working subjects collaborated on many common products, with each subject carrying out a different and independent part of the production process. This process therefore unfolded at many points in the working day and in diverse locations.

With the advent of capitalism, this process was radically transformed. The division and cooperation in domestic labour were significantly reduced, with the consequence that the reproduction of the individual became the product of the individual houseworker. In other words, every houseworker was now divided from the others and, as the comprehensive worker of a specific labour process, incorporated what had previously been many partial labouring subjects. There was a concentration and accumulation of the different operations previously carried out by many working subjects. Domestic labour became a combination of various independent parts of the labour process concentrated in a given time and space. In the transition to the capitalist mode of production, therefore, not only did the reproduction of the individual, once a common social product, become the individual product of a single woman, but the domestic work provided by the houseworker became the labour of production and reproduction of the individual worker as well as the labour power of children.

But why is the development of cooperation and the division of domestic labour inconvenient for capital? We will answer this question indirectly by demonstrating how the underdevelopment of domestic labour serves the interests of capital. Paradoxically, it is precisely through such underdevelopment that capital achieves the increased productivity of domestic labour, forcing the houseworker to produce more in less time:

1. Under capitalism, the houseworker carries out the operations required of reproduction in less time because they perform these

tasks throughout life largely on the same worker, whereas the pre-capitalist worker was collectively produced and reproduced by many partial workers through common production and an alternation of tasks. It should also be noted that, while in pre-capitalist societies the work of many workers contributing partially to reproduction was governed by tradition, under capitalism domestic labour came to be governed by capitalist planning.

2. Domestic labour becomes more productive because there is both a progressive decrease in the unproductive part of the consumption of the houseworker's labour power and a growing intensity of domestic labour. Both factors are the result of the intervention that has taken place at various levels by the capitalist mode of production to restructure the organisation of reproduction. In pre-capitalist societies, the alternation of the various working subjects who carry out the diverse procedures for the production and reproduction of individuals involves different locations, since such work is dispersed and decentralised. Furthermore, it involves a temporal dispersion through various moments of the working day and a diversity of the various partial work processes, which are specific to the individual to be reproduced. The passages not only from one operation to another, but above all from one individual to another, interrupt the course of work and render the workday porous. These openings are closed in the working process of the capitalist housewife, however, who passes from one operation to another within a single working process, carrying out lifelong domestic work focused on the same individual. Furthermore, the spatial separation between the different phases of the production and reproduction of labour power decreases and, with this, the time between one stage and another is shortened, because domestic labour is increasingly condensed within the home. And finally, considering that the houseworker must carry out the housework in a given time and place, in allotted sections of the workday, there is also an increase in the expenditure of labour power in those given periods of time.

3. The productivity of domestic labour can neither be determined by the improvement of its instruments nor by the introduction of machinery, as such development occurs for the waged worker in the period of manufacture, and subsequently in the factory in the

period of heavy industry.[3] Behind factory labour, there is a different historical transformation and a different history of struggle. Any pronounced use of technology would run counter to capitalism's claim for reproduction as a natural production process. Reproduction functions, in fact, with another kind of machinery: natural machinery. This process, therefore, can only be understood as a production of labour power that is itself mediated through the consumption of labour power. In this process, these *natural machines* work at full speed, functioning directly in relation to the machines in the factory.

The expenditure of labour by the waged worker is the process that precedes and initiates the houseworker's labour. Machines that, in the production process, function as the objective and systematically applied means of extorting a greater quantity of labour from the worker, also operate with respect to the process of production and reproduction of labour power. That is, they force the worker as a *natural machine* both to consume a greater quantity of domestic work within a prescribed period of time and thereby to increase the intensity and productivity of such work in the same periods. The direct interconnection of the labour-producing commodities and domestic labour, as well as the direct connection of the respective workers involved, means that the domestic worker is also subject to factory discipline in the sense that she has to use only the necessary time to perform her domestic tasks. This influences both the regularity and particularly the intensity of domestic labour – in contrast with the characteristics of domestic labour in pre-capitalist modes of production.

This 'technological' discovery and its capitalist use certainly did not arise with heavy industry, but with the advent of the capitalist mode of production. However, heavy industry perfected this development in the discovery that the overall productivity of labour increases if the machinery of domestic work can be made to function longer and more consistently.

---

3   The distinction here between *strumenti* (instruments) and *machine* (machines) follows the common Italian translation of Marx's distinction between the mere tool (*Handwerk*) and machinery (*Maschinerie*) in the transition to capitalism. Marx, *Capital*, vol. 1, 492–642.

The massive use of 'natural' machines for reproduction is precisely what explains the limited production of relative surplus value in this process. A simple comparison between the machinery of the factory and the tools and that of the household (the washing machine, the dishwasher) does not help. If one wants to compare the situation of the factory with that of the household, it is necessary to compare the heavy machinery of the former and the natural machinery of the latter.

The development of the productivity of domestic labour does not categorically exclude the use of tools and machines in this production process. On the contrary, even if such use is not fundamental to the production process, it still brings about increases in quantitative and qualitative terms (though much more gradually and in a more limited fashion than in the factory).

Throughout the period of manufacture, there was certainly a refinement and multiplication of the tools of domestic labour (cutlery, for example) which undoubtedly led to a certain increase in the productivity of such labour. Relatedly, a later stage of industrial development, one preceded not by chance by the establishment of a fixed working day, saw the development and use, however limited, of machinery in the form of household appliances.

4. Lastly, increased productivity of domestic labour cannot be achieved even through the increase in surplus labour time obtained by lengthening the domestic working day. This is because it already coincides with the entirety of the woman's lived day. There is a continuous tension in this mode of production, however, aimed at imposing an infinite extension of time for housework against any struggle for its reduction. Indeed, this is the most productive battle for capital, even if its intervention here is difficult for two reasons. First, the relationship between labour time and the value of labour power is based on a working day which tends to coincide with the entire lifetime of the woman, but which, for this very reason, is imprecisely determined at a temporal level. This can be an advantage or a disadvantage for capital, depending on whether it succeeds in a subterranean lengthening of this workday or women secretly succeed in shortening it. Second, the relationship between housework and waged labour is 'inter-sectorial' given that the value of labour power is determined in the production process, having the negative consequence that

the value of the houseworker's means of subsistence remains the same whether she works ten, eight, nine or six hours each day. Once the minimum value of the wage is established in the production process, capital is obviously interested that such minimal value correspond to the maximum amount of time spent in domestic labour – preferably the entire lifetime of the woman. The interest of women on the other hand is that the minimum amount of domestic labour correspond to the maximum value of her labour power and, in this regard, she has a better chance of success because this value is not directly related to her own work time.

Conversely, how is the productivity of the work of prostitution increased? In the history of capital, two approaches have been taken to such development.

The first is quite similar to that followed in the development of housework. It involves the organisation of micro-processes of production, each separated from the others: the dispersion of sex workers, the individual consumption of the means of production and the underdevelopment of cooperation and division of labour. In the latter case, there is underdevelopment of the cooperation and division of labour within the individual working process, while, at the social level, there is a development of a division that corresponds to an increasingly specialised division of sexual labour. In this regard, women who work in prostitution often specialise, some working primarily with masochistic clients, some with sadists or voyeurs and so on.

As with domestic work, here too there is limited use of instruments and machines because the fundamental machine remains the woman's body, generally reduced to its most basic sexual functions. Incidentally, it can be claimed that it is precisely the limitation of the use of machines in this sector that has caused the parallel production of films, photos, newspapers and pornographic ephemera to expand enormously alongside it, a type of production which requires much less living labour and more machinery. This, in turn, leads to the increased consumption of sex on an immaterial level.

Even in prostitution, the capitalist mode of production seeks to impose and maintain the longest-possible working day and increase the intensity of the work itself. It also seeks to reduce to a minimum the unproductive consumption of the sex worker's labour power.

The second way to increase the productivity of the labour of prostitution is much closer to that taken by capital in the production process and is based on the fact that this work lends itself to be subjected to a further leap of its productive power. The fact that the value of the sex worker's labour power is represented in monetary terms implies that her labour can be organised by capital within a social relation of production that is strictly regulated by exchange value – that is, as a waged work relationship.

Throughout its history, capital has travelled both these roads and still travels both depending on how the balance of social relations of production is configured at any given time. Each has different disadvantages. In terms of the production of surplus value, the second path is undoubtedly more productive than the first, but it is not always preferable in terms of reproduction of capital as a social relation. On the one hand, it is true that this leap obviates the structural danger inherent in the exchange between the sex worker and the pimp. Such an exchange, as has been noted, represents an inversion of roles with respect to that between the waged worker and the houseworker. If, in the relationship between the worker and the houseworker, it is the man who holds the money and purchases the woman's domestic labour, in the relationship between the sex worker and the pimp it is the sex worker who holds the money and purchases the pimp's labour. On the other hand, the factory of sex involves such contradictions for the state at the social level (including the accusation that the state itself is the 'big pimp') that when it is faced with the emergence of countless protests, it often cannot take the second path and opts for the first.

The subsequent leap in the productive force of prostitution (in eros centres, brothels and similar organisations) takes place through the restructuring of the exchange between the sex worker and the pimp. This can happen in two directions: either it is completely reversed, or an attempt is made to oblige the sex worker into a forced exchange with the state itself.

In the first case, the pimp is transformed from an employee, paid by the sex worker to provide her with services, into an entrepreneur – that is, a boss who pays her to work for him. In this case, the exchange that takes place is one between illegal or black market capital and the labour power of prostitution, between the pimp-capitalist and labour power as the capacity for sexual reproduction of the waged male worker.

This step curbs the unproductive consumption by the pimp of the money deriving from prostitution. The pimp, as an entrepreneur, is compelled to make productive use of his money, reinvesting it to a greater or lesser extent in the production process. His other expenditures (luxury cars, champagne, nightclubs and so on), which evoke other unproductive proletarian consumptions about which capital complains, thus fall within a properly capitalist framework.

In the second case, however, the state abolishes the pimp and presents itself as the only direct employer, as the only legitimate entrepreneur involved in prostitution. In this case, the exchange takes place between the state as guarantor of capital and the work of prostitution – between the pimp-state and the sex worker. In both cases, however, she is transformed into a worker once more. That is to say, the further leap in the productivity of prostitution consists in the fact that, already productive, it becomes increasingly productive by transforming itself into waged labour. In this case, whether we are talking about local brothels, the German eros centres, the brothels of Mediterranean Africa or the *zonas rojas* (red light districts) of Latin America, there is an accumulation of sex workers, the common consumption of a part of the means of production and a certain development of cooperation and division of sexual labour. In all these cases, however, we still find very little technological development.

What, then, is the form of production of surplus value in the process of reproduction? In the production and reproduction of labour power, there is no development of cooperation, nor division of domestic labour, nor common consumption of the means of production. On the contrary, the increase in productivity derives precisely from underdevelopment of cooperation and the separation of consumption. There is a certain use of machines, but only in a context in which production fundamentally occurs through exchange of labour power for labour power. The real battleground remains that of maintaining the domestic working day to coincide with the entirety of a woman's life.

The same thing can be concluded for the process of sexual reproduction of male labour power, whichever path capital might take in developing it.

To answer our questions above, surplus value in reproduction is a rather strange form of absolute surplus value. It remains unique even if we acknowledge that, starting from the historical moment of capitalist development in which the development of relative surplus value prevails in production, absolute and relative surplus value become somewhat intertwined.

How far we progress in increasing or restricting the production of relative surplus value in reproduction through the introduction of higher levels of technology or how much it is restricted through opposing forces will depend on what power relationships and mass forms of behaviour develop between the state/capital and women. What is certain is that, while the level of technological development is relevant with respect to domestic labour, it is less relevant with respect to prostitution.

Here, technology cannot free anyone from anything. The only thing that can free us from the labour of prostitution is the united struggle of housewives and prostitutes for the destruction of their unwaged work relationships. This is a radically different perspective from that proposed by a large part of the left that reduces the solution to the forced abolition of prostitution, which means the violent erasure of the prostitute herself as a social figure. Such an approach has led to the barbaric persecution of those prostitutes who do not agree to abandon the role, or to their forced education and rehabilitation (as, for example, in Vietnam, where former prostitutes were transformed into salaried workers, obviously at much lower wages).

In the process of production and reproduction of labour power, the problem of technological development is a strategic one because the possibility of getting rid of a substantial share of material domestic labour depends on how it is resolved. Whether it takes place inside or outside the house will depend above all on women's choices. In the United States, along with a decrease in the purchase of household appliances there is an enormous increase in meals consumed outside the home, and clothes washed and ironed at the drycleaners. This translates into the unburdening of domestic labour operations outside the home, and therefore their socialisation. But there is no homogeneity in these trends, at least up to now, at an international level.

What is undeniable is that the refusal of domestic labour, expressed in a thousand forms and in the constantly increasing entry of women into waged work, has considerably lowered the levels of productivity in reproduction. Today, the domestic workday that tends towards a total twenty-four hours is progressively disappearing: either because women use a salary to buy their way out of excessive domestic labour, or simply because they refuse to work full time as housewives. Although there is no official bargaining by women for the reduction of the domestic working day, domestic working time has massively decreased. The turning tide in this battle indicates a fundamental defeat for capital, though it simultaneously presents a great political and organisational challenge for women.

If feminism means the struggle for liberation from unpaid domestic labour, women's command over science and technology is an urgent political issue – not only with respect to the objectives common to the whole proletariat (the problem of energy) but also with respect to women's objectives, specifically concerning reproduction, which, given its structure and functioning, has a very low level of technological development. Just think of the antiquated contraceptive methods still in use today, or how the house is cleaned.

This problem does not concern the production process to the same extent, where both capital and workers share an interest in technological development, albeit for opposite reasons. The aim of capital was, and remains, the contraction of its expenditure on variable capital; that of the workers was, and is, the reduction of working time. Even if, in the short term, this development has resulted in mass firings of workers, or, at least, in the decrease of their quantitative consistency in production, it has also represented a step forward (for everyone) because it potentially foreshadows the liberation from waged labour.

In the reproduction process, not only has the level of technological development remained low, but the potential for future technological investment remains scarce given that, among other factors, there is no coincidence of interest between capital and women. Technological advancement and investment in reproduction would not lead to a contraction of variable capital in the form of reduced wages but would only serve to reduce domestic labour time in the short term and potentially to prefigure the liberation of women from indirectly waged labour. In conclusion, the capitalist command over technology has progressed in very different ways in each realm.

For women, unlike for waged workers, the problem is that of subjectively determining, through the organisation of our struggles, a technological leap that would liberate us from at least a segment of domestic labour through automation and machinisation. This is undertaken, of course, with the awareness that the only way to preserve for ourselves the time that we free up from unwaged work is to strengthen our ability to organise and attack capital. The political initiative for the expression of a proletarian command over reproduction is ours. Let us seize it, putting all the weight of our political power as women behind the struggle for our liberation.

11

The Family as a Form of Capitalist Development

The primary centre from which the domestic labour process flows, the productive nucleus in which the houseworker operates, is the family. The family represents the central nervous system of the process of reproduction.

Throughout the history of capitalist accumulation, the production and reproduction of labour power has been a primary function of the family, although not its only function. This is clear from the capitalist history of the family, which can be broken down into two distinct phases.

In the first phase, corresponding to the extraction of absolute surplus value, the family presents itself at once as a site for commodity production and for the production and reproduction of labour power. In the second phase, corresponding to the extraction of relative surplus value, the family appears primarily as a unit for the production and reproduction of labour power.

With the advent of factory-based production the passage or, more properly, the *leap* from the first to the second phase occurs. The factory acts as a watershed between these two types of family. Only when capital, faced with the struggles of the industrial working class, must confront the problem of the perpetual preservation and reproduction of labour power, does it begin to introduce the sexual division of labour in addition to a physical and spatial separation between production and reproduction. It is only at this moment that the factory emerges as the primary site of production in opposition to the home as the domain of reproduction. It is only at this juncture that the male wage earner becomes the counterpart to the woman of the house, who receives no direct wage. Consequently, the family is now transformed from a unit for both the production and reproduction of labour power and commodities into *the fundamental unit of production and reproduction of labour power*.

This analysis will be limited to the second phase. It can be observed that, like other elements and agents of reproduction, the family presents a dual character, a double life: an apparent life as the centre of the reproduction of individuals as use values; and a second life, a real one, as the centre of the production and reproduction of labour power, in which a great mass of surplus value is produced by the domestic worker. It is precisely this double life that allows the family to function as a primary cell of production. It can function as a centre of creation for surplus value only to the extent that it appears to be a site, unlike the factory, where no value is created, and it simply appears as the natural site for the reproduction of individuals.

The family is the place where variable capital circulates not only as income but also as capital, primarily in relation to the domestic worker and secondarily in relation to the worker and their progeny. Mothers, wives, husbands, fathers, children and brothers, while appearing as natural forms of social work, are, in reality, specific forms of labour power: the capacity for maternal (and paternal), spousal (as wife and as husband), filial and fraternal reproduction.[1] As such, they are commodities: labour power bought by capital and they produce capital. Insofar as the workers of reproduction do not belong to themselves, but to capital – they are capital.

But this much is obvious. It is common knowledge that family relationships are alienated and alienating: that the love we feel for our father, mother, children and siblings can be expressed (in the fate to

---

1 Maternal reproduction is included among these aspects of reproductive labour power although it is not automatically performed in the capacity of production and reproduction of labour power. Primarily, the worker buys labour power from women as the capacity to reproduce his labour power, and generally also to produce and raise children as new labour power. However, the capacity of women to produce new labour power is subject to many variables and may not be performed. When this relationship of exchange and production is performed and the woman becomes mother, then another exchange forms, in addition to that which exists between the paid worker and the domestic worker.

which capitalism condemns us) only through domestic labour, which is therefore commodity production. For example, although we know that our son has unlimited desires, needs to play and does not want to go to school, we drastically limit his desires, we discipline him and send him to school: we force him, in short, to become a commodity. Our love for him cannot defend him from the tentacles of capital. We are all aware that the family is ostensibly a place of love, but in reality of labour, the provision of an enormous pool of labour on which capital can draw. It is a place of total alienation and commodification. One may spend decades of life in common but remain a stranger, unknown, unable to communicate or to be truly supportive.

What has not yet entered common consciousness is how the family functions for the production of surplus value. In our opinion, this must be the starting point: the commodity character of the father, the husband, the wife, the children and siblings. Let us begin by noting that these commodities, these forms of labour power as capacities of spousal, marital reproduction, be they paternal, maternal, filial or fraternal capacities, are comparatively more complex in their varied forms of relation than domestic labour power.

Unlike domestic labour power, these forms of labour power cannot circulate as commodities in the free market, but only within the family to which the individual bearers of these commodities belong. In other words, the family constitutes the obligatory labour-market within which they must circulate. This familial circulation is the presupposition and condition of existence of the so-called *free exchange* between the paid worker and capital, and of that between the domestic worker and capital through the intermediary of the paid worker. It is precisely in the *compulsory nature of their circulation*, and therefore of the exchanges and relations of production to which they give rise within the family, that the slave-like aspect of this productive structure lies. This aspect is also the presupposition and condition for the properly capitalistic form of the *other* fundamental centre of production – the factory.

Of all these forms of labour power which must be confined to the family, a unique and partial exception is that of the marital relation, which, even if it may present itself *officially* as labour power within the family, consistently manifests outside of its confines. The long tradition of husbands' lovers and mistresses has never invalidated the institution of marriage – it has strengthened it. The same cannot be said for the adulteries of the housewife, whose infidelity has always plunged the marriage into crisis, precisely because of the lesser power she possesses, not being directly waged.

In terms of material behaviours and, to some extent, in the legal context, this male privilege has been greatly eroded, particularly over the last decade. The primary impetus for such change has been women who have forcefully claimed those same freedoms possessed by the husband, and a second reason is that extramarital relationships of both spouses have become progressively less cause for crisis within the marital arrangement. Indeed, it is not unusual for such relationships to be seen as a means for the couple to survive, saving them a deeper crisis of monogamous asphyxia. Let us be clear: especially in Italy, where the *delitto d'onore* was legal until only recently, this does not mean that the situation has fundamentally changed, only that it has undoubtedly begun a process of profound transformation.[2]

Apart from this case, however, any other articulation of labour power as a reproductive capacity can be posed as a commodity assuming exchange value only to the extent that the subjects of the exchange are determined by compulsion – that is, both the *owners* and *buyers* of such labour power are in a reciprocal relation. Non-adult labour power as capacity of reproduction can pose itself as labour power only to the extent that it is exchanged either between children and parents or between siblings. In other words, this labour power can become a commodity only for two subjects: those who materially produced it (the parents), or siblings produced by the same parents. It can pose itself as a commodity only if it poses itself as a capacity for *filial* or *fraternal* reproduction, as there can be no official free market for children's reproductive labour.

At the same time, the paid worker and the houseworker, although they require children's reproductive labour for their own reproduction, obviously cannot buy such a commodity as it cannot circulate in the labour-market. Parents cannot present their reproductive labour as a commodity except to the extent that it is positioned as a maternal or paternal capacity within the family. These capacities cannot generally

---

2   The *delitto d'onore* (honour killing) in which a husband/partner murders his wife/partner for infidelity was officially granted special leniency in the Italian judiciary system until 1981.

circulate beyond the family as commodities, since those who would purchase them (children) obviously cannot do so. For adults, therefore, the only way to make their reproductive labour power active as a commodity is to become parents themselves. The adult must materially produce the other subject of the exchange, forcing him or her to exist and, thereby, to exchange.

There is, however, one aspect that these forms of labour have in common with domestic labour: they persist in the individual for an indefinite period, both with respect to a single working day and to the entire span of their working days. Indeed, labour power as the capacity for filial and fraternal reproduction of the workforce inheres and is expressed in the individual from birth, even if, at first glance, this claim seems implausible. Newborn children *reproduce* their parents, because, at an immaterial level, they produce enormous use value (just think of the effect of their smiles) for their mother and father and for all those around them.

All these forms of labour power, moreover, given the concrete necessities of the work cycle of reproduction, must *diversify in the performance of different operations according to age* and, in the case of labour power as filial and fraternal reproductive capacities, also according to sex. Newborn children, in fact, reproduce their father and mother in a different way than a six-year-old child does, and so on. On the other hand, a male child reproduces its parents in a different way from a female child and vice versa – they are differently reproduced by the parents.

The family, then, is the place where variable capital and all articulations of reproductive capacity are operative, with the exception of part of the sexual reproduction of male labour power.

Obviously, the lion's share of the work within the family is performed by the domestic worker, who is the pillar, the foundation on which the family rests. It is her domestic labour that makes the family a productive structure. But this is a subject we know well by now, having thoroughly examined the exchange relation between her and the paid worker, as well as the relations of production based on this exchange. In the treatment of the family archipelago, therefore, this relationship, although fundamental, will remain somewhat in the shadows for the time being.

We prefer for now to address the analysis of the secondary subjects of domestic labour, their exchanges and relations of production, because they are also important elements within the overall picture of the familial reproduction of labour power.

The capitalist *family* appears historically *with the assumption of five different types of exchange*, involving as many *relations of production which are not directly waged*. These relations can be enumerated as follows:

1–2. the relation between the domestic worker and capital mediated by the paid worker and vice versa;
3–4. that between the paid worker and the domestic worker – as parents on the one hand, and capital on the other, mediated by the newly produced labour power of children, and vice versa;
5. and the relation between siblings as newly formed labour power and capital.

This is an assemblage of extremely complex exchanges and relations of production, which almost mirror the characteristics of the relation between the domestic worker and capital mediated by the paid worker, previously analysed. To understand their functioning, therefore, it is sufficient to extend what we have said about such exchange and productive relations to these, while highlighting those elements that distinguish them.

First, unlike the exchange between the paid worker and the domestic worker, which is posed as a free form of exchange, that between parents and children and that between siblings are presented as compulsory exchanges. As mentioned, these subjects are necessarily obliged to exchange among themselves insofar as their exchanges are tacitly enforced. Moreover, unlike the other exchanges presupposed by the family, that between parents and children has the characteristic of being partly immediate and partly deferred, given that the children's reciprocation is postponed until they have become active in the workforce.

None of these are direct relations like that between a houseworker and paid labourer; each is mediated by capital. Not only does each member of the family as reproductive labour power function as *capital*, but they are also its *simulacra* – that is, its representation and mediation. Husband, wife, father, mother, son and brother: each not only directly produces surplus value within the family but also serves as the instrument through which capital forces the other members of the family to produce surplus value, to work productively in the sphere of reproduction. Each family member is therefore a mediator of the productive relationship between each other family member and capital.

Let us take the husband-wife relationship as an example. We have seen that there is no relationship between the wife and the worker that is not also a relationship between her and capital mediated by her husband. Let us now add that, in relation to the houseworker, the worker also functions in another *secondary fashion* that is nevertheless necessary. He functions as a seller of domestic labour, as this act of selling entails his labour power as the capacity for marital reproduction. In this case, it is the wife who functions as mediator of the relation of production and exchange between the husband and capital, mediating on the real level the latter's opposition to itself, to the value of its labour power as productive capacity. In their role as husband and wife, they do not reproduce themselves as individuals, but as commodities, as labour power. This is true of all other family relations, which are all possessed of this twofold character.

Likewise, there is no such thing as a direct relation between parents and children – that is, this relation is formed by two distinct relations of production: one between parents and capital mediated by children; and the other between children and capital mediated by parents. This applies, of course, to the relationship between siblings as well. Each family member must confront variable capital within the family acting as capital that commands the familial exchanges and relations, forming them according to its own will and laws, as exchanges and relations of production of the commodity labour power.

The process of capitalist exploitation is, therefore, not impeded by the more or less elastic walls of the factory but continues in an even more mystified and hidden fashion in the home. It pervades familial relationships, which are relationships of production, and therefore of exploitation – capitalist relationships which have preserved only the appearance of interpersonal relationships. Of course, family members are only *conductors* of capitalist exploitation. The son does not exploit the mother for himself, but for capital, and vice versa – the mother does not exploit the son for her own gain but for capital. The mother and son are, naturally, not interested in the production of surplus value within the family but in their survival, their reproduction.

Obviously, these relations do not present themselves as dualistic, nor, of course, do they present themselves as capitalist in nature. On the contrary, they are covered in the least capitalist-seeming veneer: the worker, in his role as husband, appears to be anything but a worker, although, even as a husband, he is a worker in reproduction. Even as a husband, he is exploited by capital to produce surplus value within the family. In fact, it is an illusion, as we have seen, that his is a direct relationship with his wife. His relationship is, rather, one of production with capital mediated by his wife. Capital uses the wife to extort from her husband the maximum amount of reproductive labour, after exploiting him as a producer of commodities. The same happens for the worker as father, for the household worker as mother and for future labour power as sons or brothers.

What is variable is the subject who serves capital as a mediator for the exploitation of other family members: for the father and mother, it is the children; for the children, the parents; and for the siblings, it is one another. Indeed, it is precisely these relations of exploitation within the family that guarantee there is far less opposition to capital's exploitation. If the worker sets a definite limit to his exploitation in relation to the boss in the factory, such limits do not apply in the family. What worker could be more felicitous and inexhaustible than a mother towards her child? Which worker is more loving and available than the grandmother towards her grandchildren? What relation presents itself as less capitalist than that of a son in relation to his mother, even if the mother, by reproducing the son, reproduces a commodity and therefore reproduces capital? In this way, such exchanges also assume a double character, presenting themselves in a certain fashion on the formal level while being something quite different in the reality of capitalist social life.

As for the exchange between husband and capital through the wife, capital presents the marital reproductive capacity as a natural force of social labour. The worker appears as a husband rather than a worker, and the marital reproductive labour appears to be a personal service rather than indirectly waged labour.

If we consider the exchange between parents and children as it is mediated by capital, the father figure formally relates to the children as a wage earner and provider of paternal domestic labour. In reality, the father relates to capital as labour power in his capacity of paternal reproduction, although this relation requires mediation through the development of the labour power of children. The mother figure relates to her children as the provider of domestic labour, while she relates to capital, through her children, as maternal labour power. In both cases, the children function as mediators of the exchange and the productive relationship that operates between worker as father and houseworker as mother in their relation with capital.

Children are thus the mediators in the exchange between the waged worker as capacity of paternal reproduction and the value of the male worker's labour power as capacity of production that functions as capital. They are also mediators in the opposition between the houseworker as capacity of maternal reproduction and variable capital that functions as capital. Formally however, they simply posit themselves as the subjects of these exchanges: as children.

In the exchange between children and capital mediated by parents, the future workers relate to their parents throughout the period of their development as providers of filial domestic labour, while in reality they confront capital through their parents and the latter's role as labour power – a filial reproductive capacity. Once they have become recognised as labour power, they will also enter into direct exchange with capital as wage earners, at least when such labour is deemed necessary. In this case, it will be the parents who function as mediators of the exchange and productive relation between the newly minted labour power and capital. In this sense, they mediate, on the level of the real, two relationships. When the children are young, the parents mediate the exchange between the filial capacity for reproduction and the value of one of the parents' own labour power (the father/worker). Once the children have grown, the parents mediate the exchange between the filial capacity for reproduction and the value of the labour power of the children themselves. In both mediations, parents position themselves formally as the other subject of the exchange.

In the exchange between siblings, one formally relates to the other as the provider of fraternal domestic labour, while in reality they engage capital through their new fraternal labour power: the capacity for fraternal reproduction.

Such exchanges, like that between the housewife and capital mediated by the worker, are not, in reality, exchanges of equivalents, but neither are they represented as such in a formal sense, despite the fact that they entail an economy of relative exchange values. Within each exchange, capital appropriates the labourer's time as husband and father, as houseworker and mother, and the newly minted labour power of children and siblings. This process is not mediated through direct exchange but indirectly, through exchange with labour power as the capacity for production. Again, each worker, within the realm of reproduction, produces much more than he receives in return, which is, at most, mere survival.

Just think of the work performed by the mother for her child, or a grandmother for her grandchild. What do they receive in return? Or rather, do they receive some sort of equivalent in return for everything they do? The answer, of course, is no. But they do not care, at least within certain limits, because they perform under the illusion that they are doing the work for their children or grandchildren so that they will be happy and that they might enjoy their happiness. However, as we know, happiness does not pay – it has no price! In reality, the surplus they produce, in terms of the commodity of labour power, is produced, as we have seen, for the benefit of capital, which appropriates this value when it purchases the labour power of that son or grandson. Perhaps that son or grandson will also be happy, so to speak, but this does not mean that his happiness is not also the result of the capitalist exploitation of his mother or grandmother.

Family exchanges are therefore *all* dualistic and unequal exchanges between unequal individuals. Within them, the substance of capitalist exchanges persists, although, superficially, they appear in a non-capitalist veneer. In the eyes of the paid worker, the houseworker and future workers, these relations present themselves as individual, interpersonal exchanges that take place in a sphere extraneous to capital – as exchanges in which what one gives is equivalent to what one receives in return. This is their crucial aspect: in the eyes of family members, they must appear convenient, as the most *economical* way to structure reproduction. It is here, instead, as we discuss below, that the mechanism of such exchanges and relations of production become enchanted and no longer function except for capital. It is precisely through their presumed convenience that they increasingly reveal their true character as a convenience only for capital and not for the proletariat.

In the case of these exchanges, their dual character implies that the acts and the essential conditions that dictate them are formally different from those necessary for the exchange between workers and capital. These acts and essential conditions must be complementary to those relating to the exchange between the houseworker and capital mediated by the waged worker. The peculiarity of these relations is even more pronounced than that characterising the exchange between the houseworker and capital mediated by the waged worker. Rather than proving that these relations are outside the capitalist labour-market, this particularity must be considered as a presupposition for and condition of existence of the normality of the underlying exchange between workers and capital. The exchanges between husband and wife, parents and children and between siblings are forms of dual exchanges that, in reality, occur between these subjects and capital, and as such they are forms of capital.

Both husband and wife produce surplus value in the domestic labour process, though the surplus value produced by the waged worker as husband is incomparably smaller than that produced by the house-worker. Or at least this was the case until women's massive struggles over reproduction, especially following the Second World War, produced some redistribution of domestic labour within the family throwing some of it onto the shoulders of the paid worker. Although unequal, up until this point, the exchange between the worker and the housewife had, in their eyes, appeared as preferable to solitude (an approach which doesn't allow an economy of scale in daily life). After this period of struggle in the so-called advanced capitalist countries, this exchange however began to appear to the houseworker as less and less equal.

What her husband had given her (basically, the wage) no longer seemed sufficient compensation for the domestic labour she provided, so she gradually demanded an *ever-larger provision of spousal and paternal labour* from the paid worker. This was one of the first areas on which women concentrated their struggle. It was indispensable that they first reassess their exchanges within the family, so as subsequently to transform them with regard to capital and the state. On this ground, the battle that had begun after the war took on a mass and overt form only in the 1970s.

It is in this decade that female insubordination within the family has had the effect both of demystifying the apparent equivalence of the exchange between husband and wife, as well as of transforming the roles of *husband* and *father*. Women's struggles have forced men to recognise the monstrosity of their capitalistic relationships with partners and children, and to experience, on the one hand, the potential for sentimental, emotional and sexual wealth inherent in such relationships, and on the other, the extent to which these relationships are dependent on domestic labour. With this realisation came the related awareness that the destiny of reproduction does not depend on women's struggles alone

but is a problem of struggle and organisation for those who are reproduced as well. In short, women's struggles have forced men to reinvent
themselves as husbands and fathers.

The extent to which the new husband and father function productively or disrupt the capitalist organisation of labour is a question, as
always, of struggle and organisation. For its part, the state, in response
to women's struggles to restrict their domestic labour, has attempted to
give their husbands new tasks and responsibilities, in an attempt to make
them function for the production of surplus value.

Since the 1970s, the state has attempted to propose (or impose) a new
model of the husband and father, inviting men to share in domestic
labour and domestic joys – new experiences in an arena from which they
have previously been excluded. Men are promised that these adventures,
unlike those experienced in the world of commodity production, can
hold pleasant surprises. The whole world of love has now been opened
to these men – subjects who are still inexperienced regarding capital's
profound mystifications of the terrain of reproduction, and are full of
new energy. Just as it is no longer automatic that the woman makes the
beds and cooks the food, it is no longer automatic for her to be the
one to take maternity leave. The man is now allowed to stay home from
work to take care of the newborn child. But this is not the end of the story.

The rejection of the inequality of the familial exchange has also
turned into a rejection of the exchange itself, even in situations where
children are involved. As is well known, there are now an increasing
number of families consisting of single women with children. This is the
1980s family – one that *has no male mediation* between state and women:
a family, therefore, that is not a family in the traditional sense and in
which the state faces the open problem of reconstructing the capacity for
command over domestic labour and the grids of control over women
and children.

In the same vein, both parents and children are producers of surplus
value in the domestic labour process. Capital appropriates this value for
its own self-valorisation in spite of both parents and children, who are
interested not in the value produced, but in the satisfaction of their
needs. These needs are twofold. Parents need to be reproduced at least
immaterially by their children while the latter's labour power is forming.
Once this process is complete and the parents' labour power is declining,
they need to continue to be reproduced immaterially by their children,

and eventually to benefit from the children's material reproductive labour as well. The children need their parents to reproduce them both materially and immaterially while they are forming their labour power, and once they are economically active they need the parents to reproduce them in more immaterial than material fashion. Even when they age, parents can rarely afford not to work materially for their children in some capacity, however, because as grandparents they contribute to the rearing of grandchildren, or they help their children in their new ménage in many ways.

Those who actually decide whether or not such an exchange relation is convenient are the parents themselves, since this exchange is partly mediated and partly deferred in time. Between the two subjects then, only the parents are in a position to decide whether or not to establish the exchange; the children have only the choice of whether to reciprocate. Consequently, the fact that this exchange presents itself as equivalent and therefore convenient in the eyes of the parents is a prerequisite for it to take place.

In the history of capitalist production, the exchange between parents and children includes two distinct phases, characterised both by the different needs that drove the former to produce the latter and by the different way in which this exchange is represented from the perspective of the parents. It has been argued that capitalism has made the production of children compulsory for both the paid worker and domestic worker, because filial reproductive labour constitutes an essential element in the reproduction of their labour power. This is fundamentally true in both the first and the second phase. In terms of this dual exchange and relationship of production, what distinguishes one phase from the other is that, in the first phase, this need is also related to the *material survival* of the worker and the houseworker.

This initial phase, which roughly corresponds to the extraction of absolute surplus value, is the one in which children, from infancy, reciprocate their parents with reproductive labour. This reciprocity may be material, as well as immaterial, and sometimes entails the child's own salary. The further back one looks in the history of capital, the greater the accumulation of reproductive labour, including material labour, unloaded by the mother onto her children, especially if those children were female. The simpler the workforce was to reproduce, the more it was possible for the mother to share domestic work with her daughters and possibly with her sons as well. Today, the division of domestic work in the home between mother and children is more difficult for the latter, given the average level of complexity of the workforce to be reproduced, at least in the so-called advanced capitalist countries. In fact, it is not easy to make a child do even domestic labour after five to six hours (or more) of school, after-school clubs, sports and other activities. While it is true today that children are only secondary working subjects within the family, the further back we go in time, the less this is the case.

In the earlier stage, the exchange between parents and children appears, to the former, as *equivalent*. The cost immediately required of parents by the production of a child is soon recuperated when the child, commencing work at a young age, earns a wage and/or looks after his brothers and sisters and keeps the household running. Given this apparent equivalence and the common consumption of certain means of subsistence by members of the working-class family, it becomes more convenient for parents to exchange with as many children as possible. The lower the wage (the price of labour power) the more necessary it is for the working-class family to *produce* labour power – that is, future workers – in order to collect wages. In other words, the lower the wages, the greater the overall ability of the entire family to work must be. Of course, the trade-off is the risk of starvation if future workers cannot quickly join the active industrial army.

The proletarian face of population increase is represented by the accumulation of wages within the single family. This is the only possibility of either individual survival or increase in the rates of survival itself. For children, the opposite occurs: the more numerous they are, the less they can consume, because the available fixed capital remains unchanged and, at the same time, the variable capital does not grow in proportion to their number. The complaints about the insubordination of the child worker who does not fulfil its duties to parents, and the numerous accounts of gangs of runaway children wandering around stealing or begging, speak clearly to the popular opprobrium that falls on children who enter into such an exchange with their parents. In the history of capital, therefore, this phase, in which having numerous children becomes a guarantee for the parents with respect to their material reproduction (not so much into old age, which few of them ever reached, but rather to their basic survival), also reveals an overall weakness of the proletariat. Here, the proletariat is forced to guarantee its survival by making the maximum number of deferred exchanges with the maximum number of children.

The second phase, which corresponds with the extraction of relative surplus value, is characterised by an inversion of these elements. In the eyes of the parents, this new form of exchange appears increasingly inconvenient and unequal. Both objective and subjective factors weigh on this radical shift in parental perspective. The objective factors, which increasingly defer the exchange in time and render it increasingly random and unpredictable are:

1. the progressive *increase in the costs of the formation of the work-force*, a burden which falls on the wages of the adult male worker;
2. the progressive *increase in the time of formation of the workforce*, which tends to end just when the latter, entering the labour and/or marriage market, begin to produce a family of its own;
3. the progressive increase, in extent and intensity, of the time of domestic labour, which falls primarily on the shoulders of the female houseworker.

Subjective factors include, on the other hand, the emergence of mass struggles of children and parents against what each represents for the other as a means of capitalist exploitation and discipline. The primary result of these anti-family struggles, aimed to destroy compulsory familial exchanges, has been partially to force on the state the cost of reproducing labour power, in terms of both money and labour. We allude here to those vast processes of struggle for the expansion and free provision of social services (kindergartens, schools, hospitals) as well as struggles to obtain increasingly substantial shares of income to pay for domestic work, including care for disability, mental illness and old age.

This phase of family relations is characterised by a progressive acquisition of power by the proletariat in relation to the quantity of labour power it is required to produce. The production of a given number of children in the working-class and proletarian family, while remaining beneficial for capital, is now scarcely convenient from a material point of view for the waged worker and the houseworker. This is the moment when the relative increase in the working-class population would mean not the accumulation of wages within the individual working-class family, but the dispersion of the only wage – that of the adult male worker – and of the working day of the houseworker among a given quantity of new labour power, with which the waged worker and the houseworker would have no beneficial exchange. From this point on, there is an increasing tendency to reduce the number of future workers. The fall in the European birth rate since the second half of the nineteenth century is a clear result of this trend.

This contraction of the birth rate meant the reduction of the number of children per family. The filial reproductive labour necessary for the reproduction of the waged worker and the houseworker remains, but the exchange with children is no longer a beneficial one. Therefore the tendency of parents has been to reduce these exchanges to a minimum, often to a single child. Nor should we underestimate the new, increasingly common trend of having no children at all. This testifies to the fact that the current composition of individual relationships has been articulated in such a way as to render superfluous (or at least no longer indispensable) the labour which, until only quite recently, was necessary for the reproduction of the worker and the housewife.

In this second phase, starting from the formation of the working-class family and in the course of its various restructurings, it is not only the proportion of what is given and received that changes, increasingly to the disadvantage of the parents, but also the content itself, the object of the exchange. In fact, we are witnessing not only a *progressive increase* in the volume of use values exchanged between parents and children, but also, within this exchange, an increase in *intangible* use values. This increase, disproportionately burdening parents, does not reduce the unequal nature of the exchange, but accentuates it. In other words, it changes the *quality* of that exchange and relationship. In short, much more labour is required in parenting, and therefore the immaterial sphere covered by this relationship is much expanded and qualitatively different. Obviously, the fact that this is *commodity-producing* labour weighs heavily within this relationship and shapes it in a capitalist fashion in terms of unhappiness, hatred and death.

But this is only one side of the equation; the other is a relationship that today is potentially much more loving and affectionate. The distance that existed between parents and children, and which approached that between employers and workers, has to give way to forms of closeness. Paternal and maternal authority has been diluted, continually eroded by disobedience and increasingly purged of physical violence; it was rendered unproductive by the struggles of children before being condemned as backward by contemporary pedagogy. These forms of authority are weakened by the ever-growing and increasingly frustrated need for love, sedated by the profound transformations that have affected the life cycle of the capitalist individual. The consequence is that today children in some ways become adults very quickly. There is nothing left of parental authority but confetti: the father and mother are increasingly less the masters, and the children are increasingly less the servants. Through a thousand paths of struggle, both have eroded the capitalist quality of their relationships. The new generation's struggle within the family is so intense that it is often the parents who seem, by and large, to be the slaves or servants of their children and not vice versa. But of course this reversal of the relationship, while significant for the rupture of capitalist command that it expresses, is not a sustainable course for proletarian struggle, which tends rather towards the removal of power from such relationships.

The mediation to which parents and children are subjected as individuals who participate in exchange is not modified by historical transformations. The act of exchange always takes on a particular form because it is an exchange that is obligatory and, in part, deferred in time. Parents and children do not enter a reciprocal relationship as possessors of goods with equal rights, nor as individuals who are legally equal, because they are not: first and foremost, the relation between paid worker and domestic worker is an unequal one; and there can be even less equality between parties in their role as parents and children.

If the adult male worker as a free wage earner relates differently to his children than the domestic worker, who does not earn wages (but can only consume a portion of them), the children's relations differ more still. As newly minted labour power, they are even less equal than the domestic worker with respect to the father/worker, because they can neither sell nor do what they will with their labour power as a productive capacity, since it is only labour power in training. This is a *potentiality* of dispensing labour, which they will dispose of only when it has been actualised.

Nor can they use their labour power as an immaterial reproductive capacity, which, being implemented from birth without involving any period of training, is necessarily placed at the disposal of the parents.

On the other hand, the paid worker and the domestic worker as parents can neither freely choose the other subject or subjects of exchange. They are obliged to exchange their respective goods within the family itself: the parents are obliged to do so with their children and vice versa.

Although these relations appear to be the *negation* of free capitalist exchange, since the subjects and objects of the exchange are rigidly determined, they are, in reality, the presupposition and condition of existence for the production of new labour power by the paid worker and domestic worker, as well as the forming the basis for the free exchange of the latter and the exchange between paid workers and capital.

With respect to duration, both parents and children are required to exchange their respective commodities for an indefinite period, both with respect to the single working day and with respect to the entire span of working days, which coincides with the entirety of their lives. As we have said, if we examine closely the concrete cycle of this exchange, it turns out to be composed of two phases, determined by the specificity of the commodity that must be produced in the second moment of the exchange – labour power.

The first phase corresponds to the period in which new labour power is in training. The second corresponds to the period in which the labour power of the waged worker and the houseworker are in decline and in which that of new workers is fully actualised. Due to the specific way in which this exchange is concretely articulated, its non-equivalence can reveal itself to the parents so gradually as to delay triggering behaviours that refuse exchange itself. On the other hand, it can also happen, as it has in the last few decades, because of transformations that have affected the concrete cycle of the reproduction of labour power, that the period of maximum productivity of the worker and the houseworker as parents is greatly extended.

There is an ever-increasing awareness among young couples or, more generally, future parents, that it is best not to expect anything from their children – an assessment which obviously has a significant influence on the decision whether to have children at all. At the same time, on the part of the children, there appears to be an increasingly clear refusal to repay their parents for bringing them into the world and raising them. Being indebted just for existing – living with the constraint of owing something to someone – does not please the younger generations who, with increasing strength, take up the right to live as a right, beyond any familial exchange.

Similarly, siblings are all producers of surplus value within the family. However, this exchange is under scrutiny, as is that between the house-worker and capital mediated by the paid worker, because the latter is understood, in the eyes of the sisters, as increasingly unequal. What brothers provide sisters has been revealed as a marginal quantity of reproductive labour relative to what the sisters give in return: this reduced value reflective of the power relationship between the worker and the houseworker extends to newly minted labour power. It is tending, however, towards equality as a result of women's struggles as unwaged labourers within the family, which unmask the power relationship between them and men. Women are beginning both to recognise and denounce the fact that the amount of reproductive labour, both filial and fraternal, required of them is greater than that required of their brothers, and to struggle against it.

Even the concrete cycle of this exchange, articulated, like that of the exchange between parents and children, in two phases, is gradually being transformed. This transformation has not occurred so much in the first phase, characterised as it is by the continuity of this familial exchange and constituted by the time of the training of new labour power, in which the siblings fundamentally produce immaterial use values for each other and together consume the use values necessary for their training as labour power. The transformation has occurred rather in the second phase, constituted by the actual working time of the new labour power, in which they have, in turn, founded their own family and in which they no longer have a continuous common con-sumption with siblings and parents of the use values necessary for their reproduction. This phase, which had been characterised in recent times by some degree of *loss of the continuity of exchange* between siblings, is now disappearing despite the lability or inconsistency to which relations between siblings are subject once they leave their family of origin.

Although the family, in the second phase, is the centre only of the production and reproduction of labour power, it is also a *unit* of pro-duction. Why? Because, as we have seen, the work necessary for the reproduction of labour power is composed of multiple segments of household labour time provided by various labouring subjects: the paid worker as husband and father, the houseworker as wife and mother, the future workers as sons/daughters and brothers/sisters. The family, it has been said, is the nucleus of the five types of relations of production that are indirectly waged and stands as the fundamental centre for the production of surplus value in the process of reproduction. As such, even with the transformations attending the change of power relations within it, it is positioned on par with the factory as the *nerve centre for capitalist accumulation*. Along with the factory, it has been and remains a *location of intensive class struggle*, a place where various sections of the class continuously redefine their mutual relationship, according to the power they are able to express vis-à-vis capital.

But what are the reasons for the coexistence of these determined exchanges and this composition of relations of production within the family? These reasons respond to the need for a productive organisation of reproduction. The exchange and the relations of production between the houseworker and capital, mediated by the worker, as we have already seen, are *fundamental but insufficient*. To function for capital, the process of the production and reproduction of labour power needs other exchanges and other relations of production – primarily, the exchange of the worker as husband with capital mediated by the houseworker as wife. This further exchange is required because the reproduction of the houseworker cannot consist exclusively in the consumption of the use values into which wages can be transformed. It also necessitates the consumption of those use values that only the worker as husband can and must produce.

On the one hand, the houseworker is plausibly posited as a non-worker, and the relationship between her and her husband as a non-work relationship. Certainly, it is understood that the salary fundamentally *pays* for domestic work. Yet the exchange cannot be represented in such a simple and brutal fashion; it cannot be reduced simply to the handing over of a part of the pay cheque to the wife. In this case, it would be impossible to mystify this relationship as a loving one. The husband, in addition to providing money, must also express love for his wife in other forms.

Without such demonstrations of love, it would be impossible for capital to accomplish the immaterial reproduction of both parties given the realities of their relationship.

But the exchange and relationship between husband and wife can only be the beginning. The further exchange and relation of production which the process of production and reproduction of labour power requires is that between parents and children. The purpose of the family, in fact, as we have already said, cannot be, in capitalist society, the mere reproduction of the labour power of the paid worker and housewife. It must also entail the production of new labour power. That is, it cannot consist only in the reintegration, necessary due to the limited duration of the human working life, of existing labour power, but also the maximal production of additional labour power.

The maximum production of additional labour power, which is the maximum increase of the population, becomes a crucial knot of capitalist development – all the more crucial insofar as it is posited as the result of a natural process of reproductive labour, which the individuals are forced to provide from their birth. It is more crucial still because the reproduction of the new individual/labour power, in terms of both cost and time of reproductive labour, is dumped by capital on the parents.

This discharge can take place because childbearing is also part, as we have seen, of the reproductive needs of the worker and the houseworker.

The process of production and reproduction of labour power requires, finally, another type of exchange and another productive relationship, that between siblings, which, however, is becoming less and less necessary as the number of single children increases.

The exchanges and relationships between husband and wife, parents and children, and between siblings have been rendered both necessary and sufficient for the reproduction of the family. Gradually, exchanges and relationships of other kinds (that of parents with their parents, for example) were expelled from the family fabric for two reasons. The first was the *increased exchange of variable capital and domestic labour*, which has tended to engage in the production of new families all the new labour power – that is, children. The second is the progressive lengthening of the average lifespan of individuals in their role as labour power, which has transformed the exchange between parents and children increasingly so as to exclude the entry of parents into the new families produced by their children. At the time of the children's marriages, the parents still have a long period of life ahead of them and they generally do not yet need to be cared for.

These two factors have contributed to the sedimentation of the form of family commonly called nuclear. This capitalist family, which we have defined as based on five types of exchange and relations of production, is the form that has been the most productive, at least until today. The primary factor which has gradually determined this configuration of the nuclear family, selecting which and how many relations of production were necessary such that their combination would optimally produce labour power, has undoubtedly been the continuous process of increasing the productivity of domestic labour. Because the nuclear form of the household functions as a *form of capital development* it has become *the general form of the capitalist family*.

As a unit, the centre of production and reproduction of labour power, the family is based on *the worker's possession of wages*, the *houseworker's ownership of domestic labour power and the apparently free exchange between them*. The possession of the wage by the worker does not give him direct possession of the labour power of the houseworker and children, but of their means of subsistence. For the proletarian man, this possession depends on whether he is a member of the active industrial army or of the reserve army of the unemployed. The exclusive possession of the wage by the adult male worker in this historical and social context, and not by any other member of the family, explains why, with the advent of capitalism, the power differential existing not only between men and women but also between parents and children opened up to an extent never reached before. Men's freedom to become waged workers and therefore head of their family corresponds to the freedom of women and non-adults to present themselves as wives and children, although they are indirectly salaried reproductive workers.

The relationship between man and woman and between parents and children is transformed from a relationship of exchange of labour with living labour by capital into a formal *relationship of production* established between parents: the man/husband/father and woman/wife/mother on the one hand, and their children on the other. This transformation of the relations between man and woman and between parents and children has several consequences:

1. The father – and subordinately the mother as wife – is formally delegated the right/duty to enter a productive relationship with his children.
2. Such relations are posed as relations of production only insofar as they are represented as interpersonal relationships and presuppose an exchange of commodities, which, however, is not represented as capitalist exchange on the formal level.

3. The relationship between parents and children is no longer one based on the working cooperation of both but becomes a *specific productive relationship* that formally exists between parents and children.

4. Whereas, in pre-capitalist forms of production, men and women in their role as parents and children were expropriated by the master or feudal lord of the product of their reproductive labour, as well as of the product of their labour in the production of use values, with the capitalist mode of production they are positioned as natural forces of social labour. Thus, they are formally expropriated of the product of their domestic labour not directly by capital, but indirectly by the very product of their labour, the other labour power.

The possession of wages by the worker is a decisive element for the establishment of the capitalist family. For capital, which requires a surrogate authority and command for the orderly functioning of the overall process of production and reproduction, the worker appears as the ideal solution. Because the relationship between capital and domestic labour is indirect, it is not possible for capital to express authority and command, however necessary it is, not even through the *faux frais* of production, a special sort of supervisor directly dependent on capital placed within the family itself. The only way capital can proceed in its command is through the mediation of someone who can fully embody its authority: *the worker*. Capital establishes the worker both with full rights, both legally and materially and through military discipline and repression, but also via the selection process of factory labour power. The worker is legitimated juridically, but prior to this legitimation, he is materially founded in the production of commodities, a role to which men appear 'naturally' assigned. This apparent naturalness normalises the fact that wages go to the man, who controls and commands the family. Therefore, the command of capital over the domestic labour of the members of the same family is given only insofar as it passes through the mediation of the worker and is represented as the command of the worker over his wife and children.

This command presides over the orderly carrying out of the labour process within the family. It constitutes the authority and power of planning which regulates the task allocation and cooperation involved in domestic work as it is distributed among the various members of the family. True task allocation and cooperation of labour do not occur in the domestic labour process, however. Only a simple form of the division of domestic labour and cooperation exists, distributed between a primary labouring subject and secondary others.

Even this division of labour involves an unequal distribution, however. To say that the fundamental labouring subject is the houseworker/wife/ mother is to say that this subject provides the largest and most important share of domestic labour. Likewise, to say that the other members of the family are secondary subjects is to allude to their smaller, and indeed secondary, share of such work. The division of labour within the family entails an *unequal distribution both in quantity and in quality*, not only of the consumption of use values produced in the family but also obviously of the product of reproductive labour itself – that is, of the labour power incorporated in its various members.

Unlike the division of labour in commodity production, the division of domestic labour into various segments – consisting of a set of specific operations within the overall labour process – does not automatically entail the division of roles taken on by the respective labouring subjects. On the contrary, within the individual household, the houseworker is, at the same time, both wife and mother, the worker is both husband and father, the new labour power are the children and siblings. Each working subject within the family has a dual role and must provide multiple forms of domestic work.

It goes without saying that the role is dual only within a traditional family unit. Every family is, however, part of a network such that every individual in their role as labour power is part of more than one family and has at least a dual role that is multiplied exponentially. Unlike the distribution of labour in the sphere of commodity production, individuals play all their different roles concretely. This multiplicity of roles also characterises the kind of cooperation that exists within the family, and which is grounded in the shared need of everyone, in their role as labour power, to consume the domestic labour of others and to cooperate with other family members in reproduction. Such cooperation is made particularly stringent by the fact that each individual must take on a dual role and must engage with at least two different segments of reproductive labour.

While, in the factory, the worker is subject to the command and discipline of capital, in the family the wife and children are subject to the

command and discipline of the wage earner. Or rather, they have traditionally been subjected to this discipline. In the current phase of capital,
this subjection to the command of the husband/father is shaky at best,
as described above. The worker-authority figure in its command over
wife and children, has been profoundly undermined, both by the struggles of women and young people within the family against this marital
and paternal authority, as well as by the possession of wages by a growing
segment of women. As we have seen, however, the command of the
salaried worker over the domestic work of his family, not being in aid
of his own self-valorisation but for that of capital, is a command that
arises as the *formal mediation of the real command exercised by capital*.
This command over the subjects of domestic labour appears as the only
formal consequence of the fact that the wife and children, instead of
working for themselves, seem to be working for the worker and thus to
be under his command, while, in reality, they work for capital and are
under its command. But this form of command is not only a particular
function arising from the nature of the process of production and reproduction of labour power and pertinent to that process. It is, at the same
time, a *function*, not directly one of exploitation but rather of the *mediation* of capitalist exploitation, of the different labour power employed
in that mediation process.

In the factory, 'the co-operation of wage-labourers is entirely brought
about by the capital that employs them', such that 'their unification into
one single productive body, and the establishment of a connection
between their individual functions, lies outside their competence'.[3] As
a consequence, 'the interconnection between their various labours confronts them, in the realm of ideas, as a plan drawn up by the capitalist,
and, in practice, as his authority, as the powerful will of a being outside
them, who subjects their activity to his purpose'.[4] The same happens in
the family with respect to the cooperation of labour power as a capacity
for reproduction that is indirectly waged.

In the family, the worker is also a function of the plan, of the authority of capital that subjects the activity of all the workers of reproduction
to its own ends. In the family, we reiterate, capital does not find its

---

3 Karl Marx, *Capital*, vol. 1, *A Critique of Political Economy*, trans. Ben Fowkes
(London: Penguin, New Left Review: 1990 [1976]), 449.
4 Ibid., 450.

mediation in a worker who places himself in the exclusive role of supervisor. His cannot occupy an exclusively supervisory role, because he too is a reproductive worker as well as the holder of the means of subsistence of the entire working-class family. Consequently, the mediation of capital by the worker involves a great paradox, since the worker is also the internal negation of capital; he is presented with a *space of potential refusal in the exercise of capitalist command*.

To this we can add that, just as in the factory not all salaried workers are subjected to the command and direction of capital in the same way, so in the family the wife and children are subjected to the worker in a differentiated fashion. In other words, here too, as we have seen, a *hierarchical structure* develops which assigns to each a specific place under the command of the worker. But even against this hierarchy, a fundamental element for the smooth functioning of the domestic working process, a cycle of struggles by women and young people has been unleashed that is no less virulent than that waged against the hierarchy in the factory.

Now, the family, as a unit of production and reproduction of labour power, also acts as a *unit of production and consumption of use values* necessary for the reproduction of labour power itself: a unit in which the use values produced by working subjects are consumed by one another. As we have seen, this means neither the homogeneous supply in the quantity and quality of labour by the various members, nor equal consumption in quantity and quality of the products themselves. But, aside from these differentiations which affect the various members of the family, the crucial thing in this context is that the various subjects, in all the exchanges to which the worker's salary gives rise, cannot buy money with their domestic work.

The legitimate holders of variable capital always remain those who have earned it: the workers. With respect to the consumption of children/siblings, the same argument applies as for the houseworker: with their domestic work they are only entitled to the consumption of the portion of variable capital corresponding to the value of their means of subsistence – that is, they too are always bound, with respect to the quantity and quality of their consumption, to the waged worker's consent.

It must be said, however, that the struggles of women and young people against domestic work and family discipline have also completely changed the *structure of consumption within the family*, especially since the end of the Second World War. If the adult male worker was previously not only the greatest consumer who worked the least but also the figure holding the power of decision over both the common and individual consumption of the members of his family, with the 1950s a new wind began to make demands on the wallet of the husband/father. As we have said, women have exerted enormous pressure within the family to broaden the sphere of consumption, especially on their children's behalf rather than their own. Moreover, an obvious pressure is exerted by young people themselves, who are fighting furiously to become the decision makers of their own consumption process, as well as to broaden its sphere. These pressures have forced capital to discover them as important new agents of production.

It is in this period that young people (even children) demand and achieve the agency to choose which clothes to buy, so that they often squander a salary for their own in frivolous spending, plundering a substantial part of their fathers' wages. They impose their wishes on the family: the scooter, the record player or, more recently, the cassette player and television set. In addition to the consistently high levels of domestic labour performed by mothers, it is evident how much of the paternal salary is used by them. This is a new generation, inexhaustible in its material and immaterial needs; such needs may be satisfied for many, but remain unmet for even more.

With women's rising class solidarity, they begin to manage a slice of the father's salary themselves. The father (through the mother) becomes the provider of a basic wage for children who manage to get money without having to work in return. In such a context, the denial of oneself as labour power is a practice adopted at the mass level. This is perhaps the most anti-capitalist habit learned by young people in the family: to demand access to money, however little, in exchange only for their existence as individuals and not as labour power. If someone in the family is forced to sacrifice more so that the children can sacrifice less, it is no longer just the mother, but also the father.

The mother can act as a solid support in these struggles of children: she may pave the way, prepare the ground, collaborate in the attack, and eventually cover the retreat.

This restructuring of consumption sees the dethroning of the male waged worker as the privileged figure. The relationship between the possession of wages and the quantitative and qualitative determination of consumption is severed. The worker is divested of his power of command over family consumption. He is no longer able to continue consuming in greater quantities commodities of better quality than his wife and children, precisely because of these struggles for a more equitable distribution of the family wage. They are struggles made by crying, tantrums, emotional blackmail, muzzling and enforced silences. These struggles are not organised, but they are homogeneous and occur on a mass level. Whatever else, they are capable of redefining, among other things, the map of family consumption, and of triggering a mechanism whereby new generations of workers are accustomed to a higher level of income than that which capital has assigned to them.

In the family, therefore, the movements of capital mark the different exchanges and relations of production and regulate the differences in power that are established among its members as a result of the division of labour articulated therein. This division of labour within the family obviously corresponds to a *stratification of power* among its various members. In other words, on the basis of the division of reproductive labour not only to be disbursed but also to be consumed and incorporated, there develops the hierarchical scale, mentioned above, which, based on differences of age and sex, functions as a *productive force immanent* to the capitalist organisation of domestic labour. This is both with respect to the materiality of the production process and with respect to the shrinking of the possibilities of struggle for all, as a consequence of the sedimentation of this stratification of power.

Even here, the particularity of exploitation is achieved through the differentiation of its levels, which are based on the stratification of labour power as a capacity for reproduction within the family.

In this context, it is easy to understand how the family can be a pit of vipers, a chasm of hatred and a factory of madness. In fact, it represents a tangle of masters and workers, an interweaving of exploiters and the exploited, a grid of emotional blackmail, frustrations and dependencies. The family is capital, and against it there can only be class hatred, revolt and sabotage. Parents are the most immediate enemies of the children, the first masters, and vice versa, the children against their parents, and the husband against his wife. But their real enemy, ultimately responsible for their misery, is capital.

On the other hand, it is just as easy to understand how the family is potentially also a great pool of love, affection and solidarity, and how it is a great achievement of the workers – especially those who are women. But only by deepening the organisation of the struggle against capital will it be possible to transform this potentiality into actuality, to humanise the relationships between parents and children, and to bring out all the love contained within them that the struggle against their capitalist aspect already allows us to see. Even if it is difficult to fight against capital as children, parents, husbands, wives, brothers and sisters – this is the only way out. We must become increasingly aware of this.

It is not necessarily true that the struggle against the family assumes the form only of a transformation from within. On the contrary, the tendency towards the concrete *extinction* of the family itself is becoming stronger and stronger. A large part of the proletariat no longer seeks their reproduction within families, preferring solitude or different reproductive arrangements to the 'factory of chains' that is the family. There is a strange parallel here with the traditional factory, which is gradually becoming extinct. It is not too bold to say that we are moving towards a phase of the capitalist mode of production *with neither factories nor families*. The trends show a deep restructuring of the social productive body, which already has, *in nuce*, separated much of production from these two structures, or anyway from the various standard forms each has taken, from the industrial revolution to the present day. If, on the one hand, the family is dying out as a reproductive centre, on the other hand, in the new forms in which the reproductive terrain is reconstructed, it also tends to incorporate within it processes of commodity production. The form is that of the *cooperative*, and the principle is that of *self-management*. At least, this is what capital is trying to organise as a response to proletarian struggles against both structures.

12

Capitalist Accumulation and Population

If reproduction generates surplus value, then its vicissitudes have as much effect on the accumulation process as do those of production. Therefore, it is not enough simply to analyse the organic composition of capitalist production. The organic composition of variable capital and its related dynamics, with different, if not opposing laws, must also be considered. But here a question presents itself: Is it even possible to consider the composition of variable capital from a technical point of view, and from the point of view of value – that is, is it possible to consider it in terms of its own *organic composition*?

We insist that such an analysis *is* possible, even if it presents greater difficulties in terms of an analysis of technical composition and value than that of production. In the process of reproduction, the means of production are less clearly separable from labour power, both from a technical point of view and from the point of view of value production, than they are in the production process. Even in the latter, constant capital is less distinct from variable capital than it appears, given that constant capital is ultimately only the accumulation of dead labour. Suffice it to recall that the *organisation of work*, which materially makes use exclusively of living labour, also performs the functions of fixed capital in the form of machinery. However, in the reproduction process, this connection is less straightforward.

If we distinguish, for the sake of convenience, the production of labour power from reproduction in general, we see that, in the former, it seems almost impossible to determine the composition of variable capital in terms of value, because the value of the raw materials, of the means of production and of auxiliary materials cannot be separated from the houseworker's own labour power.

Here, the raw materials and means of labour, which coincide with the bodies of men and women, have no inherent value, because they are a prerequisite and necessary condition for the existence of capital. The value of auxiliary materials, constituted by the means of subsistence of the houseworker, *cannot be separated from that of labour power*, because these values coincide in the person of the houseworker. The only part of the value of the means of production that is not included in that of labour power is the value of those auxiliary materials which do not simultaneously constitute themselves as means of subsistence of the houseworker's own labour power.

In the reproduction of labour power, on the other hand, the value of the raw materials, of the means of production and their auxiliary materials may or may not appear separable from the value of the labour power of the houseworker. These values are, however, separable in the initial phase of the domestic labour process and separable from the production of material use values.

In this stage, the raw materials correspond to food, clothing, furniture, the house and so on; the means of production are the washing machine, dishwasher and so on; and auxiliary materials include electricity, water and gas. To determine the value of labour power and that of the means of production, it suffices to separate the value of the means of subsistence of the houseworker from that of the means necessary for the survival of the other members of the family, who also constitute the means of production for domestic labour. Subsequently, we need to divide the value of the means of subsistence consumed in common by the other members of the family by their total number. By adding this latter value to that of the means of subsistence of the houseworker, we obtain the value of the houseworker's individual labour power.

In this first phase, the value of the means of production of *immaterial use values* does not appear separable from that of the houseworker's own labour power. Proof of this is that the raw materials and means of production coincide with the houseworker's own person, and the auxiliary materials (such as make-up and clothes) form part of her means of self-maintenance. Thus, the value of the means of production made up of auxiliary materials coincides with the value of the labour power of the houseworker.

However, in a second phase of the domestic labour process, the value of the means of production is clearly separable from that of the houseworker's own labour power. Here, the value of the tangible and intangible commodities produced in the initial phase present themselves as the means of production for domestic labour. More precisely, they appear as both raw materials and auxiliary materials, with respect to which the means of production are constituted by, as we have seen, the individual as labour power.

In any case, these difficulties that arise regarding the determination of the organic composition of variable capital are easily overcome. It suffices to assume that, in terms of value production, those means of production which present themselves simultaneously as the means of subsistence of the houseworker function not as the constant part of variable capital, but as its variable part – that is, as the value of the labour power of the houseworker. Starting from here (considering only the value of the means of production that do not function as means of subsistence for the houseworker in the initial phase), it is possible to distinguish the constant and variable parts of variable capital.

Correspondingly, in terms of their technical composition, the true and proper means of production in reproduction can be assumed to be only the parts which do not simultaneously function as the means of subsistence for the labour power involved in the process. Once this has been clarified, it is simple to obtain the average of the organic composition for variable capital, simply by calculating the averages of the various compositions existing in individual domestic labour processes.

Once this initial obstacle has been overcome, the crucial problem remains of examining the dynamics of organic composition for both capital and variable capital.

Our thesis is that in the 'phase of this process, in which the increase of capital occurs while the technical composition of capital remains constant', both capital and variable capital are subject to the same dynamics in the composition of value, since the variable part increases in both.[1] In the process of production, Marx observes, 'growth of capital implies

---

1 Karl Marx, *Capital*, vol. 1, *A Critique of Political Economy*, trans. Ben Fowkes (London: Penguin, New Left Review: 1990 [1976]), 772.

growth of its variable constituent, in other words, the part invested in labour-power. A part of the surplus-value which has been transformed into additional capital must always be re-transformed into variable capital, or additional labour fund' – for which 'accumulation of capital is therefore multiplication of the proletariat'.[2]

But multiplication of the proletariat – the increase of the constitutive part of the variable capital that derives from the increase of capital itself – also means an increase of the variable part of variable capital. Consequently, accumulation of capital means not simply an increase in the mass of the waged male proletariat that valorises capital in the production process (and is discarded as soon as they have become superfluous to such a process) but also an increase in the broader mass of female proletarians (houseworkers who produce and valorise capital so long as the wage workers also do so – and who also find themselves discarded as soon as they have become superfluous to the requirements of accumulation). They do not actually become superfluous, however, as will be shown below.

For those phases, however, where, once the general foundations of the capitalist system have been established, 'the development of the productivity of social labour becomes the most powerful lever of accumulation', our argument is that, in the dynamics of their composition, the organic structures of capital and variable capital diverge.[3] In the production process, the growing quantity of capital investment corresponds to an increase in the relative size of the means of production, which is accompanied, as Marx teaches us, by the increase in their absolute value, but not to an increase in proportion to their quantity.

In the process of reproduction, the amount of capital investment grows, but only in absolute terms. Relative to the individual domestic labour process it decreases, and this decrease corresponds to the diminution in the exchange value of labour power that accompanies the progress of accumulation. Furthermore, in this context, the specific development of labour productivity is expressed in a different fashion, through the growing magnitude *not* of the means of production relative to the labour power incorporated in them, but of the total sum of domestic labour provided by domestic labourers. In other words, here,

---

2   Ibid., 763, 764.
3   Ibid., 772.

the decisive moment of the process of accumulation is to be identified in the very creation and maintenance of the domestic workday and its working subject: the houseworker.

The fact that capital focuses here not on the increase in the magnitude of the means of production but on the mass of labour power should come as no surprise. We have already spoken of this phenomenon as regards the underdevelopment of the division and cooperation of domestic labour. This divergence in the capitalist path, as we have also seen, derives precisely from the specificity of domestic labour, which is positioned by capital as the productive force of social work and by the very different paths of struggles that have taken place against such work.

In the production process, capital, finding itself faced with the struggle for the reduction of the working day, had to develop the productivity of labour, starting from the constraints of a given working day, largely through an increase in the quantity of means of production. In the process of reproduction, however, it had first to lengthen the working day, constructing a practically unlimited domestic workday. If the factory era of large-scale industry begins with the introduction of heavy machinery, in the home this era entails the *increase in the extensive scale and scope of domestic labour*, progressively forcing proletarian women to position themselves primarily as houseworkers. This means that capital usurps the woman's workday in the production process. It thereby reduces the value of her labour power to that of her labour power as a houseworker – a value totally absorbed into the male wage.

In reproduction, the lever of capitalist development is essentially based on the creation and formation of a *working class of the household*, which sees variable capital as a consequence of the transformation of the sexual and generational composition of waged labour power such that it corresponds to the value of the labour power of the entire working family.

Only later does capital increase the intensity, magnitude and, at a certain point, also the productive power of domestic labour, albeit within certain limits. Specifically, it increases its productive power through an increase not only in the magnitude, but also in the quality of the means of production deployed by the single houseworker in the home. Yet, as we have seen, the value of the latter's labour power only decreases corresponding to the increase in the productive power of labour in the production process.

This second moment, which passes through a different technical composition of variable capital, is opened by capital in response to the cycle of struggles (which, unfortunately, we cannot deal with here) for the reduction of the domestic labouring day carried out by the working class of the home in an invisible but nonetheless effective fashion. This cycle, which has as its main axis the struggle to reduce the number of new workers to be trained and raised through domestic labour, has led to a reduction in the duration of the domestic workday in the process of production of labour power. This has meant less arduous motherhood in general, and specifically in the reduction of the extent and intensity of this workday in the reproduction process, resulting in fewer hours of domestic labour per day.

The fall in the birth rate is a direct expression of the houseworker's refusal of the housework that having a child entails. Not only that, but given children's role as *natural machines*, as fundamental means of production of domestic labour, this also results in a reduction of the overall magnitude of the means of production that a houseworker at the same time and with the same intensity of labour must employ.

Capital responds to this struggle, as we have already mentioned, by:

1. increasing the relative magnitude of the means of production in the domestic labour process in relation not to labour power but to the quantity of domestic labour;
2. bringing about a transformation in the quality of the means of production in the domestic labour process;
3. re-imposing a domestic workday of infinite extent.

This does not contradict the previous analysis of the limit of the capitalist use of machines within the reproduction process. In fact, this limit does not mean that there cannot be an increase in the volume of the means of production deployed in the domestic labour process, as indeed has occurred both in absolute and relative terms, in the sense both of the development of instruments of work and, partially, of the sophistication in its technology. But it does mean that this increase must be much smaller and much less crucial than what correspondingly occurred in the production process.

To reiterate, this was an increase not only in quantitative but also qualitative terms, inasmuch as it has been the means of production of domestic labour proper which have increased to a relatively greater degree – that is, there has not been a comparable increase in the means of subsistence of the working-class family. This increase in the volume and quality of the means of production that took place within the individual labour process gave rise, on the one hand, to an increase in absolute terms of the means of production with respect to the quantity of labour power employed, and, on the other hand, to a greater concentration of these means relative to the individual houseworker. Each of these now transforms into use values directly consumable by the members of the family, a volume greater than the relative size of the means of production during a given time and with the same work intensity.

In this process, however, the increase in the volume and change in the quality of the means of production does not correspond, as we have seen, to any decrease in the amount of labour power employed, but only to a decrease in the amount of domestic labour necessary for their use. Building from this situation, capital, being interested in resuming the massive use of women as more or less precarious workers in the production process, does not oppose a decrease in the absolute amount of domestic labour provided. In cases where capital wants to continue consuming female labour power in the form of houseworkers, it ensures only that the quantity of domestic labour decreases relative to the single tasks that certain so-called improvements in the instruments of labour help individual houseworkers to perform in less time. It does not, however, decrease the number of workers or the quantity of housework they must perform – instead, it increases such labour in absolute terms by increasing the number and variety of tasks required from the houseworker.

The increase in the number and quality of these means of reproduction (domestic appliances, automobiles and so on) therefore tend not to shorten the total time of domestic labour, but only some specific tasks that require the individual houseworker to make use of more means of production. Here, the increase in the productive power of labour does not consist in producing more commodities in less time, but, starting from a limited and diminishing quantity of commodities produced, it consists in carrying out certain tasks in a shorter time only to perform others. This increase in productive power is therefore not reflected in an increased production of commodities, or a lowering of their price, but in the expansion of the content of domestic labour, which is continually complicated by new practices and procedures.

One additional note should be added here. In reproduction, as in the production process, as the volume of the means of production increases, their value simultaneously decreases (that is, their value increases in absolute terms, but not in proportion to their quantity). The increase, therefore, of the difference between the constant and the variable parts of variable capital is much less than the increase of the difference between the quantity of the means of production into which the constant part of variable capital is converted and the mass of female labour power into which the variable part of variable capital proper is converted. It goes without saying that, if the progress of accumulation decreases the relative proportion of the variable part of variable capital, it by no means excludes an increase in its absolute magnitude, since, as Marx says, the uninterrupted retransformation of surplus value into capital is represented as the increasing amount of capital which enters the production process and therefore the reproduction process.

The different dynamics of the organic composition of capital and that of variable capital within the process of capitalist accumulation transform the workforce in the factory and at home in different ways – indeed, according to opposite laws. Marx sees very clearly the laws governing the movement of labour power in the production process, even if he regards them as general laws of capitalist accumulation and not as laws governing only the production process. Among these laws he includes the following, which he considers the absolute law:

> The greater the social wealth, the functioning capital, the extent and energy of its growth, and therefore also the greater the absolute mass of the proletariat and the productivity of its labour, the greater is the industrial reserve army. The same causes which develop the expansive power of capital, also develop the labour-power at its disposal. The relative mass of the industrial reserve army thus increases with the potential energy of wealth. But the greater this reserve army in proportion to the active labour-army, the greater is the mass of a consolidated surplus population, whose misery is in inverse ratio to the amount of torture it has to undergo in the form of labour. The more extensive, finally, the pauperized sections of the working class and the industrial reserve army, the greater is official pauperism. This is the absolute general law of capitalist accumulation.[4]

---

4   Ibid., 798.

However, the laws which govern the process of reproduction remain obscure to him. In any case, the latter demonstrate opposing trends and, as we have already seen, this process does not involve the same sort of industrial reserve army and its relative surplus population.

The reason for this difference is already clear: the increase in the workers employed in the production process, albeit in a constantly decreasing proportion in relation to the increase in total capital, is represented as an increasing magnitude of variable capital entering the reproduction process. Such increasing magnitude, in turn, implies an increase of the variable constituent part of variable capital. The demand for domestic labour therefore increases in proportion to the growth of variable capital, which, however, as we might recall, presents itself in a constantly decreasing proportion with respect to the increase in total capital.

While, in the production process, working-class overpopulation is necessary for the development of capitalist accumulation, in reproduction it would be superfluous, because any increase in the population of houseworkers means an increase in a totally useful population, all indirectly exploitable and valorised by capital. There is no aspect of necessary domestic labour that capital is required to suppress in order to posit it as surplus labour. If, in the production process, dismissal, unemployment and rehiring are the expression of the double movement of capital, in that of reproduction it is full employment that expresses the only movement capital determines. As opposed to the dual tendency of capital to increase the working population in the process of production and incessantly transform a part of it into relative overpopulation, here there corresponds a single tendency to increase it. In other words, the necessary labour supplied in the production process, which is rendered superfluous by capital, does not automatically render the domestic labour driven by it superfluous.

At most, domestic labour runs the risk of presenting itself as superfluous to the unemployed worker who can no longer exchange a salary with the houseworker for her domestic labour. But such a risk does not arise in reality, as addressed below, for this is the same moment in which labour power (in the traditional sense within production) presents itself as '*outside the conditions of the reproduction of its existence*; it exists without the *conditions of its existence and* is therefore a mere encumbrance;

needs without the means to satisfy them'.[5] Even if such domestic labour survives, this is not because it is reproduced through the dual exchange between labour and capital and between wages and domestic labour, but because it is maintained today by collective capital, and ultimately by the state. It can easily be understood, even in this situation, how domestic labour does not become superfluous for the worker. Even the unemployed worker still has the problem of satisfying the basic minimal needs of existence: to survive, he still needs domestic labour.

This work continues to be necessary not only for the worker but also for capital. Capital also desires that the houseworker continue to carry out domestic labour for the unemployed worker, because it thus contributes to sustaining this potential means of labour, keeping it in reserve for later use. In this case, domestic labour no longer values a salary, but welfare and unemployment benefits, and it becomes the work of reproducing the worker not as actual but as potential labour power. The absolute increase in the working population relative to the production process (which consistently increases faster than variable capital itself, or rather faster than the means which gives the latter employment) therefore produces, through the process of reproduction, an absolute increase in the working population. This increase is consistently produced at a rate greater than that of variable capital – that is, at a rate exceeding the means of its own employment. This does not mean, however, as we have seen, that a relative population of houseworkers is created, one exceeding the average needs for the valorisation of capital that is therefore superfluous. Indeed, the opposite occurs: namely, that all female living labours remain necessary for capital.

The absolute law of capitalist accumulation in the process of reproduction therefore works as follows: *The greater the social wealth, the greater the capital in operation, the volume and energy of its increase, therefore also the absolute mass of the proletariat and the productive power of its labour and thus the greater the absolute size of the working population in reproduction.*

However, the analysis of how the dynamics of the organic composition of capital and that of variable capital differ in their deployment of labour power in their respective processes does not end here. So far, we have seen

---

5 Karl Marx, *Grundrisse: Foundations of the Critique of Political Economy*, trans. Martin Nicolaus (London: Penguin Books, 1993), 609.

the use of labour power in both realms and the different laws that regulate this use, depending on whether it is for the purpose of producing commodities or reproducing labour power; but we have to explore further upstream. It is necessary to assess how they deploy the production of labour power – that is, how the *population* is produced in capitalist society – which presents itself, in its confrontation with the production process, as a presupposition and condition of the latter's existence. Obviously, these are intertwined levels of discourse, ones which may also be addressed separately. A preliminary problem presents itself in the very concept of population. Marx's use of this term revealed a great uncertainty: sometimes, he talks about the working population, sometimes of the population *tout court*, and other times of the working-class population. However, he shows a lively concern to distinguish the concept of population – as the mass of actual or potential labour power – from that established by the bourgeois economists, for whom its meaning is simply the mass of individuals, within which there are bosses, workers and so on. Indeed, he is right to keep this concern alive, because the concept of population has historically been an expression of the economists of capital.

Today, however, in the phase of the social worker, at this level of mass proletarianisation, the current concept of population can be recovered in Marxian terms since the extent to which it is not a mass of labour power is statistically negligible.[6]

If, as we have seen, the houseworker is the party responsible for the production of future workers and the family is the space to which this production is assigned, the laws that regulate domestic reproduction and the struggles waged on its terrain obviously influence the development and structuring of population. To analyse the problem of population, therefore, it is not enough to consider its increase, as Marx does, as one that is a natural force of social labour.

Population must be considered in relation to the overall cycle of capital: on the one hand, that is, as a result of the domestic labour process, and on the other, as a presupposition and condition for the existence of the production process. Only from this perspective is it possible to

---

6   Here Fortunati uses the phrase 'nella fase dell' operaio sociale', referring to the influential distinction, common in *operaismo*, describing the transition between the mass worker and socialisation of labour. See Antonio Negri, *Dall'operaio massa all' operaio sociale. Intervista sull'operaismo* (Milan: Multhipla edizioni, 1979).

understand not only why capitalist production presupposes maximal population growth (the maximum production of living labour power) but also how this production takes place – the laws regulating its growth, as well as which type of labour processes creates this living labour power in ever-increasing quantities. From Marx onwards, it has been widely recognised by all that the capitalist mode of production and accumulation produces and requires the maximum population growth possible.

> As to production founded on capital, the greatest absolute mass of necessary labour together with the greatest relative mass of surplus labour appears as a condition, regarded absolutely. Hence, as a fundamental condition, maximum growth of population – of living labour capacities. If we further examine the conditions of the development of the productive forces as well as of exchange, division of labour, cooperation, all-sided observation, which can only proceed from many heads, science, as many centres of exchange as possible – all of it identical with growth of population.[7]

It is not sufficient for existing labour power to reproduce itself; it must multiply, generating new labour powers. It has been well established that this increase does not occur naturally. It is in the nature of this increase that the problem begins for Marx, who speaks of population growth as a natural, and therefore unpaid, form of social labour. The assumption opens the way for a gross misconception that population increases naturally, since such an increase is seen as a product that is historically given in the capitalist mode of production. He fails to understand, however, that this increase, one posited as natural by capital is, in reality, an increase in the value produced by domestic labour, which is, despite appearances, productive labour. Capital accumulation, on the other hand, is the absolute increase of the proletariat, not only because the absolute size of the variable part of capital increases, but because the quantitative dimension of the proletariat increases in absolute terms. In other words, there is an increase in the production of labour power, which must reproduce by multiplying itself, thereby increasing the production of value, and therefore of capital. This multiplication must be an increase in population to the maximum possible limit, because in

---

7 Marx, *Grundrisse*, 608.

it 'the development of all productive forces is summarised'. Population growth forms the basis for capital's unimpeded appropriation. Indeed, here, overpopulation and pauperism appear 'the result of labour itself, of the development of the productive force of labour'.[8] On the other hand, as we have seen, one of the conditions of existence of the capitalist mode of production is the continuous and maximal production of surplus value in the process of reproduction – even if this surplus value is not totally re-transformed into surplus value and thus into capital in the production process. In other words, this mode of production presupposes the continuous, maximal creation of new labour power. Although offspring are not all necessarily transformed into productive workers, they are the condition that allows capital to decide how many, where and how to transform them into productive workers – that is, to apply the laws that regulate the production of commodities.

If the effect of the development of capital is the maximum development of population, what consequences does such development have for the proletariat? Obviously, the effects are negative: the progressive devaluation of the individual, reduced to a commodity, to labour power.

This process occurs not only because 'the working population . . . produces both the accumulation of capital and the means by which it is itself made relatively superfluous; and it does this to an extent which is always increasing'.[9] In other words, this occurs not only because the relative overpopulation increases more and more and therefore determines in the proletariat 'an accumulation of misery . . . a necessary condition, corresponding to the accumulation of wealth . . . In proportion as capital accumulates, the situation of the worker, be his payment high or low, must grow worse'.[10] But it also occurs because the *multiplying*, of the proletariat, has the intrinsic meaning of *devaluing oneself*. The more labour power produces and reproduces, the greater the self-expropriation of the value produced in the process of reproduction. Furthermore, in multiplication, the consumption of the exchange value of labour power is managed in accordance with capitalist expectations of population growth, which foresee the production and development of a certain average quantity of new labour power. When this management of

---

8 Ibid., 604–5.
9 Marx, *Capital*, vol. 1, 783.
10 Ibid., 799.

consumption complies with capitalist planning, in the sense that each individual as labour power corresponds to a predetermined level of subsistence, the value of the workforce determined in the production process finds its confirmation in that of reproduction. Only the effective production and reproduction of a calculated quantity of labour power can confirm it as an average value, corresponding to the labour power of a working-class family in which an average number of new labour powers is calculated. There will, of course, be many families below such an average and others, though fewer, over it. For the latter, the greater availability of means of subsistence potentially increases the use value of individual labour power. In establishing the exchange value of labour power, however, capital disregards the differences in excess or deficiency of its use value, precisely because it is interested in the average use value of labour power.

For capitalism, the troubles begin when the exchange value of labour power corresponds to that of a working family who's average size is much lower than that established and required by capital. In this case, the reduction in the number of new workers entails an increase in the value of the means of subsistence that must be extended to each unit of labour power, and therefore an increase in the use value incorporated in labour power beyond the level which capital requires for its valorisation. Historically, in fact, this trouble for capital began quite early, precisely from this weak point in the mechanism through which the increase in population is produced: the somersault of exchange value of labour power from the production process into that of reproduction. This determination of the magnitude of labour power's use value is only the first stage of the struggle.

The other stage of the struggle occurs in the realisation of the value of labour power. Here, the struggle is above all that of women who have a privileged position of sorts, because in this context it is the worker and especially the houseworker who determine the size of the family. If, on a mass level, they do not produce the average proletarian family, the value of the individual's labour power increases. The struggle for a lower birth rate, and the reduction of the domestic workday in the process of production of the workforce, arose and developed precisely based on this weakness in the mechanism of exploitation. The collapse of the correspondence between the exchange value of labour power and its quantity as projected by capital has indirectly impelled an increase in the exchange value of labour power. If a young labour force in training has achieved a certain level regarding its means of subsistence, it is unlikely to accept any decrease in the level of its own consumption – and therefore its exchange value – as it enters the workforce.

This demographic contraction, however, not only exerts pressure on the exchange value of labour power but also, as we have seen, exerts immediate pressure on the use value of labour power, which tends to increase beyond the needs of capital, as well as on the increased scarcity of workers available for wage labour, and, last but not least, on the structure of the population itself.

The unforeseen increase in the use value of labour power is meagre consolation for capital, which, in the meantime, is forced to solve the problem of the fall in the birth rate with the import/export of labour power, whose use value might be lower but is nevertheless available for factory work.

Just as, in the process of production, the struggle for the reduction of the working day forced capital to use machines, so the struggle for the reduction of the working day in the process of reproduction forced capital to develop an international labour-market – to build multi-national working classes, with all the political consequences that such operations entail. Whether these transformations are designed to remedy the insufficiency of the working population in the centres of historical capitalist power or to remedy the lack of a skilled workforce in the countries of the so-called Third World, the contradictions opened by the immigration/emigration of the workforce are enormous.

If the power relationship established between the working class and capital in the production process has been represented in the political determination of the price of labour power – that is, of wages – in addition to working hours, then in the sphere of reproduction, it was initially represented in the political determination of the number of new labour powers produced – that is, in the slowdown of population increase.

This reduction has had a decisive effect, reconfiguring the structure of the population in an increasingly unproductive fashion. Within much of the so-called First World, for example, the proportion of older adults is increasing significantly, while that of new recruits to the workforce is clearly diminishing. This aging of the population is a stab to the heart of capital because it can clearly no longer extract surplus value from an ever-growing proportion of the labour force while demands for public spending, if anything, expand.

This assumption – that the more the proletariat multiplies, the more it self-valorises – is equally valid if we view proletarian reproduction as a diachronic movement, and if we consider it in a synchronic fashion, through the different contributions that its various sections make to the absolute increase in population. In fact, this assumption is also valid if reversed: the lower the value of the labour power of a section of the proletariat, the greater the contribution it generally makes to the increase in population.

In this regard, Marx had already observed that the reproduction of a stagnant relative overpopulation was comparable in capitalism to 'the boundless reproduction of animals individually weak and constantly hunted down'.[11] We have already discussed the causes that determine this inverse relationship between the value of labour power and its capacity for growth. What should be added here is that this assumption is also represented by the inverse relationship between the level of the wage and the quantity of new labour power produced. The lower the former, the greater the latter, and vice versa.

When wages are repressed, the means of subsistence for the working family's labour power (which are also the means to produce labour power in production) are also diminished; and also diminished are the means of production that function exclusively as such. The only means of production in this case that does not simultaneously function as a means of subsistence is the uterus. Under these conditions, the continuous functioning of the womb represents the specific productive force of domestic labour. The higher the wage, the greater the mass of means of subsistence that also function as means of production, and above all that which functions exclusively as means of production for domestic labour.

But even this dynamic within the various sections of the proletariat has not remained unscathed by the women's struggle. Nor has it remained unchanged historically, because, from a certain point onwards in the so-called advanced countries, the decrease in the birth rate began to affect even the poorest strata of the proletariat. Nor, currently, is the decrease limited to these nations, as can be seen clearly from the international situation: in the so-called Third World, where a lower concentration of capital creates a population surplus, the decrease in the

---

11   Ibid., 797.

birth rate still occurs, even if the production of labour power is strenu-
ously enforced. This is not only the result of demographic campaigns
conducted increasingly through violence rather than incentives, but also
represents the *consequences of a political will among women.*

This inverse relationship between wage levels and the number of
labour powers produced by the single working family was also grasped
by Marx, who understood its real function and scope, since he defined
it as the 'law of capitalist society'. Unfortunately, he barely mentions
this inverse relationship, only to highlight the different proportions in
which the various elements of the working class participate in its overall
increase. The stagnant overpopulation, he says,

> forms at the same time a self-reproducing and self-perpetuating ele-
> ment of the working class, taking a proportionally greater part in the
> general increase of that class than the other elements. In fact, not only
> the number of births and deaths, but the absolute size of families,
> stands in inverse proportion to the level of wages, and therefore to the
> amount of the means of subsistence at the disposal of different cate-
> gories of worker. This law of capitalist society would sound absurd to
> savages, or even to civilised colonists.[12]

Marx limits himself to enunciating this law as if he had deduced it from
empirical observation, supported in this by analogous assertions,
expressed in a much cruder fashion, by Adam Smith: 'Poverty seems to
favour procreation'; and by S. Laing: 'Poverty, driven to the extreme
point of famine and pestilence, instead of preventing the increase of
population, tends to favour it.'[13] Marx fails to grasp that this 'law' is also
valid from a diachronic point of view with respect to the history of
capitalist development, as demonstrated by European history from the
second half of the nineteenth century onwards: that the accumulation of
capital has led to an absolute increase in the population, but also to a
decrease in its relative growth.

Behind this inverse relationship there are subjective factors – as mentioned above, women's struggle over the birth rate – as well as objective
factors by which struggles continue to be triggered and radicalised. These

---

12   Ibid., 796–7.
13   Ibid., 797, n.22.

include compulsory primary education and the prohibition of child labour, among others. These factors have had various consequences, including the lengthening of childhood as the period in which new labour power is raised and, at the same time, an increase in the cost of reproduction, due to the prohibitions of child labour and the attendant fact that children and young adults no longer bring home a wage.

Beyond any discussion of causes, it is important to emphasise that the inverse relationship between the level of the wage and the quantity of new labour power produced represents the internal mechanism of the reproduction process, which contributes to regulating the development of the population. This development is affected by the increase of the wage in absolute terms, albeit in a constantly decreasing proportion with respect to the increase in total capital, but also by the general movement of wages determined by the relationship between the entire working class and social capital in its totality.

The movements of this relationship reverberate in population shifts. The population is initially subjected to growth in absolute terms, due to the dynamics of the total wage, as Marx underlines. This corresponds to the absolute growth of variable capital (even if the latter occurs in constantly decreasing proportion with respect to the increase of total capital). From a certain stage of accumulation onwards, the population is subject to a constant fall in its relative growth rate due to the dynamics of the wage.

One of the fundamental aspects of the general law of capitalist accumulation, therefore, is that it is accompanied by the growth of population in absolute terms, exceeding the average needs of the valorisation process but that this proportional growth of population progressively decreases.

13

For a Workers' History of Reproduction

What is the history of reproduction within the process of capitalist accumulation, its role in the process of the production of absolute and relative surplus value? What paths of struggle have forged this history? How can we write a *workers' history of reproduction*? These questions are posed not in order to give them a comprehensive answer, which would require infinitely more time and space, but in order to establish some points urgent to examine.

The thesis presented here is that, in reproduction, capitalist development has proceeded in a manner opposite from that of production. The reading of workers' history proposed by Marx, though written in grand strokes, applies to the production process and not to the overall capitalist accumulation cycle. The very fact that he did not see reproduction as a process of value creation created blind spots even in his reading of the history of production.

According to Marx, the production of absolute surplus value is fundamentally characterised by the lengthening of the working day. To say this does not exclude the fact that, in the initial stage of its development, capital simultaneously seeks or applies particular methods of producing relative surplus value, such as the development of new forms of cooperation and division of labour. But it is to claim that the increase in the productivity of labour is primarily founded in the dilation of the time of surplus labour up to the natural limits of the working day, and *not* through the restriction of necessary labour time achieved by making workers a cheaper commodity. Clearly, Marx's discourse refers here solely to the production process.

In reality, the expansion of surplus labour time has occurred beyond the lengthening of the working day in terms of the necessary labour time involved in production. Surplus labour time has also invested all the labour time necessary for the reproduction of the worker that is not included in the production process, by making it *superfluous*, and thus unpaid.

Production of absolute surplus value therefore means the incorporation of reproduction, in its totality, into the realm of surplus labour. Reproduction is separated by the dividing line of value from the production process, and domestic labour is established as a natural force of social labour. But, although domestic labour is an appendage of the realm of surplus labour with respect to the overall capitalist cycle, it nevertheless also functions as a process of commodity production. As such, it is a process as self-enclosed as the others, in which labour is divided into necessary labour and surplus labour.

Within reproduction, what are the processes that the production of surplus value initiates? There are two distinct processes. First, the production of labour power (procreation and pregnancy) is subject to the same fate as the production of commodities: the development of the sector through the lengthening of the working day. The reproduction of labour power (material and immaterial care) is, on the contrary, underdeveloped through the curtailment of its working day. Why are these two different and opposed tendencies operative in the two distinct moments of the reproduction process? The first moment is developed while the second faces the opposite fate, because the development of the first does not impede the commodity production process, while that of the second would counteract it. But let us take the two processes in order.

As we have established, there is a lengthening of the working day in the process of production of labour power. This is a rather unique workday, since it must be calculated in months (pregnancy lasts about nine) and with respect to the length of the period of fertility whose natural limits are set by the appearance of menstruation and the onset of menopause – a period that corresponds to the *length of a woman's working life* in this process. The prolongation of such a working day to its physical and moral limit implies that:

1. if this working day is considered from a temporal point of view, it coincides with the duration of fertility;

2. if it is considered from a spatial point of view, as the result of the juxtaposition of all the working days, it consists of the maximum number of working days.

The more numerous the working days, the *greater the simultaneous valorisation of capital*. The prolongation of this total average working day entails the reduction of the necessary labour time required to produce labour power. The individuals as labour power are not only forced to reproduce themselves in less time, but, simultaneously, in the same amount of time, they are forced to produce more individuals. In other words, not only is the adult woman obliged to procreate without interruption throughout the period of fertility, forced into perpetual motherhood, but every woman has this obligation – every woman must become a mother. This is also why capital encourages the maximum exchange between variable capital and domestic labour. It is in its interest that everyone should marry and become fathers and mothers, because the more general this exchange – the greater the number of those who bear and produce children – the more surplus labour can be appropriated.

The expansion of motherhood that emerges under capitalism exists in conjunction with the prolongation of the workday of commodity production because pregnancy does not necessarily prevent women from working in the latter process as well. The labour of making a child (apart from the moment of the delivery) does not foreclose the simultaneous provision of wage labour, although certain restrictions apply. The expansion of motherhood therefore poses no obstacle to capital's craving for surplus value.

Indeed, if it is true that the development of the production of labour power becomes possible on a large scale only in the capitalist mode of production proper, it nevertheless emerges, at least as a tendency, at an earlier stage. This is specified as an emergent tendency because it does not yet seem to have been proved that the pre-capitalist period ever saw an increase in population attributable to an increase in the birth rate significant enough that we can speak with certainty of such a phenomenon.

In any case, the fact that the increase in population is a crucial node, as the 'the mathematical limit to the production of surplus-value by the total social capital' even in this phase of the capitalist mode of production, is incontrovertible.[1] Obviously, in manufacture, a form of the capitalist mode of production where the division of labour predominates, population increase must be quantitatively proportional to the amount of capital invested. But, in any case, population increase on the general level is nevertheless fundamental with respect to the total workday of society, because 'the increase in population increases the productive force of labour, since it makes possible a greater division and combination of labour, etc.'[2]

This correspondence is particularly fundamental in the period of heavy manufacture, where, as already stated, a division of labour predominates which requires 'a division of labour within society should have already attained a certain degree of development' and which conversely 'reacts back upon that in society, developing and multiplying it further'.[3] But, while the division of labour and cooperation are posited as particular methods of producing relative surplus value that develop the productivity of labour power by shortening the labour time required for the production of a given quantity of commodities, the increase in population is obviously not posited as such. As an expression of the development of domestic labour, although it is presented as a result of the productive power of capital, it is, in reality, the effect of the spatial and temporal lengthening of the domestic workday required for the production of labour power. As the effect, therefore, of the absolute lengthening of surplus labour time, it is the result of a process of production which is positioned as the production of *absolute surplus value*.

On the other hand, in the sphere of reproduction, during this phase capital curtails the workday and increasingly underdevelops its working process, as mentioned above. It is the need to extend the time of surplus labour in the process of commodity production that, in this case, forces capital to shorten the domestic workday, even if, in its entirety, it is posited as *surplus labour time*. This is a tactical choice, not a strategic one. Tactically, it usurps not only free time, but also that part of the working time necessary for reproduction which *appears* as non-labouring time. But how is it that the capitalist mode of production can proceed so

---

1   Karl Marx, *Capital*, vol. 1, *A Critique of Political Economy*, trans. Ben Fowkes (London: Penguin, New Left Review, 1990 [1976]), 442.

2   Karl Marx, *Grundrisse: Foundations of the Critique of Political Economy*, trans. Martin Nicolaus (Penguin Books: London, 1993), 400.

3   Marx, *Capital*, vol. 1, 473.

rapidly in this usurpation, not only by overcoming the barrier constituted by the working time necessary for reproduction, but by tending progressively to reduce this time to the limit of the mere time necessary for the production of the means of subsistence? How does it succeed here, where pre-capitalist forms of production had failed?

We ask this question because it seems at first contradictory that capital's lust for surplus labour in the production process comes to usurp even the time of domestic labour and consumption. This is not a contradiction if we consider that the economic purpose which drives pre-capitalist forms of production is profoundly different from that which drives the capitalist mode of production, and in each form of production, therefore, an inherently different need for surplus labour develops.

In pre-capitalist modes of production, the economic purpose is the production of use values – the reproduction of workers, the reproduction of the holders of the means of production and the reproduction of the social relation which subjects the former to the latter. In this arrangement, the need for surplus labour does not derive from the character of production. Rather, the limit of surplus labour is determined by a double relation: by the greater or lesser extent of the needs of the holders of the means of production, which is in turn delimited by the greater or lesser duration – relative to the single working day – of labour necessary for the worker to produce and consume his means of subsistence. This time constitutes an insurmountable barrier to the need for surplus labour, since the reproduction of the holders of the means of production depends on the reproduction of the workers themselves, as means of production.

The need for surplus labour is thus influenced by the extent of the needs of the holders of the means of production and by the necessary labour time required by the worker to produce and consume his means of subsistence. This relation is demonstrated by the fact that, when the need for surplus labour expands, there is a limit on the increase of surplus labour that cannot be overcome temporally with respect to the single working day, but can only be overcome spatially, through the combination and multiplication of working days. This is why the number of slaves and serfs is so important because, the more numerous they are, the more surplus labour the master and feudal lord can count on to satisfy their needs.

In the capitalist mode of production, where the economic purpose becomes the creation of value for value's sake, the need for surplus labour is unlimited insofar as it arises from the very character of production. This generally unlimited nature is further expressed in relation to the working day of the individual worker. The novelty which the capitalist mode of production introduces lies in the fact that it proceeds to the extension of surplus labour, even with respect to the single working day. But it proceeds in a completely different fashion.

The worker has become *free* as the bearer of labour power, the commodity the capitalist buys for a determinate period. *The process of reproduction thus appears completely separated from that of its consumption*, and the necessary labour time for reproduction appears to be split into two parts: one in the consumption of labour power in the production process, where it appears as the labour time required to produce the value necessary for reproduction's subsistence; the other, in the process of reproduction, the necessary labour time provided in the home by the houseworker, in which the worker's individual consumption is also incorporated. The part of reproduction's socially necessary labour time that relates to the production and consumption of intangible use values seems to disappear.

Capitalist production appears only as the material production of physical commodities. It is in material production that capital finds its fundamental possibility of direct application, because the moment of production of material use values is clearly separable from the moment of their consumption, and such a time separation enables their circulation as saleable goods.

By contrast, the production of those immaterial use values that do not possess an independent and separable form from their producers and consumers, and consequently cannot survive a prolonged interval between their production and consumption, were slow to be appropriated by capital. For example, it will be with the first extraction of relative surplus value that the production of information – the immaterial commodity *par excellence* – will become crucial in the production process and that the production of other immaterial commodities of this type will become part of the worker's consumption.

But, throughout the period in which the extraction of absolute surplus value prevails, the capitalist mode of production does not seem to find a foothold in such immaterial production, to the point that it apparently disappears – *apparently* because, in reality, such production does not disappear at all but is reintroduced as a fundamental part of the process of reproduction and, in particular, reproduction of the family, where such labour is incorporated into domestic labour, and is constituted as a natural force of social labour. In this case, the initial contraction of the domestic workday leads to an immediate reduction. It is, above all, this time of immaterial use value production that is sacrificed for the purpose of absolute surplus value (see, for example, all the repressive measures concerning sexuality, idleness, play and so on).

The advent of capitalism thus entails not only the dehumanisation of the individual, as Marx states: 'Production does not produce man only as a *commodity*, the *human commodity*, man in the form of a *commodity*; it also produces him as a *mentally* and physically *dehumanised* being.'[4] The advent of capitalism also entails the increased materialisation of the individual, a stripping of its capacity to produce immaterial use values.

Moreover, the moment of production of the worker's means of subsistence is separated from the moment of their consumption, just as the labour time necessary for their production is separated from the time required from the worker for their consumption. But the most relevant aspect here is that this separation is not only temporal and spatial; it is a separation marked by the dividing line of value, such that the first segment of time is presented as labour time, being that time for which the capitalist has purchased labour power (indeed this becomes the ultimate measure of the value of the labour power itself). The second segment is represented as non-working time, or as *free time*, in which the labour power belongs to itself. Incidentally, it is only with capital that this paradoxical situation arises whereby *the time required for consumption is represented as non-labour time*, even though the individual consumption of the worker is a moment of commodity production: the production of labour power.

Since workers have now been reduced to the commodity of labour power, the measure of labour time required to reproduce them is no longer derived from the need to reproduce them as individuals, but exclusively from the need to reproduce them as labour power, with the consequence that this labour time is drastically reduced. Everything that

---

4   Karl Marx, *Early Writings*, trans. Rodney Livingstone and Gregor Benton (London: Penguin, 1992), 336.

is not strictly related to their own reproduction, which returns them continually to their position at work, is now superfluous. 'Life is only a function of work' is the slogan that capital invents and imposes on the proletariat at this stage.

The first consequence for the worker is that he is not only exploited more in the process of production, but he is also exploited in the process of reproduction because he is now forced to reproduce himself for only as long as it takes to reproduce his capacity for work.

If the worker is a woman, then this is only the initial consequence, because the production of absolute surplus value *not only lengthens the time of surplus labour* in the production process (for both men and women) but *lengthens it much more for women in general*. The *woman*, in fact, positioned as the fundamental working subject of the process of reproduction, is also responsible for the domestic workday, although the latter has been stripped to the bone. This operation succeeds because capital simultaneously *deepens wage discrimination* against women by making their time insufficient for survival from the necessary labour disbursed in the production process alone.

As noted, the production of absolute surplus value involves an underdevelopment of reproduction. But it should be specified that this underdevelopment is only relative to pre-capitalist forms of production. If, instead, we consider the capitalist mode of production itself, we discover that, within its overall cycle of production, underdevelopment does not occur; it represents exactly the kind of development that capital needs during this phase – and it is, therefore, *productive*.

In fact, in this situation, capital would not be interested in a higher use value of labour power than that allowed for proletarian reproduction, achieved as quickly as possible. It is the increase of productivity in the production process, which passes through the lengthening of the workday, that renders *unproductive* the labour time necessary for any form of reproduction other than that of directly producing commodities. The reasoning is simple. Given that the worker is now reduced to the commodity of labour power, the interest capital takes in it, as with any other commodity, is to reduce its production to the shortest-possible interval of time. However, since it is impossible, given the development of the productive force in the factories, to produce in less time the value of the means of its own subsistence, and since it is not possible to reduce its exchange value by reducing the necessary labour time within the production process, it must instead reduce the time of the workday of reproduction, and therefore the time of surplus labour in the process of reproduction.

This reduction means that capital, even though it does not extort *relative surplus value*, still succeeds in determining a change in the ratio of the two constituent parts of the working day – necessary labour and surplus labour – required for the production process. This change is brought about by an extreme shortening of what used to be the working time necessary for reproduction, by including only a small portion of it within the workday of the production process and relegating the rest to the process of reproduction, the time of unpaid work and, as such, the time of surplus labour. In other words, capital succeeds in lowering equally both the labour time necessary for the reproduction of the worker, which is now reduced to labour power, and excluding from the working day a good part of the labour time necessary for the reproduction of labour power and thereby devaluing labour power in terms of its use value. The non-development or underdevelopment of the production of use value in the process of reproduction presents itself to capital as the only way to enable *the development of the production of absolute surplus value in the process of production*. For capital, throughout the period of manufacture, it is crucial that *the development of value production take place in terms of exchange value and not in terms of use value*. Given that, in the development of productive forces, the only way to accomplish this is to increase the time of surplus labour in the process of commodity production. Capital does not hesitate, on the one hand, to subordinate reproduction to commodity production and, on the other hand, to decouple the consumption of labour power from its adequate reproduction. Capital can afford to do this because the autonomous existence of labour power at an ever-broader level allows capital to free itself from the need for an adequate production of use value in the process of reproduction – that is, it allows it to prevail in its basic position as a buyer of the labour power commodity. As a buyer of labour power, it is therefore interested, on the one hand, only in the maximum consumption of labour power and, on the other, in ensuring the possibility of buying more and more of it.

With the growth of heavy industry, the production of absolute and relative surplus value is even more closely intertwined, until capital is forced by workers' struggle for the reduction of the working day to make a fundamental leap into the production of relative surplus value. In this phase, the process of production is now also separated spatially from that of reproduction. In the factories, the use of machinery, and with it the increase in the productivity of labour, is accompanied by a further extension of the working day – and therefore an increase in the quantity and intensity of work. In this phase, the sexual, racial and generational composition of labour power changes, and the *increase in the productivity of labour in the production process* becomes a trend powerful enough to engulf the working day, already stripped to the bone, of the other process, seriously affecting its production.

'Après moi le déluge' is the motto that informs the behaviour of every capitalist and that echoes through the murderous consumption of labour power within the factories. Here, capital's lust for surplus labour not only reduces the labour time necessary for reproduction practically to subsistence levels, but *also swallows the labouring subject of the reproduction process, the woman.* By forcing her into the factory as a worker it *almost totally excludes the possibility of exploiting her capacity for reproduction.*

The development of the capitalist mode of production requires at this stage the complete sacrifice of the reproductive sector for the development of production. At first, therefore, the domestic workday, already severely limited, tends towards extinction. The consequence however, *is that any female or male worker is now insufficiently reproduced and inadequate to the needs of capital.* The struggle for the reduction of the workday on the part of the working class not only puts an end to the particular form of surplus value extraction constituted by the production of absolute surplus value in the process of production, but at the same time imposes a turning point, a reversal of the trend in the realm of reproduction. Having hit rock bottom in its destruction of reproduction, capital is now forced into its development.

It is now in capital's interest to increase productivity in the process of reproduction by lengthening its working day. Faced with the struggle for the reduction of the working day in the factory, capital is confronted with the fact that the rate of surplus value can only be increased if, in the production process, the relative proportion of the constituent parts of the working day (necessary labour and surplus labour) are varied. This increased surplus value extracted from production also requires, in the process of reproduction, a parallel valorisation of labour power: the extension of labour time necessary for reproduction occurring *outside* the workday. This lengthening should be understood not only as an expansion of the time of worker consumption – that is, of the time that is set aside as the free time, of non-work which happens automatically with the reduction of the working day in the production process; above all, it should be understood as a lengthening of the domestic working day itself.

By now, in order to raise productivity in the production process – that is, to lengthen the time in which surplus value might be generated by lowering the quantity of necessary labour, capital is forced to invest more and more domestic labour in reproduction. Now the labour power involved in reproduction must in turn be valorised, given that development of the productive forces is necessary in order to create relative surplus value within the production process. It is understood that there will be *no more productive consumption of labour power in the factory unless the individual consumption of the worker is also consumption of the labour power of the houseworker.* Thus, in order to raise the rate of surplus value in terms of exchange value, capital must also develop the rate of surplus value in the process of reproduction. Relative surplus value does mean a lowering of the value of commodities, and therefore of the value of labour power, but only in terms of exchange value, because, as we have seen, the use value of labour power increases as a result of the lengthening of the domestic workday. But this lengthening is only one aspect of the transformation taking place in the capitalist mode of production.

The production of relative surplus value also provokes a new leap in the development of the sexual division of labour, initially by determining a new sexual and generational composition of labour power in the production process. If a major demand of industrial capitalism, before it was faced with the struggle to reduce the working day, had been that *women and children work*, after this struggle it became a demand for *adult male work*. The production of relative surplus value means *the concentration of capital's interest on the exploitation of women predominantly as a capacity for production and reproduction of labour power*, rather than on a form of dual exploitation. Consequently, it means *the transition from the domestic workday positioned as the extension of the factory workday* to a domestic workday characterised by the fact that the latter has no limit other than the duration of the day itself.

With this transformation, a new figure of labour was born: the *housewife*, or rather the houseworker. If the workers of the early industrial revolution included women and children and if this great industry accumulated its workers in the space of the factory, the worker-figures involved in the production of relative surplus value are two: one – the salaried male worker – inside the factory; the other – the indirectly salaried houseworker – outside the factory, in the house.

Marx describes the struggle of the working class against capital for the reduction of the workday. In the Marxian reading of this struggle, the *how* of working-class struggle has remained rather obscure. The history of this struggle, in fact, cannot be read solely as a struggle between the working class and capital, but must also be understood in terms of the class relations implemented within the working class. It is the class struggle, and not the class relation itself, that is limited to the two fundamental classes. The complex class relationships that occur during and around this struggle between the working class and capital provide a kind of photographic evidence for the argument presented here. Marx fails to grasp this complexity either in his analysis of the class struggle or in his historical writings where he discusses the political composition of the working class. In both cases, he remains anchored to an abstract concept of the working class – insofar as it derives directly from the concept of abstract labour, and is abstractly human – which, while it works perfectly well in a theoretical analysis of capital, does not work at all on the concrete level, on the level of historical analysis, where he can no longer solve the problem of class composition.

Likewise, we can consider the definition of labour power that Marx provides in *Capital* – 'labour-power, or labour-capacity, the aggregate of those mental and physical capabilities existing in the physical form, the living personality of a human being, capabilities which he sets in motion whenever he produces a use-value of any kind'.[5] Here, I more or less concur with Marx's definition and it might be appropriately integrated with the arguments made above. In terms of the topic at hand, however, this definition is no longer adequate. The set of physical and intellectual engagements, being the result of natural circumstances and of those acquired and historically determined, is not homogeneous in all individuals. In men and women, as in peoples of different cultural backgrounds, as in adults and children, these characteristics are different. In fact, the position historically held by each of them, and the

---

5   Marx, *Capital*, vol. 1, 270.

experience of each of them within the pre-capitalist division and organisation of labour in the specific forms of social production, has differed widely. As a result, they all presented themselves differently before capital. They did not present themselves as an undifferentiated mass, but separated into different *sections*, based on their different histories of subjection and resistance, and which capital has attempted to appropriate, repurpose or diversify in order to establish relations of control with each sector of the class.

Precisely because he did not begin his analysis with such complexities, Marx found it impossible to acknowledge the different sectors that constitute labour power – the differences that distinguish and divide the category, and that are subsequently expressed as power differentials within the working class itself. Marx was also trapped, as we have seen above, in a failure to grasp the full history of the liberation of labour power because he considered only male, white, adult labour power.

Marx was blind to the different processes of apparent liberation within which capital has entrapped other sectors of labour power, as well as how the liberation process of some sections of the class proceeded at the expense of the liberation process of others. Marx does not see this, despite the fact that capital's will to prevent unique liberation processes for different class sectors was macroscopic. In fact, it was not in the interests of capital to free labour power from its internal power differentials, because the stratification of labour's bargaining power within the class composition allowed capital both to differentiate heavily in the disbursement of wages – and thus to acquire a greater quantity of surplus value in the realm of reproduction – and to curb the struggle of the working class in general. This was not its only achievement. Indeed, stratification is an essential condition for political command and control over the class as a whole.

This limitation in the Marxian reading of the history of capital, a limitation that can be found in all Marx's articles for the American press as well as in the *Neue Rheinische Zeitung*, was also reflected in the broader Marxist tradition, which, when it had to take note of the various class relations, the result of the different processes of liberation among the class sections, defined them as 'vestiges' of pre-capitalist relations that the capitalist process would progressively eliminate. This idealistic interpretation of the capitalist process arose precisely from a Marxian misapprehension that a particular process is a general one, leading to a

general deficiency in understanding the history of capitalist development. The consequent political limitations were:

1. A failure to recognise the differentiation and discrimination within
   labour power that capital has adapted or re-established, and a
   resulting failure to recognise the way in which capital has determined the formation and determination of class composition over
   time.
2. A failure to understand capital's capacity to pit men against women,
   whites against Blacks and vice versa: to face a class enemy engaged
   in infighting was the only way to freeze or curb the power of the
   workers' struggle.
3. A failure to see capital's requirement to have at its disposal an
   articulated supply of labour power and to guarantee, according to
   the specific needs of the production process, the necessary amount
   of female, male, child, white or Black labour power.
4. A failure to understand that command over labour for capital
   necessarily becomes command over the class composition – sexual,
   generational and racial – of workers, and that, in a parallel fashion,
   the struggle of the working class is also a struggle against capitalist
   command over its composition.
5. A lack of awareness that the working class was born with the deep
   internal divisions of capitalist class relations and that the terrain of
   the class composition of the workers has itself always been a terrain
   of class struggle, both within the class itself and by the working
   class against capital.

Likewise, if Marx's point of view on the labour-market, appropriately
integrated with the arguments above, holds true on the theoretical
level, it falls apart when we turn to its history and concrete transformations. There we discover that, in the particular section of the
commodity market that is the labour-market, there are no generic free
workers, but only workers with different generational, racial and sexual
characteristics. The hierarchy of power founded within the working
class on the difference in the exchange value of the labour power of its
various sectors, and on the different access each has to the wage, has
also heavily affected the possibilities of political organisation of the
working class.

As soon as the exchange in the buying and selling of labour power no longer had as its protagonists the individual worker and the individual capitalist but two social aggregates, the working class posed itself from its inception as the organisation of a single section of labour power – that of white, adult, male workers – neglecting the specific class interests of women, children and Black people. Since then, the struggle in the labour-market has become even more unfavourable for the collective worker than it appeared to Marx and the Marxists – not only because this is a terrain inherently more favourable to the bosses, but also because at the moment of buying and selling, the workers are already divided internally, as we have said, by their different capacities to bargain with capital. Faced with this class division among the workers, the union comes into being as an organisation of struggle which fails to contest this capitalist hierarchy within the working class and selects the interests of the strongest section – that of the adult, male workers, whose interests it alone organises against those of capital. The other class sectors, from this moment, cannot initiate the struggle against capital from their own specific interests, but from the interests of adult male workers that are smuggled in as the general interests of the working class.

But these are well-known facts that belong to the archives of feminist debate, and they may be further demonstrated if one investigates class composition preceding and following the struggle for the reduction of the workday. It is important to investigate this history because it is only by appreciating how complex that struggle was that one can understand the complexity of the capitalist response. It explains not only the necessity for the introduction of machines into the production process, but also the *development of reproduction*, the organisation of domestic labour and the formation of the working-class family home.

While, in the period of manufacture and early industry, capital fails to determine a sexual and generational class composition of wage-earners adequate to the needs of the production process because of the resistance put up by the proletariat, with large-scale industry the political initiative on this ground passes over to capital. The wage labour of women and children becomes, as Marx puts it, 'the first result of the capitalist application of machinery'.[6] Capital becomes voracious for women's and children's flesh, because 'so far as machinery dispenses with

6   Ibid., 517.

muscular power, it becomes a means for employing workers of slight muscular strength, or whose bodily development is incomplete, but whose limbs are all the more supple'.[7] Throughout the period of manufacture, capital had been able to make use of such labour and 'preferred to employ semi-idiots for certain operations which, though simple, were trade secrets', but their use had been statistically negligible.[8] It is only through the technology of heavy machinery that capital managed to determine a class composition of wage workers that was radically different from a sexual and generational point of view. The workers' lack of discipline, about which continuous complaints were heard throughout the early-industrial period, became intolerable for industrial capital, which found a way to eliminate it, by removing large swaths of adult male workers from the factories.

On the one hand, it was machinery that rendered the artisanal ability and physical strength of the adult male worker superfluous, and gradually redundant; on the other hand, women and children, already accustomed to discipline within the family, presented less resistance to the authority of the factory and became new, more malleable salaried workers. But discipline was not only the problem that capital solved with the new composition of the working class.

Equally important was the *cost* of labour: the wages received by women and children were lower than those of men. The lesser physical strength of women and the immature physical development of children were the pretext for capital to use these workers of the industrial revolution in conjunction with machines, and to pay them less. A woman has fewer *needs* than a man; she even eats less; likewise, a child has fewer needs than an adult, capitalists argue. The value of labour power, since it tends to represent the labour time necessary to produce the means of subsistence of the individual worker, obviously declines in the case of female and child labour power. The new class composition of the workers immediately implies a *devaluation* of labour power, because, if the value of labour power previously tended to correspond to the value of the means of subsistence necessary for the reproduction of the working-class family, now it tended to correspond to that of the individual. But the sum of wages within the working-class family, even if it corresponded to a

---

7   Ibid.
8   Ibid., 483.

higher capacity for consumption of commodities, did not automatically correspond to a higher level of reproduction.

The capitalist voracity for absolute surplus value gobbled up not only the worker's time of consumption, but also the time of domestic labour, which Marx calls 'the family labour necessary for consumption'.[9] Or rather, while capital usurped the time of consumption from the male worker, the same time was also usurped from the female worker, but with it the time of domestic labour she performed to make the wages consumable by the whole family.

> Since certain family functions, such as nursing and suckling children, cannot be entirely suppressed, the mothers who have been confiscated by capital must try substitutes of some sort. Domestic work, such as sewing and mending, must be replaced by the purchase of ready-made articles. Hence the diminished expenditure of labour in the house is accompanied by an increased expenditure of money outside. The cost of production of the working-class family therefore increases, and balances its greater income. In addition to this, economy and judgement in the consumption and preparation of the means of subsistence become impossible. Abundant material on these facts, which are concealed by official political economy, is to be found in the *Reports of the Inspectors of Factories,* the *Reports of the Children's Employment Commission,* and particularly in the *Reports on Public Health.*[10]

As can be seen, Marx notes this appropriation of domestic labour very lucidly even though it is significant that this is the only point in his entire treatise where he explicitly mentions such labour and, moreover, does so only in a footnote. That is to say that Marx can see domestic labour only when capital destroys it. Here Marx's analysis was largely drawn from government reports, which had already grasped the problems such appropriation entailed, but recognises the issue only for a moment without fully understanding it. What Marx called 'economy and judgement in the consumption and preparation of the means of subsistence' was nothing other than the domestic labour necessary for the production and reproduction of labour power and therefore indispensable to a productive

---

9   Ibid., 518, n.38.
10   Ibid., n.39.

consumption of wages. Proof of this is that the leap to a significantly higher level of productivity in the process of reproduction – and, consequently, also in the individual consumption of the worker – occurred only through the construction of the housewife as the primary subject of domestic labour and the widespread diffusion of the exchange between wages and domestic labour.

The fact that it is specifically housework that, through the management and spending of wages, makes the individual consumption of the worker much more productive for capital, can be clearly seen when we examine the period of its transformation in which domestic labour and its exchange were all but destroyed. There are many testimonies to the collapse of the productivity of the worker's individual consumption. Marx references one such report frequently:

> During the cotton crisis caused by the American Civil War, Dr Edward Smith was sent by the English government to Lancashire, Cheshire and other places to report on the state of health of the cotton operatives. He reported that from a hygienic point of view, and apart from the banishment of the operatives from the factory atmosphere, the crisis had several advantages. The women now had sufficient leisure to give their infants the breast, instead of poisoning them with 'Godfrey's Cordial' (an opiate). They also had the time to learn to cook. Unfortunately, the acquisition of this art occurred at a time when they had nothing to cook. But from this we see how capital, for the purposes of its self-valorization, has usurped the family labour necessary for consumption. This crisis was also utilised to teach sewing to the daughters of the workers in sewing schools. An American revolution and a universal crisis were needed in order that working girls, who spin for the whole world, might learn to sew![11]

But, since the higher costs of production of the working-class family often exceeded the increased incomes, the devaluation of labour power arose not only in absolute terms with respect to the individual, but also in relative terms in relation to the entire working-class family.

The prolongation of the working day, precisely because it is combined with this particular class composition of the workers, has negative

---

11 Ibid., 517–18, n.38.

consequences – far greater than those Marx identifies – not only for the working class but also for capital: namely, the increase in the production costs of labour power. Given the organisation of the production process, the extraction of a greater magnitude of absolute surplus value comes into conflict with the production and reproduction of the commodity of labour power – that is, potential capital. The attack against the reproduction of the working class becomes so strong that it exhausts labour power itself.

What happens as a result is not only the shortening of the average length of labour's working life, but also the substantial decrease in the use value of labour power and therefore of its consumption by the capitalist. It is not only that capital now consumes in six years the labour power which should have lasted forty, but also that, in these six years, the consumption of this labour power in the production process is not matched by an adequate reproduction of labour power itself, so that even this capitalist consumption of labour power is in danger. The *'race of workers'* is in danger of extinction, not only because surplus labour kills the worker in a few years, but also because *surplus labour eliminates the domestic worker* and consequently destroys her workday. In addition, *the conditions of the exchange between male wages and female domestic labour are eroded* because the value of labour power as a whole now corresponds to the value of the means of subsistence of the individual as labour power, and therefore the exchange of domestic labour for the wage becomes increasingly unprofitable for the woman.

At first, all this does not affect the individual capitalist, however, who is not only disinterested in the average lifespan of the worker, but also has no concern for the overall conditions of his production and reproduction because, as the buyer of labour power, the capitalist is only concerned that the commodity is available on the market in sufficient quantity.

Subsequently, however, the devaluation of labour power has grave consequences that necessitate a capitalist response. The most destructive is the almost complete absence of domestic labour, brought about on the one hand by capitalist appropriation of women's labour time in production, and, on the other, by the rebelliousness of women who, with direct access to their own income, have much less need to perform domestic labour for the worker and their children.

Capitalist disinterest in the conditions of production and reproduction of labour power also becomes worker disinterest and women's resistance to domestic labour. The destruction of such work consequently, in addition to having a capitalist cause also has a working-class face – that of women's refusal.

Official surveys speak clearly about the factors contributing to the higher level of mortality among the children of workers in their early years. The 1861 survey, reports Marx,

> showed, moreover, that while, with the described circumstances, infants perish under the neglect and mismanagement which their mothers' occupations imply, the mothers become to a grievous extent denaturalized towards their offspring – commonly not troubling themselves much at the death, and even sometimes . . . taking direct measures to insure it.[12]

Even in the agricultural districts, where 'the revolution in cultivation had led to the introduction of the industrial system', 'all the phenomena of the factory districts are reproduced here, including a yet higher degree of disguised infanticide and stupefaction of children with opiates'.[13]

However, this refusal to bear and raise children is not only a refusal on the part of women to accept the domestic labour that a child entails, but also a refusal of the costs involved, which fall entirely on the shoulders of the parents. An image that testifies clearly in this regard is the steep curve of the increase in the rate of abandoned children that, in the words of Necker quoted by Marx, transforms the European cities of the industrial revolution into 'enormous warehouses' of children.

Faced with this phenomenon, the state is obliged to assume the costs of bringing up a large share of new labour power. At this juncture, it discovers at its own expense the extent to which the presupposed naturalness of women's instinct for procreation and reproduction of the species is transformed, demystifying itself, when capital's lust for surplus labour prevents the exchange between male wages and female domestic labour, thus revealing the not-natural but historically determined social relationships existing between man and woman, and between these and their children. When the conditions presupposed by this relationship break down, the supposed naturalness is transformed into an equally unexamined unnaturalness. Again, in Marx we read:

---

12   Ibid., 521, n.46.
13   Ibid., 522.

As was shown by an official medical inquiry in the year 1861, the high
death-rates are, apart from local causes, principally due to the employment of the mothers away from their homes, and to the neglect and
maltreatment arising from their absence, which consists in such things
as insufficient nourishment, unsuitable food and dosing with opiates;
besides this, there arises an unnatural estrangement between mother
and child, and as a consequence intentional starving and poisoning of
the children.[14]

Here Marx is blinded by capitalist ideology in failing to understand that
the question here is not to do with the naturalness or unnaturalness of
mothers, but rather of the material transformations to which the relationships between man and woman and parents and children are subject
at this historical juncture. In the period we are examining, the conditions
of existence of these relationships have largely been destroyed, and with
them the conditions of existence of the working-class family in its role
as a centre of production and reproduction of labour power.

The only relation of reproduction that does not undergo a transformative leap, but is rather augmented by the almost complete disappearance
of the exchange between waged worker and houseworker, is that of
prostitution. The labour of prostitution becomes the only form of reproductive labour that capital does not seize for its self-valorisation in the
production process. One of the major reasons this relation is not transformed is that, on the formal level, it is more markedly organised as
commodity production. In fact, it has been noted that prostitution, with
the advent of industrialisation, undergoes a great increase. As it develops, it involves such a lengthening of the workday that the labour power
of these sex workers is consumed in a few short years.

In a subsequent moment, it has been noted, the state in its role as
collective capital must take note that the lust for surplus labour in production has expressed itself in such a way as to affect its interests in
reproduction. The state learns that it must direct capital's craving for
surplus value in such a way that it does not affect reproduction – indeed,
in such a way as to make it functional in the long run to the needs of
production – or else let it proceed down the road of its own self-destruction.
The state also comes to understand that a certain generational and sexual

------

14   Ibid., 521.

composition of labour power, while paying more in the short term, is much less productive in the long term than a composition that favours adult male workers.

This is not the place to retrace the dynamics of the historical struggles, even within the class itself, which took place at this juncture – struggles over the class composition of salaried workers, the reduction of the workday in the process of production, or struggles, particularly by women and children, against domestic labour and family discipline. Nor is this the place to reconstruct the dynamics of the conflicting interests between the capitalist class (as producers of commodities and buyers of labour power, who are interested in it only as a commodity to be bought at the lowest-possible cost and exploited to the utmost) and the state (which, as an expression of their command over society, must guarantee the preservation and constant reproduction of the working class, a condition necessary for the reproduction of capital).

Instead, we are interested in reconstructing the complexity of the capitalist response to this cycle of workers' struggles around the reduction of the working day – that is, the response of the state, which also implies a profound transformation of the state itself. If, during the period of manufacture, the state subordinated the sector of reproduction to that of production – that is, it subordinated the reproduction of the labour force to the formation of the proletariat, managing the underdevelopment of the former to launch the development of the latter – in the era of industriali-sation it poses itself as the planner of the *development* of reproduction. Among other things, this is what constitutes the *transition to the modern state* proper, expressed, on the one hand, in the emergence of the section of the class comprised of housewives, in the organisation and development of domestic labour, in the reconstruction and re-foundation of the working-class family, and, on the other hand, in the creation of the fun-damental structures and instruments for the social reproduction of labour power. In other words, on the one hand, it directly plans the production and reproduction of labour power in the individual sphere as well as the sexual production of male labour power, and, on the other hand, it con-stitutes itself as an entrepreneur of the reproduction of labour power in the social sphere.

The state's need to function, from the outset, as a site of planning with respect to reproduction, derives from its particular organisation as a productive sector. In essence, it emerges from the indirect form of the relationship of production between women and capital; a relation which requires the mediation of the worker. It is precisely this form of relationship that determines the domestic labour process, as well as the process of sexual reproduction of male labour power as characterised by two peculiar phenomena.

The first is that capital cannot use wages as an instrument capable of directly controlling the houseworker and sex worker, since neither earns a direct wage. Nor can it coerce them into that self-discipline and self-determination in which the waged worker is forced to become fluent.

The second is that, within the process of reproduction, capital cannot directly control the consumption of women's labour power, which passes indirectly through the individual consumption of the worker. In other words, capital no longer formally establishes itself as the owner of the means necessary to give life to its own process (the workers become the bearers of this responsibility); capital is no longer the owner of the means of production. Capital therefore cannot directly control the quantity and quality of production, though it remains interested not only in the quantitative dimension of the new labour power, but also in the magnitude of its use value.

It is from this situation that the role of the state as the materialisation of collective capital differs from the one it assumes with respect to production and becomes crucial for the functioning of reproduction. With respect to production, given that there is a direct relationship between the individual capitalist and individual worker, it is sufficient for the state to function as an expression and instrument of the command of collective capital. With respect to reproduction, on the other hand, where this relationship is indirect, the state must come to function as the primary and direct planner and organiser. It ends up managing reproduction in its totality, and therefore in the absence of any competing mediating force, the state, as the *expression of the command of collective capital*, must take on a specific role, one involving two primary functions:

1. It must take responsibility for the socialisation of the domestic labour process – as well as that of prostitution. Otherwise, it would not be possible, because of the individualised nature of these relations, to determine an average and necessary socialised form for both domestic labour and prostitution. The process of socialisation is not directly handed over to the immediate process of reproduction: it either

passes through the state or it cannot exist as such. While in production, the formation of the state as an agent of the general interest of capital is a long and contradictory process because the socialisation process is directly handed over to the immediate production process (generally in the factory), in reproduction the state presents itself from the outset as a fundamental and immediate agent of command.

2. Second, the state must control the worker in his role as disciplinarian of the houseworker and sex worker. This is necessary because, forced to resort to these roles in order to organise capillary control over women, the state's power inadvertently opens up a contradiction. As we have seen, this contradiction involves the fact that the worker, who is also a negation of capital, has been handed a large potential space of refusal in which to exercise this control. The coexistence in him of these two oppositional tendencies – exploited and exploiter – requires, in order to be rendered productive, that he exercises a form of control and discipline that goes beyond the control and discipline that capital can organise and impose within the production process itself: a control which, as such, can only be guaranteed by the state. The state's function with respect to reproduction is not to do directly all that capital is not allowed to do, but it is to control the extent and intensity of domestic labour (as well as the work of prostitution) – that is, to control the quantity and quality of the commodity produced – labour power – such that it always corresponds to the needs of capital.

What are the instruments that the state gives itself to achieve this control and command over the reproduction of labour power?

With respect to the quantitative dimension of labour power, the state adjusts its production to conform to capitalist needs by placing itself as the de facto owner of the means of production of labour power itself – the uterus – which it expropriates from women, leaving them in possession of the uterus but without ownership. It is within this context that we can understand the regulation of contraception and abortion access and their strategic importance with respect to the material production of this commodity.

With respect to the qualitative dimension of labour power, the state's intervention is articulated on various levels, although the socialisation of the production process, on the one hand, and that of the process of social reproduction of labour power, on the other, contribute materially and fundamentally to the determination of average social domestic labour. First, it plans and controls the homogeneity of domestic labour through diverse investments, be they related to productive areas and/or areas of struggle – in other words, it engages in *social services*. These services, in addition to functioning as poles of *control* over the duration and intensity of domestic labour and thus as tools for *determining* its average standards, also function as *centres of family support*. They provide for the distribution in the social fabric of quotas of reproductive labour where its provision (mainly by the houseworker but also by other family members) is either considered insufficient by the state with respect to the average standards required or is considered insufficient by the proletariat with respect to its needs.

The terrain of state intervention in this context also entails the *material organisation, regulation and management of the exchange of variable capital and domestic labour*. It is not by chance that the capitalist history of this exchange develops through:

1. the institution of marriage, which the bourgeois state has controlled since its inception, making its formalisation compulsory for the entire proletariat;
2. *the exchange of variable capital and prostitution* in all its aspects, ranging from the quantitative regulation of prostitutes to ensure their optimal proportionality with respect to housewives, to the organisation of the ways, times and places of this exchange;
3. the relations of production resulting from these two exchanges, which include the continuous normative restructuring of the relationship between man and woman as husband and wife and as client and prostitute as a response to women's struggles against reproductive labour – and, more generally, the organisation, regulation and management of the family, as its primary and fundamental cell, as well as the functioning of various institutions and social services for the family's support, control and complement.

Given that the advent of mass production, on the one hand, and mass consumption, on the other, concur in a primary way to determine the standards of average social consumption, the state must *plan and control the levels of homogeneous proletarian consumption*, through numerous instruments that we cannot fully examine here, because, among other things, they vary historically.

Finally, among the few functions of the state analysed here, we have observed that the state *organises, manages and controls the average standards of mass information*, which include, on the one hand, the organisation of socialised compulsory education and, on the other hand, the construction, assumption and continuous dissemination of bourgeois ideology of the material relations of existence. Particular attention is paid here to the relations of reproduction, and on the other hand, the related organisation and management of the so-called mass media (radio, television, press).

Reproduction therefore faces, on the one hand, a significant concentration and condensation in the state of power and command over women (established as the counterpart to the struggles of the houseworker and sex worker), and, on the other hand, a great deal of decentralisation and atomisation of this power and command is distributed among the male workforce.

The *macrophysics* of capitalist command over women cannot be understood if we do not simultaneously consider the *microphysics* of male power over women. Thus, if we are to recognise the *capitalist* face of the working class, we must also recognise its *state* face.

All these functions of command are necessitated by the fact that *the simple subordination of reproduction to production has been thrown completely into crisis*. Specifically, what throws this policy into crisis, and with it the old figure of the state, is the passage from the production of absolute to relative surplus value, behind which lies the workers' struggle for the reduction of the working day. State management of this passage implies, at least initially, a mechanism of reversal, namely the subordination of production to reproduction. The worker-imposed reduction of the working day in the process of commodity production has precisely this meaning, just as the state intervention in the progressive lengthening of the working day during the period of manufacture had the opposite meaning.

The state was forced to grant the working class a reduction in the working day, but, soon afterwards, it rapidly changed the political composition of salaried workers, with an increase in the presence of adult male workers at the expense of women and children, who were progressively expelled. The working-class woman who, together with children, had constituted the backbone of the working class in the era of heavy industry, was forced progressively to transform herself into the wife-mother, the primary subject of domestic labour – into a housewife. The young, once labourers themselves, progressively became labour power in development – that is, *children*. Both were newly entangled in the relationship of indirectly paid work within the family that was re-founded as the privileged site for the provision of domestic labour, and where the woman, as a houseworker, faced a frighteningly long workday. The production of absolute surplus value migrates from the factory to the home and therefore becomes secondary only in relation to the production process. In the overall cycle of capitalist accumulation, the transition to the production of relative surplus value in the factory is accompanied by the corresponding transition in the home to the production of absolute surplus value in reproduction.

Afterword:
Reading *L'arcano* Today: 1981 to 2025

Leopoldina Fortunati

Much has changed in the forty years since this text was written. The theses offered here have been shared, developed and debated by both a new wave of feminist movements (Non Una Di Meno in particular in the Italian context) and by numerous scholars from various disciplines who deal with domestic work and reproductive labour.[1] The question of reproductive labour has also become contested across the political spectrum more generally in a way it was not in the Cold War era when the 1959 'Kitchen Debate' between Nixon and Khrushchev represented state-level discourse over what constituted the ideal Fordist home and heads of state from the major superpowers could exchange pleasantries regarding the subservience of women in their unwaged role of the reproduction of labour power.

Does this mean that *L'arcano* is now outdated? After all, the work describes the functioning of the capitalist system, above all the production

---

1 Non Una Di Meno (literally Not One More) is a social movement founded in Rome in 2015, taking its name from the Argentinian movement Ni Una Menos that began earlier the same year. Both groups formed in direct response to the prevalence of women's deaths from domestic violence, and developed comprehensive policies that extended an analysis of violence in the home into calls for transformative changes to social services, workplace protections and the law. For an example of recent scholarship on the *Arcana*, see the excellent review by Natalia Hirtz, 'À propos de *L'arcane de la reproduction*', *Ouvrage*, 12 January 2024, revue-ouvrage.org.

and reproduction of labour power, in what was still largely a period of Fordism. Today, by many accounts, we have entered a *brave new world*, one encumbered with various terms for post-Fordism: a global system understood as both transformed and transforming while fundamentally sustaining all-too-familiar modes of expropriation and accumulation.[2] At the same time, this system has been altered quite radically under the pressure from women's struggles and by the political initiatives of social movements in both their irreducible specificity and inevitable convergence in new forms of class composition and political initiative.

L'arcano della riproduzione, composed throughout the upheavals of Italy in the 1970s, is, in certain ways, a product of its era with all the foreclosures, openings and unrealised potential that the era afforded. I and my comrades in Lotta Femminista, and the Wages for Housework movement more broadly, did not have the benefit of recent anticolonial critique, recent Black feminist critiques of the legacies of chattel slavery in a US and Caribbean context, nor the recent flowering of queer and (trans)feminist engagements with a Marxian tradition. There was, of course, great passion in the analysis of such projects as they would develop historically. Mariarosa Dalla Costa in particular published some of the important early analysis of immigration and global capitalist development. The enthusiasm for Fanon, Cabral, Rodney, Mao, Black Power in the US and Third Worldist discourse and analysis in general coursed through the Italian political landscape; while the women of the Wages for Housework movement, particularly Selma James with her 1975 work *Sex, Race and Class*, and Black Women for Wages for Housework members such as Margaret Prescod, Wilmette Brown and Andaiye developed a critical intervention that would help form a basis for subsequent theories of racism, colonialism and misogyny as central to and inextricable from capitalist development. Finally, Silvia Federici's and my own subsequent works would extend the historical analysis of the group into an encounter with the new rounds of what Marx had called 'Primitive Accumulation' that characterised the origins of capitalist development.[3]

---

2 Prabha Kotiswaran, 'Laws of Social Reproduction', *Annual Review of Law and Social Sciences* 19 (2023).

3 Silvia Federici and Leopoldina Fortunati, *Il Grande Calibano. Storia del corpo sociale ribelle nella prima fase del capitale* (Milan: Franco Angeli editore, 1984), and Silvia Federici, *Caliban and the Witch: Women, the Body and Primitive Accumulation* (New York: Autonomedia, 2004).

Keeping in mind the complicated context in which the original text was written, I will try to reconstruct some of the most relevant changes that have taken place in the sphere of reproduction in recent decades. As Kathi Weeks wrote in her thoughtful critical reinvestment in the Wages for Housework movement, feminist historical inquiries must strive to avoid a vulgar dialectical account of progressivist development in which feminist or queer theories are understood to supersede and eclipse one another in a teleological fashion, as well as any sentimental attachment to the task of redeeming a past that has been 'lost'.[4] I think that *L'arcano* remains generative of certain analytical tools, and is still useful for understanding how the capitalist system as a whole is structured at present and the current role of the sphere of reproduction in particular. It can only be my hope that *L'arcano* continues to be a source of inspiration for constructing an expanded feminist theory, programme and political strategy for the coming decades. The text below is divided into eight sections, each addressed to a particular way in which capitalism, and the realm of reproduction in particular, has been transformed in recent decades relative to the analysis presented in the original text.

1. How has the capitalist system changed?

Let us start from the initial thesis of *L'arcano*. Contrary to what Marx had maintained, the production of surplus value is not confined within a single sphere in the capitalist accumulation process – that of commodity production alone. Rather, it is formed by two interlocking spheres: that of the production of commodities; and that of the production and reproduction of labour power. These two spheres are inextricably linked and interdependent, the first being the presupposition and condition of existence for the second. In recent decades, the power relations between these two spheres have shifted, as have their respective roles within the capitalist system. In the post-war era up to the 1970s, the sphere of commodity production had appeared as dominant and that of the reproduction of labour power as ancillary. This dominance of commodity production resulted from the fact that

---

4   Kathi Weeks, *The Problem with Work: Feminism, Marxism, Antiwork Politics, and Postwork Imaginaries* (Durham, NC : Duke University Press, 2011).

the exchange value earned through the wage in this sphere generally commanded and controlled the organisation of reproduction. Furthermore, the factory was the site of the capital's maximum technological investment. In the sphere of reproduction, some second-rate technology might occasionally arrive but this was generally considered a 'hand-me-down' or even a waste of the more profitable and 'noble' technologies developed for the factory.[5]

Gradually, over the last few decades in particular, the centre of gravity for the production of surplus value within the capitalist system has shifted to the sphere of reproduction – that is, the sphere of the production and reproduction of labour power. The energies of capitalist development in the innovation and proficiency in the use of technologies have also begun to migrate from businesses to homes and spaces outside of the official workplace; big-tech markets have become increasingly domesticated. In this process, we are again encountering a certain kind of seepage of power from those with dominion to those who are dominated. Today, the sphere of reproduction can be considered as dominant, in that it is the realm in which the most surplus value has come to be directly extracted.[6] Furthermore, the general lack of workplace protection in the sphere of reproduction has been instrumentalised by capital to erode protection in the sphere of commodity production, even as the former has taken on an increasingly dominant role in the production of surplus value.[7]

The extraction of value in the sphere of reproduction has been greatly enhanced over the past thirty years. In addition to the classic production of value described in *L'arcano*, which consists in the creation of labour power (the most precious of commodities for capital), another process of value production has been initiated through the use of digital technologies.[8] The scope of the latter process entails an attempt to machinise, or 'outsource to the machine' the immaterial part of domestic work,

---

5   Alain Gras, 'Grandeur et dépendance, Sociologie des macro-systèmes techniques', *Sociologie du travail* 36, no. 3 (1993), 405–7.

6   Leopoldina Fortunati, 'The Reproduction Sphere as the Site of a Double Production of Value', paper presented at the international conference 'Law and Social Reproduction: The Misconceived Value of Care', Rome, 4–5 May 2023.

7   Arlie Hochschild, *The Time Bind: When Work Becomes Home and Home Becomes Work* (New York: Metropolitan/Holt, 1997); Romano Alquati, *Sulla riproduzione della capacità umana vivente. L'industrializzazione della soggettività* (Bologna: DeriveApprodi, 2021).

8   Leopoldina Fortunati, *Telecomunicando in Europa* (Milan: Franco Angeli, 1998).

involved in the process of reproduction.[9] The first is the direct expropriation by multinationals such as Facebook (now Meta) or Google and their parent company Alphabet of the data of mobile phone and computer users (the vast majority of the world's population) and their subsequent sale to companies or governmental organisations, which, in turn, use this data to exercise better planning and control over markets and citizens.[10] The word 'expropriation' is appropriate in this context because users are not remunerated for this data, although it is a very precious commodity.

The second process is the elaboration of online user-generated content by digital companies which expropriate value directly from such content while paying little or no economic recompense to its creators. The production of online content has been defined as 'digital work' and an extensive debate has developed on this issue over time: one which has generally neglected investigating the sphere of reproduction as the primary site for such unpaid work.[11]

This double extraction of value from the sphere of reproduction has contributed to positioning it as the current primary strategic sphere of capitalist development. What is more important to underline, however, is that this sphere not only provides a more intensive production of value than it has previously, but that the specific companies that exploit digital labour outside any market exchange also generally do not pay taxes to the states where this extraction of value takes place. Consequently, not only are women and other workers of the reproductive sphere subject to double exploitation (joined particularly in this second exploitation by children, adolescents, adults and older adults of all genders), but, at the same time, in many countries, they suffer from a worsening of welfare

---

9　Leopoldina Fortunati, 'Immaterial Labour and Its Machinization', *Ephemera Theory and Politics in Organization* 7, no. 1 (2007), 139–57; Kylie Jarret, *Feminism, Labour and Digital Media: The Digital Housewife* (London: Routledge & CRC Press, 2016).

10　Vassilis Charitsis and Mikko Laamanen, 'When Digital Capitalism Takes (On) the Neighbourhood: Data Activism Meets Place-Based Collective Action', *Social Movement Studies* (2022).

11　Christian Fuchs and Sebastian Sevignani, 'What Is Digital Labour? What Is Digital Work? What's Their Difference? And Why Do These Questions Matter for Understanding Social Media?', *Triple C* 11, no. 2 (2013), 237–93; Trevor Scholz, *Digital Labour: The Internet as Playground and Factory* (London: Routledge, 2012); Leopoldina Fortunati and Arlen Austin, 'Digital Labour and the Domestic Sphere', in Jack Qiu et al., eds, *The Handbook of Digital Labour* (IAMCR and Wiley Blackwell, 2025).

provisions, due in large part to the non-payment of taxes by these companies to the various nation-states.[12]

As for the export of a model forged in the sphere of reproduction into the sphere of commodity production, it has been frequently observed that the relations of unpaid labour that typify the domestic sphere have begun to spread through various forms of commodity production, particularly among a new generation of workers. At first, such labour relationships were specifically targeted towards younger workers, and then were later extended to adult and older workers. Work with little or no pay began to be offered as long-term apprenticeships or internships, as precarious work, low-paid work, undeclared work or double work in exchange for a single wage, with the consequence that people, while working and receiving a wage in supposedly advanced industrialised nations, could remain poor – even while working two to three jobs to survive.[13] The deconstruction of the wage-labour relationship and decline in real wages was a process which, in the years from 1970 to 2000, initially involved the proletarianisation of the middle and lower middle classes and, subsequently, in the last two decades, the working class itself, which has been greatly impoverished. In this context, capital has used the relative weakness of organisation in the sphere of reproduction to counter the power previously conquered by the working class through struggles in the sphere of commodity production.

What is referred to as *lavoro povero* in Italian, indicating poorly paid work requiring the worker to take on multiple jobs to survive, and its related forms of contract (or lack thereof), has also been central to an ideology linked to domestic work.[14] Here, the ideology of the labour of

---

12   Fortunati, 'The Reproductive Sphere as the Place of a Double Production of Value'.

13   Annabelle Berthiaume et al., *Grèves des stages, grève des femmes. Anthologie d'une lutte féministe pour un salair étudiant (2016–2019)* (Montréal: Les éditions du rémue-ménage, 2022); Maud Simonet, '"Wages for". Une approche féministe du salaire comme puissance subversive', *Salariat* 1, no. 1 (2022), 87–100. See also Ross Perlin, *Intern Nation: How to Earn Nothing and Learn Little in the Brave New Economy* (London: Verso, 2011); Norene Pupo and Ann Duffy, 'Unpaid Work, Capital and Coercion', *Work Organisation, Labour and Globalisation* 6, no. 1 (2012), 27–47; Barbara Ellen Smith and Jamie Winders, 'Whose Lives, Which Work? Class Discrepancies in Life's Work', in Katie Meehan and Kendra Strauss, eds, *Precarious Worlds: Contested Geographies of Social Reproduction* (Athens: University of Georgia Press, 2015), 101–17.

14   Weeks, *The Problem with Work*.

love or 'marrying' one's own work is paramount.[15] This change in the meaning of the work is the latest in a long series of transformations attributed to the meaning of work throughout history. As Sarti, Bellavitis and Martini remind us, the meaning of work has consistently shifted throughout historical epochs: from being a biblical curse, it became the forced task of slaves, then serfs and the lower classes.[16] Thereafter, it was subsumed within the ideology of the capitalist system, which advocated the so-called freedom of workers to sell their labour power. When poverty became a problem for the social order, work was redefined as its remedy, up to the Protestant tradition, which considered it as a divine calling (*beruf*) and finally to the modern glorification of self-sacrificing, uncompensated and perpetual work.

It must be remembered that the meaning of work in various social eras was not only imposed from above, however, but was also a social co-construction and result of class resistance. There is much of the subjectivity and strength of the working class (as the term might be understood in a general sense) within the current culture of work, in that it has managed, over time, to transform work into something less harmful, abhorrent and alienating than in the past. Work has been transformed over time, under the impetus of epoch-defining struggles of the working class, which has helped to redesign it so that today many jobs can prove interesting and instructive, and less and less factory-like in their organisation. But such co-construction should not detract from the fact that work itself remains a primary site and source of exploitation.

2. The capitalist division between the production of commodities and the reproduction of labour power

The separation between the production of commodities and the reproduction of labour power had, in the classic Fordist model, previously been configured in the factory and the home as two distinct and often

---

15 Giovanna Franca Dalla Costa, *Un lavoro d'amore* (Rome: edizioni delle Donne, 1978). See also, for example, Sarah Jaffe, *Work Won't Love You Back: How Devotion to Our Jobs Keeps Us Exploited, Exhausted and Alone* (New York: Perseus Books, 2021).

16 Raffaella Sarti, Anna Bellavitis and Manuela Martini, eds, *What Is Work? Gender at the Crossroads of Home, Family, and Business from the Early Modern Era to the Present* (New York: Berghahn, 2018).

incommensurate spaces. Such a distinction of realms has become increasingly fragile and blurred over time. This is true even in the so-called Global North, where the extreme difficulty of separating production from reproduction that had long been a predominant experience in much of the Global South has become increasingly prevalent.[17] In this sense, the existing differences in the organisation of the capitalist system between the North and the South of the world are shrinking. I adopt here Sirisha Naidu's conception of 'circuits of social reproduction', which include the paths of the Global North where production and reproduction are becoming increasingly difficult to separate, and those of the Global South, where production and reproduction often have been and continue to often be spatially indistinguishable.[18]

In the old, core industrialised nations, the realm of production has established itself within that of reproduction in recent decades, adding new forms to the classic small-scale manufacture of home-based work and now appearing under such flashy branding as 'smart working', 'distance learning' or 'hybrid-remote work' – all such terms implying familial and small-business digital work performed at various levels within business hierarchies and the overcoming of home–workplace distinctions. Reproduction has increasingly incorporated certain formal characteristics of corporate office work, a phenomenon that has been accentuated by the COVID crisis. During and after the pandemic, the family has become, in many countries and contexts, what the factory once was. There are an estimated 260 million home-based workers in the world today, accounting for approximately 8 per cent of global employment.[19] This process has represented a marked convergence between the global regions of North and the South. The spaces of global production

---

17   Maria Mies, Veronika Bennholdt-Thomsen and Claudia Von Werlhof, *Women: The Last Colony* (London: Zed Books, 1988); Samita Sen, 'The Problem of Reproduction: Waged and Unwaged Domestic Work', in Achin Chakraborty, Anjan Chakrabarti, Byasdeb Dasgupta and Samita Sen, eds, *'Capital' in the East* (Singapore: Springer, 2019), 173–93; Alessandra Mezzadri, Susan Newman and Sara Stevano, 'Feminist Global Political Economies of Work and Social Reproduction', *Review of International Political Economy* 29, no. 6 (2022); Donatella Alessandrini, *Value Making in International Economic Law and Regulation: Alternative Possibilities* (London: Routledge, 2016).

18   Sirisha Naidu, 'Circuits of Social Reproduction: Nature, Labour, and Capitalism', *Review of Radical Political Economics* 55, no. 1 (2022).

19   International Labour Organization, *Women and Men in the Informal Economy: A Statistical Picture* (Geneva: International Labour Organization Report, 2018), ilo.org.

are today occupied by a multitude of *family* units, a form omnipresent throughout society, increasingly understood as a large family and modelled according to explicitly corporate parameters. Even in the light of these structural transformations, the ideological orchestration of the naturalness of domestic work and stereotypical female roles has lost both its persuasive and coercive capacities, making the neo-capitalist rhetoric regarding women less and less credible.

Let us now turn to the second thesis advanced in *L'arcano*: one which stated that it is possible to understand how capital works only if we start with a hypothesis that acknowledges its duplicity. In other words, although reproduction presents itself as the creation of non-value, it is, in reality, the creation of value, an integral part of the capitalist system. Despite being *integral*, it necessarily presents itself as its opposite. While the representation of production corresponds in a linear and coherent fashion to what the process actually entails, that of reproduction is more complex and contradictory because, on a formal level, it is regarded as a sort of *nature*, while, on the plane of the real, it is what was referred to in *L'arcano* as an 'inverted photograph' of production. For this duplicity of reproduction to be sustained over time, it was necessary to separate it strictly from production, even on the level of its formal representation; excluding it and hiding it from the *surface* of the painting that represented a scene of domestic bliss. It is only thanks to such duplicity that capital has been able to function more productively than previous modes of production. To sustain this duplicity however, it had to be supported by a very powerful and complex ideological orchestration which made use of the mass media, advertising and the fashion system to develop and convey a socialised figure of the housewife that corresponded to the specific and highly ambivalent characteristics of the sphere of reproduction.

Within such a framework, the separation between the production of commodities and the reproduction of labour power also configured the status of two distinct workers separated by a precise division of labour along gendered lines: the man assigned to factory work and the woman to housework. For this to happen completely, male workers were increasingly dispossessed of their ability to reproduce, while female workers were only partially dispossessed of their ability to be conscripted into waged labour as capital required. Over time, the expropriation of the ability to reproduce (to manage a home, daily life, household chores and raise children) that male workers have been bestowed within the Fordist nuclear family has turned out to be both a *privilege* and a *trap*. Both terms, however, should be interrogated.

Such an arrangement could be described as a 'privilege', given that, in exchange for the eight hours of work in the factory or in the office, men long considered themselves exempt from the obligation to contribute to domestic work. In the classic Fordist nuclear family, when male workers returned home after work, it was their 'privilege' to take well-deserved rest: sit in an armchair, perhaps read the newspaper or watch television. For women, the well-deserved rest was more a mirage than a real possibility, as the work of reproduction tended to be unending.

This arrangement was a trap for two fundamental reasons. First of all, it has implied an erosion and emptying out of any role for men either as father figures, or otherwise engaged in their children's lives. In the long run, this expropriation proved to be intolerable, with the number of fathers who began to take care of their children more consistently, sharing important moments in their growth, gradually but steadily increasing, as evidenced by countless studies.[20] Second, the expropriation of men's reproductive capacities entailed an attack on their personal autonomy, one staged at a historical moment in which the social drive towards forms of hypercapitalist individualism was increasing exponentially.[21] Such expropriation was irrelevant when they could count on a stable relationship with a woman they lived with (in marriage or cohabitation). When, however, for whatever reason, they were left alone, such expropriation could prove burdensome.

In the 1970s, the consequences of this expropriation became particularly evident in Italy, amongst other places, when a man became a widower. But these were relatively few cases, because generally, in the old, core industrialised nations, men had a lower average lifespan than women and their age at marriage was, on average, higher than that of

---

20   Suzanne Bianchi, Melissa A. Milkie, Liana C. Sayer and John P. Robinson, 'Is Anyone Doing the Housework? Trends in the Gender Division of Household Labour', *Social Forces* 79, no. 1 (2000), 191–228; Suzanne Bianchi, Melissa A. Milkie, Liana C. Sayer and John P. Robinson, 'Housework: Who Did, Does or Will Do It, and How Much Does It Matter?', *Social Forces* 91, no. 2 (2012), 55–63.

21   Louis Dumont, *Essais sur l'individualisme. Une perspective anthropologique sur l'idéologie moderne* (Paris: Seuil, 1993); Charles Taylor, *Modern Social Imaginaries* (Durham, NC: Duke University Press, 2004).

their wives.[22] Finding themselves alone, without any knowledge and training for domestic work – without having an idea of how to run a house or how to take care of themselves – meant that widowers found themselves living in difficult and uncomfortable situations.

Awareness of this dispossession on the part of an increasing number of men has exploded in recent decades, in which the traditional Fordist nuclear family has dissolved and, as a result, many men have found themselves living alone: divorced, separated, single, in open relationships, living as a couple but not cohabiting, sometimes due to the mobility imposed by work – as well as those who are widowed. The majority of such men were forced to cobble together competence as workers in the sphere of reproduction of labour power, learning to reproduce themselves and take care of children when they had to look after them. For many men, this new condition has been burdensome, as shown by research that highlights the higher mortality rate of unmarried men (compared with married men) or shows that, in the United States in 2019, for example, more widowers than widows rushed to rebuild the couple form and found a family with another woman.[23]

3. How has the sphere of reproduction changed?

In the context of its composition, *L'arcano* highlighted the formation of the sphere of reproduction by two fundamental processes: those of domestic work and of prostitution. Domestic work as a category was understood to consist in two distinct processes: the production and reproduction of the workforce. The first process is constituted by procreation, gestation and childbirth, and is 'used up', as the Marxists would say, in the final product (the newborn). The second process consists in three distinct operations:

---

22   In 2016, among over-seventy-five year-olds in the US, 58 per cent of women were widowed compared to 28 per cent of men. Yerís Mayol-García, Benjamin Gurrentz, and Rose M. Kreider, *Number, Timing, and Duration of Marriages and Divorces: 2016* (Washington, DC: Census Bureau, 2021), 70–167, census.gov.

23   Y. Ben-Shlomo, G. Davey Smith, M. Shipley and M. G. Marmot, 'Magnitude and Causes of Mortality Differences between Married and Unmarried Men', *Journal of Epidemiology and Community Health* 47 (1993), 200–5; Administration on Aging and the Administration on Community Living, *2019 Profile of Older Americans* (Washington, DC: Department of Health and Human Services, 2020), acl.gov.

1. the reproduction of the existing workforce (that is, all those tasks
   of domestic work which allow it to restore the energy consumed in
   the work process and which therefore allow it to go to work in the
   factory day after day);
2. the reproduction of reproductive labour power; and
3. the reproduction of future generations.

The work of prostitution accompanies that of reproduction, but it
is generally focused on sexuality, broadly speaking, and is fundamentally aimed at the male workforce. Identifying the most important
changes that have occurred in this sphere in the last forty years would
require a book of its own – one which I would largely defer to others
to write and would require the participation of scholar-activists with
experience of sex work as an industry as well as the day-to-day practice of reproducing oneself and one's familial and kinship relations.
For the Wages for Housework movement, events such as the 1975
occupation of Saint-Nizier Church in Lyon by a coalition of prostitutes were galvanising. The emergence of the sex worker/prostitute as
both political subject and object of global capitalist development,
particularly in the context of a mass internet apparatus and infrastructure that has allowed much sex work to be conducted through digital
platforms, is one that requires extensive investigation beyond the
scope of this text. For reasons of space, I will try here to establish only
a few points regarding the two processes that make up the sphere of
domestic reproduction.

3.1 The production of labour power

To understand the changes taking place in the first process – that of
procreation and gestation – we need to begin our analysis by acknowledging the battle that is taking place globally over women's bodies. In this
regard, L'arcano was prescient in criticising Marx when he defined labour
power as 'above all else, the material of nature transformed into a human
organism', given that labour power is always already a 'raw material',
incorporating nine months of work by the mother.[24] Similarly, L'arcano
was foundational in arguing that capitalism had completely transformed

---

24 Karl Marx, *Capital*, vol. 1, *A Critique of Political Economy*, trans. Ben Fowkes
(London: Penguin, New Left Review: 1990 [1976]), 323, n.2.

the relationship between a woman and her body, as the female body in particular has become a means of production, a machine, from whose control the woman has been expropriated. As regards the renewed expropriation of such bodies in recent decades we have only to glance at abortion legislation, the belated and inadequate development of contraception for women, welfare policy and so on . . .

It is important to reiterate once again that, as stated in *L'arcano, this machinisation of women's bodies was the greatest of the technological inventions introduced by capital,* since the reduction of the female body to a machine implied that it was no longer the woman who used her own body; rather, it was rendered available for use, becoming a source of extraneous expropriation (that is, subject to the command of others), and therefore a source of alienation. In this context, the body consumes its own alienation as the ferment of its own vital process.

But why, we might ask, has capital preferred to machinise the woman's body rather than the domestic labour process in general? It has done so because the human body is the formal link between the spheres of production and reproduction, as it is both a product of the domestic sphere, but also the condition for the existence of the realm of production. The process of expropriation of women's bodies has many names in various parts of the world, but it responds to the same objective: to make their bodies function as productively as possible. Virtually all aspects concerning women's bodies are currently under attack in what can be defined as a real war against women globally: from procreation to pregnancy, from sexual mutilations to rapes, from femicides to the violence against trans or gender non-conforming people to prohibitions on the very appearance of the female body.

As regards procreation, it has inexorably continued to be the subject of a massive struggle by women who have demanded control of their bodies: claiming for themselves the decision whether to have children, as well as when and how many. This was a political programme that emerged from the feminist movement of the 1970s, which reaffirmed a series of core principles:

1. a woman is a woman, even if not in any immediate and obvious sense a mother, because we are all mothers of other people's children;
2. women have the right to decide if and when to have children;
3. women have the right to decide how many children to have.

This programme has given rise to a series of forms of mass behaviour by women. The number of women who have decided not to have children has grown, thus debunking the toxic rhetoric that a woman is only a woman if she is a mother. Given that, primarily in the historically industrialised nations, the working time necessary to raise children increased over time, along with the expense entailed in the process, women have generally decided to have fewer children. Both abortion and contraception are, however, precarious achievements, as the legal status of abortion has been contested in many nations and is now illegal in much of even the most supposedly advanced capitalist countries – the US primary among them.

Thanks to the mass claim to the right to birth control pills (first marketed in 1965) and to abortion, women have been able to decide when to have a child. Many women have decided to postpone having their first child, often to the deadline set by the so-called biological clock, or have lengthened the interval between the first and second child. In many nations, these decisions have had the effect of reducing the birth rate. But, even in the face of a gradual decline in the birth rate due to the will of women, and in general of young couples, there has continued to be a serious shortage of social services. Furthermore, in cases where funds were allocated to increase maternity rates, these were generally directed not into the hands of women as mothers, but into the breadwinner's pay cheque. In response to this decrease in births – that is, the reduction of productivity on the terrain of the production of new labour power – a series of technologies have been developed (including assisted fertilisation and surrogacy) in an attempt to ensure that the refusal or reduction of childbearing does not result in general decline in available labour power.

In recent years, attacks against women by states and institutions have intensified with the aim of regaining control over their bodies. A sensational example is given by the recent ruling on abortion by the Supreme Court in the United States, but there are more creeping and pernicious processes, less likely to garner media coverage but just as harmful to women. The medicalisation of procreation, which has occurred following the reduction in the birth rate mentioned above, has not only drained and continues to drain immense amounts of money from the already meagre resources of women but has also re-introduced the toxic social rhetoric which claims that a woman only qualifies as such if she is a mother. This toxic rhetoric, which had been demystified by the feminist movement of the 1970s, later reappeared in the mystifying terms of the supposed *right* of anyone to have a child, even if biologically unable to for various reasons.[25] In the logic of capital, the more individuals or couples have children, regardless of the means, the more the sphere of the production of labour power functions at full capacity. With the support of the most powerful biomedical lobbies, the right of all couples to have children, even in the face of sterility of one or both of the parties involved, can be exercised equally. Whether that means free or paid surrogate pregnancy is irrelevant to the capitalist system.[26] The most important thing for capital is that the highest number of wombs are put to work, capitalising on the ever-increasing impoverishment of women in general. This discourse also generally applies to some biological processes of bodies and tissues, which become places of value extraction.[27]

Surrogate pregnancy is a recurring theme in the history of humanity. For example, various cases are reported in the Bible, as Murgia relates.[28] Even in Roman times, this practice existed, as a woman's infertility was perceived as a social waste. When a man's wife was barren, he resorted to the wife of a friend, who placed her at his disposal for a few months.

---

25   Anna Curcio, 'Il femminismo marxista della rottura', in Anna Curcio, ed., *Introduzione ai femminismi. Genere, razza, classe, riproduzione: dal marxismo al queer* (Rome: DeriveApprodi, 2021).

26   I welcome here the correction to the terminology employed in Italy around surrogacy. Rather than speaking of *maternità surrogata* I prefer to employ the term *gestazione per altri*, where the experience of maternity is not reduced to the period of gestation. See Michela Murgia, 'Non chiamatela maternità surrogata', *L'espresso*, 1 February 2016, lespresso.it.

27   Kalindi Vora, 'After the Housewife: Surrogacy, Labour and Human Reproduction', *Radical Philosophy* 2, no. 4 (2019): 43–7; Cinzia Brunati, 'Produttività Incarnata. Il biolavoro svolto dai corpi femminilizzati' (Master I Livello, Studi e Politiche di Genere, Dipartimento di Filosofia, Comunicazione e Spettacolo, University of Rome, 2021).

28   The first case is that of Abraham, whose wife Sarai gives him her slave Hagar to join him and bear a son whom she will consider her own. Hagar will generate Ishmael, but then Isaac, the son of the promise, will arrive from Sarai, and then both, mother and son of the flesh, will be driven away to make way for the mistress's child. The second case is that of Jacob, married to the two sisters Rachel and Lia, each of whom offers her husband her slave Zilpa and Bila. The question of class, continues Murgia, is inescapable: Sarai, Rachel and Lia are the mistresses and Hagar, Zilpa and Bila are their slaves, and it is only by virtue of this power relationship that pregnancy by proxy is acceptable. See Murgia, 'Non chiamatela maternità surrogata'.

Marco Porcio Cato Uticense (Cato the Younger), for example, offered his wife Marzia to his friend Hortensio Ortalo, who very much wanted to have a child but had an infertile wife. Plutarch recalls:

> A Roman who possessed a sufficient family of his own might be pre-vailed upon by a friend who had no children to transfer his wife to him, being fully empowered to give her away, by divorce, for this purpose; but a Lacedaemonian was accustomed to lend his wife for intercourse with a friend, while she remained living in his house, and without the marriage being thereby dissolved. Many, we are told, even invited those who, they thought, would beget fine and noble children, to converse with their wives.[29]

In the history of the proletarian family, the high number of children to feed combined with meagre incomes had often led, over time, to the practice of entrusting one or more children to relatives who perhaps could not have any. There was no contract but an agreement of mutual solidarity.

What is peculiar about the current industry in paid surrogacy is that it passes through the deepening of social hierarchies, the colonial structuring of the world economy and the further racialisation of the process of procreation itself.[30] Federici underlines that one of the key requirements of surrogacy contracts is that children born are immedi-ately handed over to the new parents, a legal clause that has traumatic consequences, especially for newborns who are separated from the maternal body in which they grew for nine months, whose rhythm, voice and smell they recognise and from whom they expect nourish-ment.[31] It is also very likely that, when they grow up, these babies will potentially want to know the biological mother who brought them into the world. At the same time, there are political positions on surrogacy which see it as a potential queer-feminist project in which the current organisation of the practice is evaluated as leverage against the capital-ist discipline of the family form and as potential for the creation of new

---

29   Plutarch, *Plutarch's Lives*, vol. 1, trans. Aubrey Stewart and George London (London: George Bell and Sons, 1894), 243–4.

30   Vora, 'After the Housewife', 43–7.

31   Silvia Federici, 'Social Reproduction Theory: History, Issues and Present Chal-lenges', *Radical Philosophy* 2, no. 4 (2019), 55–7, radicalphilosophy.com.

practices of parenting and kinship structure in which reproductive labour might be transformed and destroyed as a capitalist commodity.[32]

On a structural level, all this means that, in the sphere of the reproduction of labour power, capital has reacted to the transformations of marriage and the family, managing to create a parallel and alternative labour-market with the help of biomedical research and new reproductive technologies dependent on regimes of capitalist power. Thus, it attempts to detach the process of the production of new labour power from that of the reproduction of the labour force itself and from the marriage market. This has led to a certain biomedical conquest of the processes of procreation and gestation – one which obviously conflicts with the so-called naturalness of the domestic sphere. While the Fordist organisation of the family entailed that the woman, as a pregnant houseworker, worked for capital within a non-salaried relationship mediated by the waged worker, in the new parallel market, women are paid for the work they perform by customers with which they have only a commercial connection. Alternatively, they are uncompensated because they perform such labour in solidarity with women who cannot have children. In these latter, relatively rare cases, the work of producing a newborn is presented as a voluntary social activity; a gesture which reconfirms and relegitimises the non-remuneration of domestic work. The crucial aspect of this arrangement for capital is that women have been reinscribed as reproductive machines and that this capacity can be divorced from any emotional bond with the product of their work: specifically, the baby they give birth to. Equally important for capital is to *reaffirm the concept that women can, at most, be paid for the housework they carry out only if they perform this work for others* and *not* for the children they choose to have and/or care for. Such has long been the case with work performed by immigrant women and racialised minorities within core capitalist nations; here, such logic is extended through an industry and technology of surrogate labour.

Sexual harassment, rapes and femicides are the other face of violence against women.[33] Globally, data from 2000–18 shows that more than one

---

32   See Sophie Lewis, *Full Surrogacy Now: Feminism against Family* (Verso: London, 2021)

33   'Violenza sulle donne, il rapporto del Viminale: in aumento femminicidi e violenze sessuali', *La Repubblica*, 8 March 2023, repubblica.it.

in four women aged between fifteen and forty-nine have experienced physical or sexual violence, or both, at the hands of their partner.[34] Meanwhile in 2017 (the latest year for which we have such statistics, which however are not wholly reliable or systematically collected), about 90,000 women were killed by men, mostly their partners or family members.[35] Cepeda, Lacalle-Calderon and Torralba have proposed a global index to measure and monitor violence against women, as reliable information tends to be elusive.[36] All these forms of violence are actually forms of male mediation between capital and women that may seem dysfunctional, but in fact serve to keep the female social body in check when it becomes too rebellious. Misogynist violence attempts to restore men's power over women's bodies and to re-instil in them subordination to male power and control. Not by chance, women's bodies are still considered private property by many men ('I love you, therefore you are mine') or simply as a site to be defaced and devalued. The practice of genital mutilation (the partial or total removal of the external genitalia of girls and boys, generally performed by a circumciser with a blade and no anaesthetic) continues to be perpetrated in many African and Middle Eastern countries. Such practices have spread throughout the world through the flow of migrant labour: 600,000 women living in Europe have been victims of this practice and another 180,000 are at risk in thirteen European countries.[37]

Finally, we must consider the simple appearance of the female body, which is not only a cultural and social entity, but also inextricably linked to the functionality and productivity of the body in the sphere of reproduction. Faced with the inalienable need for beauty that individuals often express and to which women in particular have historically been bound – a duty in large part required by their work within reproduction – media and advertising campaigns have both proposed and imposed

---

34   Lynnmarie Sardinha et al., 'Global, Regional, and National Prevalence Estimates of Physical or Sexual, or Both, Intimate Partner Violence against Women in 2018', *Lancet* 399 (2022), 803–13.

35   Shalva Weil, 'Two Global Pandemics: Femicide and COVID-19', *Trauma and Memory* 8, no. 2 (2020), 110–12.

36   Isabel Cepeda, Maricruz Lacalle-Calderon and Miguel Torralba, 'Measuring Violence against Women: A Global Index', *Journal of Interpersonal Violence* 37 (2021), 19–20.

37   'Mutilazioni genital femminili: in quali paesi vengono praticate? Perché? Quali sono le conseguenze?', Parlamento europeo, 11 February 2020, europarl.europa.eu.

models of feminised bodies. Historically, these have largely been based on commercial beauty standards; clichéd, stereotyped and enforced youthful ideals. These relentless campaigns have dug deep into the atavistic insecurity instilled in women towards their own bodies. Such insecurity derives from the fact that, for a woman who has to sell her reproductive labour power in a market of sentimental and social relationships, the judgement of others about her body is crucial. The social evaluation of the adequacy or lack thereof of one's own body always weighs heavily on women – especially during adolescence – and therefore on their general sense of well-being and safety. This profoundly misogynist ideological orchestration has managed to convince and exercise influence over many women (and increasingly people of all genders), enforcing a notion that their body is inadequate, either through imperfection or as the result of aging or other diminution. In a sense, the image of women has become a machine of its own within a contemporary capitalist media apparatus. In this context, more and more people, primarily women, seek touch-ups (through both surgical and non-surgical means), much to the satisfaction of a medical industry that has found a plentiful source of income in such practices.[38] Compounding such ideals is an extensive dieting and lifestyle industry that has urged women to present themselves as some combination of professional model and model waged worker. Given that beauty and its relationship to the gendered distribution of labour must become a battlefield, we are faced with a need to restore the organisational tool of *autocoscienza* groups on the body and invent other forms of organisation and struggle to fight what is truly a war against women.[39]

---

38   Emre Tokgoz and Marina A. Carro, *Cosmetic and Reconstructive Facial Plastic Surgery: A Review of Medical and Biomedical Engineering and Science Concepts* (Cham, Switzerland: Springer, 2023).

39   I use here the original term *gruppi di autocoscienza* because, in the Italian feminist movement, this was the term used to indicate the self-help groups typical of the American feminist tradition, although the relationship between *autocoscienza* as it was developed by groups such as Rivolta Femminile in the Italian context differed in certain important aspects from the practice of consciousness-raising developed by Redstockings, the New York Radical Women's Collective and other groups in the US context. See Maud Anne Bracke, 'Between the Transnational and the Local: Mapping the Trajectories and Contexts of the Wages for Housework Campaign in 1970s Italian Feminism', in Lucy Bland and Katharina Rowold, eds, *Reconsidering Women's History* (London: Routledge, 2016), 105–22.

3.2 The reproduction of labour power

As for the second process – that of the reproduction of both the productive and reproductive capacities of labour power – in the last two decades, in historically industrialised countries, several important factors have had significant effects on this process. First, there has been an impact from the high number of women working outside the home, the fragmentation of the family, the technological colonisation of immaterial labour, the drastic increase in the investment in children in terms of domestic work, time and money (although the number of children has decreased) and the lengthening of the average lifespan. Later, consideration will be devoted to the first three factors; here, I will consider only the latter two.

To begin with I consider how women have decided to reinvest the time once spent on housework and the money they had saved by limiting the number of children they have. Generally, instead of investing it in themselves, women have reinvested in the few babies that are born, providing them with more intensive care, and better nutrition, education and access to health care.[40] This decision greatly mitigated the positive effects for women of the refusal to work that was linked to the decline in birth rate. While women generally continued to carry out more or less the same amount of domestic work, thus adding more *value* to the new generations that were dwindling, capital hastened to fill the gaps left by the fall in the birth rate in the labour-market, by attracting immigrants and enforcing migration.[41]

The other crucial factor to consider here is the lengthening of the average lifespan, which has greatly increased both the number of older adults and the number of years of life they have ahead of them. The increasing population defined by this so-called 'third age' has risen with

---

40 Matthias Doepke, Anne Hannusch, Fabian Kindermann and Michèle Tertilt, 'The Economics of Fertility: A New Era, Working Paper 29948' (National Bureau of Economic Research, 2022), nber.org.

41 See, for example, Mariarosa Dalla Costa, 'Riproduzione ed emigrazione', in Mariarosa Dalla Costa and Leopoldina Fortunati, *Brutto ciao. Direzioni di marcia delle donne negli ultimi 30 anni* (Rome: Edizioni delle donne, 1976), 11–24; Mariarosa Dalla Costa and Selma James, *The Power of Women and the Subversion of the Community* (Bristol: Falling Wall Press, 1972). See also Ferruccio Gambino, 'Composizione di classe e investimenti diretti statunitensi all'estero', in Ferrari Bravo, ed., *Imperialismo e classe operaia multinazionale* (Milan: Feltrinelli, 1975), 318–59; Sabrina Marchetti, 'Le Donne delle donne', *DWF* 1, no. 2 (2004), 68–98; Giulia Garofalo Geymonat, Sabrina Marchetti and Penelope Kyritsis, eds, *Domestic Workers Speak* (London: Open Democracy, 2017).

the entry of millions of pensioners in the over-eighties age group, which in the Unites States currently comes to 8.6 million people. Up until a few decades ago, women had always taken care of older adults, but, at a certain point, women abandoned the field. With the female employment rate as it has been emerging over time and with the increase in the average life span of the population, women have made this decision because they would have found themselves guaranteeing the impossible: providing long-term care made up of material and physical assistance, daily help with household chores and emotional support for older people for an extended period of time, would have been a task incompatible with other domestic workloads undertaken outside the home.[42] In fact, performing housework even for an increasingly aging population would have meant taking on an unprecedented burden of reproductive work. Today, many approaching retirement age have themselves begun to take care of even older adults. However, when this has not been possible, recourse is made to paid domestic work, largely undertaken by immigrant women.

Contrary to what is often assumed, it is not only wealthy families who have been forced to resort to waged domestic work but also many working-class and lower-middle-class families, either due to the lack of social services or because their cost is too high. The use of paid domestic work, particularly the labour of immigrant women, to replace domestic work by women in the old, core industrialised nations has, on the one hand, implied the deepening of social hierarchies, the colonial structuring of the world economy and further racialisation of the reproduction of labour power. On the other hand, it has continued to place the cost of domestic work on the shoulders of women and their partners. This has meant low wages for paid domestic workers and a further depletion of the family budget for the children and grandchildren of older adults.

In general, in addition to the use of paid domestic work, other strategies have been implemented by women to reduce the burden of domestic work. One has been to postpone marriage (in 2016 in the US, men were, on average, married by the age of thirty and women by

---

42   Anne Brodsky, Colleen Loomis and Christine Marx, 'Expanding the Conceptualization of PSOC', in A. T. Fisher, C. C. Sonn and B. J. Bishop, eds, *Psychological Sense of Community. Research, Applications, and Implications* (New York: Springer, 2002), 319–36.

twenty-eight) and to delay and reduce the number of children.[43] Since women have always been aware that marriage generally entailed an increase in their domestic work, postponing marriage meant prolonging the years of life in which they were solely responsible for taking care of themselves and could perhaps concentrate on studying or their jobs. The second consisted in the further development of those practices which, since the 1970s, have tried to make domestic and care work sustainable with respect to the overall rhythms of work and the needs of daily life. A whole set of minor practices – small day-to-day revolts – developed: that of no longer ironing sheets, towels and tablecloths, of cleaning the floors just enough without making them shine, of cleaning the house only when necessary, of cooking once for the whole week, and so on. Over the past forty years, domestic work has continued to be reinterpreted by women using the awareness derived from their struggles.[44]

A third strategy has been to share housework with the partner and other family members, as we discuss below, and a fourth has been to transfer a portion of domestic work to social services provided by the state. This latter strategy has met with limited success, however, given the increasing divestment by states in education, health and assistance to the disabled and the elderly. Private, for-profit social services have generally been quite expensive and often of inferior quality, as I discuss below. Finally, a fifth strategy has involved the increased outsourcing of a portion of domestic work: eating out, purchasing prepared foods, making use of laundry and cleaning services. Such a strategy has generally become a chimera for working-class and proletarian women because family budgets do not allow them to purchase finished or semi-finished goods, apart from cheap, highly processed food with long-term health risks.

Thus, compared to forty years ago, perhaps less domestic work is done (though more work is performed outside the home), and it is redistributed

---

43   Mayol-García, Gurrentz and Kreider, *Number, Timing, and Duration of Marriages and Divorces*, 70–167.

44   These 'proto-political' acts have been one among the many forms of behaviour that Wages for Housework reinterpreted as evidence of women's resistance to capital or even revolt. Maybe they are still difficult to interpret through a traditional political lens but are nonetheless important. As Silvia Federici wrote in the epigraph to her classic essay *Wages against Housework*: 'They say it is love. We say it is unwaged work. They call it frigidity. We call it absenteeism.' See Silvia Federici, *Wages against Housework* (Bristol: Falling Wall Press, 1975), 1.

somewhat more equitably among the various members of the family, with the exception of older adults. However, there is a core of domestic work that continues to be performed, because one cannot do without it. The problem is that the terrain of reproduction is increasingly degraded, because not only do states invest less and less in social services by reducing the indirect wages for domestic work, but the capitalist system drains more and more energy from homes, forcing women into extra-domestic work for a meagre wage and leaving the house unattended for many hours a day. Children's education is increasingly outsourced to technology both in the home and at school, with cell phones, televisions and computers entrusted the task of educating and socialising them in some way. There is a clear deficit of reproductive work that mothers are unable to carry out, given the overall work schedules imposed on them and the low wages of extra-domestic work.

In such a context, there has been a convergence among many feminist authors in recognising that a crisis in the sphere of reproduction is under way.[45] Nancy Fraser speaks of a 'crisis of social reproduction', which, in her view, is endemic to the current form of capitalism and which combines the scarcity of time with the exhaustion of social energies.[46] Rai, Hoskyns and Thomas use the term 'depletion' to indicate the fatigue and discomfort that pervades the sphere of reproduction.[47] Naidu argues that gendered, racialised and caste-based unwaged labour serves as the last recourse of subsistence in India often supplementing or filling in entirely for waged income.[48] Federici also speaks of a permanent crisis of reproduction.[49] Women are impoverished globally and the impoverishment at all levels of the sphere of reproduction brings one's mind back to the situation described by Marx: a history of immiseration which at points threatened its very reproduction.

Faced with this situation of *crisis* in reproduction, many remain convinced that the sphere itself is growing increasingly residual. In the

---

45   Cynthia Hess, 'Women and the Care Crisis', Institute for Women's Policy Research Briefing Paper no. 401, April 2013.

46   Nancy Fraser, 'Contradictions of Capital and Care', *New Left Review* 100 (July/August 2016); Hochschild, *The Time Bind*; Heather Boushey, *Finding Time* (Cambridge, MA: Harvard University Press, 2016).

47   Shirin M. Rai, Catherine Hoskyns and Dania Thomas, 'Depletion', *International Feminist Journal of Politics* 16, no. 1 (2014), 86–105.

48   Naidu, 'Circuits of Social Reproduction'.

49   Federici, 'Social Reproduction Theory', 55–7.

early 1980s, Angela Davis was one of the most authoritative voices advocating such a position: pointing out that, in situations of racial-capitalist exploitation (a primary example being apartheid South Africa and the history and legacies of chattel slavery in the US and Caribbean), domestic life and reproductive labour could be entirely discarded by capitalism in contexts of racialised hyper-exploitation.[50]

I disagree with this concept of 'obsolescence', however, based as it is on a progressivist strain in Marxism in which capitalism is understood to create the conditions for its own supersession. Clearly, we have seen domestic work expand exponentially in the context of the COVID crisis, and consistently reappear, in its classic Fordist form of the nuclear family, in nations undergoing intensive industrialisation.

Alternatively, some feminist scholars continue to insist that the realm of reproduction does *not* generate value – that, if anything, it produces only a commodity (labour power) that is subsequently positioned as potentially generative of value in the moment of encounter between humans in their capacity as living labour and capital. Such a distinction, however, neglects the broader cycle of accumulation in which labour power must be continuously produced and reproduced, made available both in the waged labour relationship and held in reserve, in a devalued or unvalued form. In addition to such a broad view, however, it is increasingly untenable to claim that reproductive labour does not directly generate value for the simple reason that today's major tech industries, enabled by a digital infrastructure and apparatus, intensively extract value from the work of reproduction, whether in the realm of shopping, sociality or sexuality.

In addition, I suspect that, behind attitudes that would deny the value-producing nature of reproductive labour lies an opacity around domestic work in general: it remains relatively hidden in its political, social and cultural significance, even to women themselves and others who engage in such work. In addition to representing a source of value for capital, personal reproduction is a necessity linked to the very existence of individuals. It is also a value for women, for the working class and, in a universal sense, for humanity broadly speaking – just as procreation, gestation and childrearing, social life, love relationships, friendships and

---

50   See 'The Approaching Obsolescence of Housework', in Angela Y. Davis, *Women, Race and Class* (New York: Random House, 1981), 222–44.

so on are of great value. Women are not sufficiently aware of the important thing they have accomplished with their silent and unacknowledged struggles, in continuously de-capitalising this work and retransforming it into a human and humanising work.

If we view domestic work from a Trontian perspective, which sees class as the true engine of the capitalist system, it reveals the capitalist face of exploitation, of the family as a minefield on an emotional level, of the deceptive nature of familial relationships – but it also reveals all the strength and determination of women in defending the value of caring for oneself and for others against the idea of a society governed by the logic of *homo homini lupus*.[51] What could be more beautiful and gratifying than watching a child grow up: teaching them to speak, to communicate with the world, take their first steps? Cultivating the uniqueness and unrepeatability of human beings against any homogenisation that might be derived from their position as commodities is also a question of culture and civilisation. Household work differs according to who is its object – taking care of a newborn is very different from taking care of an older adult spouse. Precisely because individuals are unique and their experiences unrepeatable, this process can only work à la carte. Reproduction is the site where the differences, inclinations and talents of individuals are cultivated. Although reduced to a labour power commodity, the individual is also reproduced as a singular human being, with their own tastes, desires and even whims. There is no other work in this society that is as potentially subversive as domestic work, because women's struggles to *liberate it from capital* are positioned as the nerve centre where capitalist logic can be completely overturned. Now, forty years later, calls for the exclusion of women from the political composition of the class for being technically 'unproductive' and therefore marginal to the capitalist accumulation process can only make us smile. The exact opposite is true: women are the political subjects most likely to undermine the capitalist system. If the left is still struggling to accept this vision today, the same cannot be said for capital. It is for this reason that it continues to devalue and impoverish domestic work, injecting in it its logic of unhappiness.

Women cannot remain impartial as, year after year, the conditions of reproduction deteriorate more and more despite their efforts: children

---

51   Mario Tronti, *Workers and Capital*, trans. David Broder (London: Verso, 2019).

grow up alone, parents are hostage to unsustainable work rhythms for an insufficient wage; mothers are increasingly exhausted, and older adults condemned to be alone or to be assisted by other women (or male caregivers whose number is growing rapidly) with whom they have no kinship; loneliness devours the lives of more and more people; violence leads an uncontrolled, random massacre of people particularly the young. The capitalist system is plundering the sphere of reproduction of labour time and money, endangering its very survival. History teaches that this system is capable of going to any lengths in order to increase profits. Women must find a way to react politically to all this, deploying the great strength of which they are capable.

4. How has the exchange between men and women changed?

L'arcano describes a separation between the production of commodities and the reproduction of labour power which clearly configured two workers separated by a precise division of labour: the man delegated only to factory work and the woman basically to housework, and secondarily also to a back-up job outside the home. An organisation of the capitalist system that was based on this male-female division of labour brought with it a strong pressure for men and women to marry: for men, who, without women, were incapable of looking after themselves, the house and daily life; for women, who, without men, had no income, and could not make ends meet. It is clear that the obligation to work in capitalist society has always been accompanied by the obligation to marry.

In capitalist society, the exchange between men and women in the form of marriage has experienced enormous developments, because marriage is the institution which in principle guarantees the maximum productivity of both men and women. Their cooperation was based on a well-defined hierarchy of power that assumed, on the one hand, male domination and allowed men to make the most of their salary while allowing women to guarantee their own survival, provided they devote themselves to their husband/partner and to the children, and, if necessary, to work outside the home for a salary that supplements that of the husband/partner. In marriage, an economy of scale is also activated (for which fixed expenses are shared – housing, bills, food and so on), which serves to reduce the per capita cost of daily life. Remaining unmarried becomes a scarcely productive condition in capitalist society, for which it is discouraged. One recalls that, under Italian fascism, for example, celibates had to pay a special tax to make up for their lower productivity.

L'arcano describes a man–woman relationship, in which the man is subject to the wage labour relationship, the capitalist relationship *par excellence*, while the woman has no formal relationship with capital but is subject to a service relationship with the worker. The waged worker in the factory and the houseworker in the house therefore have tactically (but not strategically) antagonistic interests. In reality, however, women are forced to work, through those they love, for capital. This is why their love is ultimately unable to deny themselves and others as commodities. Under capitalism the power differential between men and women reaches a greater scale than ever before, but, at the same time, the possibility of destroying the power relationship between men and women been never been so great.

This relationship model, which found its apotheosis in marriage, was shattered, as we will see below in the transformations of the family by women. Sexual identity itself has become a terrain of profound social and political upheaval and has developed in various directions, in forms of homosexuality and lesbianism, bisexuality, queerness, trans and gender nonconforming identity (and refusal of identity), among others. Given that heterosexuality is precisely the sedimentation of the capitalist organisation of individual relationships, all forms of different sexual identities must be read, in some sense, as behaviours of rebellion and refusal against the capitalist organisation of individual relationships and the social order.[52]

At the same time, the number of people who have decided not to marry or who have been forced reluctantly to remain uncoupled (singles and celibates) has grown.[53] The number of people, especially women, who have decided to bear and raise a child or children alone, outside of

---

52   On this issue, see Gianfranco Rebucini, 'Du "mariage pour tous" à la "famille pour tout le monde"? Pour une politique queer populaire de parentés dépareillées', *Eigensinn* (2022), Mariages, 1; Gianfranco Rebucini, '"Mariage pour tous" et émancipation sexuelle. Pour une autre stratégie politique', *Contretemps. Revue de critique communiste* (2012), contretemps.eu.

53   Kincade Oppenheimer, 'Women's Rising Employment and the Future of the Family in Industrial Societies', *Population and Development Review* 20, no. 2, (1994), 293–342.

a stable relationship with a partner, has also grown as has the number of women and men who have decided to maintain relationships without cohabiting. In cases where men and women have decided to marry and cohabit, their relationship has become less of a lifetime commitment. The average duration of the man–woman relationship has been shortened by the frequent occurrence of separations and divorces. Many, after the dissolution of a first marriage, have remarried several times. The number of married couples who have decided not to have children has also grown. The number of people who have decided to live together with two partners of different sexes has also grown. The number of those who have decided to marry or cohabit with a person of the same sex or outside of the man–woman gendered binary has grown exponentially along, with the number of such couples who have and/or raise children.[54]

How to interpret these changes in gendered relations? And why did capitalism's most productive relationship model break down? Clearly, the engine that propelled these changes was women's desire to acquire power within male-female binary gendered relations. This mass political initiative expressed by women has combined with four primary factors that have contributed to reshaping the relationship between men and women, profoundly changing the objects of their exchange in terms of both wages and domestic work. The first factor is that male wages, especially in the middle, middle-lower and lower classes, have weakened considerably over time, losing much of their ability to command and control domestic work. The second factor is the greater economic autonomy that a growing number of women have claimed through work outside the home, particularly in the old, core industrial nations and, as far as Europe is concerned, especially in the northern countries. For example, the employed female labour force in the US reached 75 per cent in 2000, while other countries, such as Italy, have remained much further behind: here the increase in the number of employed women in 2000, despite substantial growth, reaching only 46.1 per cent.[55] Having their

---

54   As regards the situation in Italy, see the 2023 report of the Italian Association for Population Studies (AISP): AISP, *Le famiglie in Italia: forme, ostacoli, sfide* (Bologna: Il Mulino, 2023).

55   Paula England, Ivan Privalko and Andrew Levine, 'Has the Gender Revolution Stalled?', *Economic and Social Review* 51, no. 4 (2020), 463–88; Eliana Viviano, 'Un'analisi critica delle definizioni di disoccupazione e partecipazione in Italia', *Politica economica* 19, no. 1 (2003), 161–90, bancaditalia.it.

own money and contributing on an equal or almost equal basis with men to the family budget has allowed some women to negotiate much more with their husbands/partners than in the past, even with respect to domestic work.

The third factor is constituted by the various waves of the feminist movement that have functioned as drivers of greater and more widespread social and political awareness by women of their power. The fourth factor is the growth of individualism, a process which has accompanied the history of capital and which Marx had already grasped. In the life cycle of individuals, the duration of life in which they are alone has lengthened, because the age of spouses at marriage has risen, because the periods between the end of one relationship and the beginning of another has multiplied and finally due to widowhood, especially female, with many women living through old age alone. As *L'arcano* underlined, since the individual has been reduced to a labour power commodity, individual relationships can only exist as reproductive relationships and, as such, fundamentally as family relationships. This does not mean that reproductive relationships do not exist outside family relationships (friends, acquaintances, neighbours, colleagues), but that familial relationships are positioned as the cornerstone on which the reproduction of the individual hinges: they guarantee the stability and continuity that the reproduction of labour power most needs to be productive.

The convergence of these four factors has set in motion social behaviours of rebellion and intolerance towards the gender-binary model proposed and imposed by capital, which has been perceived as increasingly unfair and steeped in exploitation. The rejection of this model has represented an attack on productivity in the sphere of reproduction, especially by women, but also by the LGBTQ+ community. The fact that the wage-housework exchange takes place between a man and a woman or between a woman and a woman or a man and a man, or persons of any gender, does not necessarily make any difference to capital. It is sufficient that the work of reproduction be carried out by someone, and that, in the morning at the factory, as in the office, as in public institutions, workers arrive, well washed, dressed and fed, able to work hard throughout the day. These changes are shaking the entire social order, however, including the organisation of the family, the birth rate and the retention of younger generations of workers, as well as the division and cooperation of labour in the sphere of reproduction. The capitalist system cannot afford a society that does not function adequately, because its excessive dysfunctionality would also undermine the regular functioning of the economic system. This is precisely the aspect that most worries right-wing political forces, which are currently supporting the capitalist system and have risen to power in many countries, such as the government of Giorgia Meloni in Italy.

The changes described above that have taken place in the man-woman relationship have also involved other family relationships. Woman continues to be the fundamental subject of the production and reproduction of labour power, but she is *not* the only subject. The reproduction of labour power, as underlined in *L'arcano*, requires a plurality of secondary reproductive relationships and therefore a plurality of exchanges: between parents, children, brothers and sisters and so on. Following the continuous redefinition and renegotiation of the relationship between men and women, these exchanges have become increasingly important. Children are involved more in domestic work, since many mothers work outside the home. There are many scholars today who not only agree on the existence of a plurality of secondary reproductive relationships but who also observe that this sphere is expanding. For example, as Pupo and Duffy underline: 'Recent research on unpaid work in the household has extended well beyond mothers and fathers. Not only are men increasing their contributions but also grandparents, children and teens (depending on social class) are with increasing frequency picking up any slack left by women's growing involvement in the paid labour force.'[56] Furthermore, according to recent Canadian research, both family of origin and background affect teens' unpaid housework. Among teens of immigrant parents, participation in housework remains clearly gendered, with girls undertaking significantly more than the one-hour national daily average, while boys do significantly less. Similarly, 'teens in blended two-parent families or with stepparents also surpass the average amongst teens in the number of minutes spent daily on housework.'[57] Particularly in the southern hemisphere, the work of reproduction is carried out by all family members.

---

56   Norene Pupo and Ann Duffy, 'Unpaid Work, Capital and Coercion', *Work Organisation, Labour and Globalisation* 6, no. 1 (2012), 27–47, 33.

57   Katherine Marshall, 'The Busy Lives of Teens', in *Perspectives on Labour and Income* 8, no. 7 (May 2007), 5–14, 11.

Its delivery is shaped not only by the dividing lines of gender but also by generation, and in India, for example, interacts in complex ways with those of caste and tribe.[58]

Overall, the changes that have occurred in the male-female ratio all point to an indication that the gender disparity that existed prior to the 1970s has been mitigated over time. The reduction in the difference in power between men and women seems to have profoundly affected male and female identities. The social body today reveals fewer significant differences between men and women. From a political, social and psychological point of view, the indices of personality, attitudes and behaviours are becoming more and more similar between men and women. Which processes affect our society more strongly: masculinisation or feminisation? It is now important, above all, to understand and interpret the signs of this lack of differences or, better, these new forms of commonality, because in this way we can understand whether, at an evolutionary level, it is a matter of the conquest or defeat of humanity and, above all, of women themselves.

5. How has the family changed?

In the past forty years, the fragmentation of the family has given rise to many different forms of domestic organisation. The remodelling of its structure was produced by the behaviours of struggle, resistance or counter-power expressed by women within and against the family, above all by diversifying and undermining the stability and continuity of the man–woman exchange, as mentioned earlier, and therefore the production of surplus value in the domestic sphere.[59] Women have courageously pursued these behaviours, even at the risk of their poverty and social marginalisation, as in the case of separated or divorced women with dependent children who often end up living below the poverty line.[60]

---

58   Alpa Shah and Jens Lerche, 'Migration and the Invisible Economies of Care: Production, Social Reproduction and Seasonal Migrant Labour in India', *Transactions of the Institute of British Geographers* 45, no. 4 (2020), 719–34.

59   See AISP, *Le famiglie in Italia*.

60   Divorced women were more likely to find themselves in poverty (at rates of 20 per cent and 11 per cent respectively). See Mayol-García, Gurrentz and Kreider, *Number, Timing, and Duration of Marriages and Divorces*, 70–167.

Let us try to summarise these behaviours, although some of them have already been mentioned in the previous discussion of transformations in the gender binary.

First, the number of families continues to grow while the number of its members decreases. Second, according to the Population Division of the United Nations Department of Economic and Social Affairs, in 2021 the average number of children per woman over a lifetime was 2.3, while in 1950 it was 5.[61] Given this drastic decrease, the same report argues that, in the next few decades, migration will be the sole driver of population growth in old, core industrialised nations. According to the OECD, there is a category of women who bears fewer children than others: women in paid work, those with higher education and incomes and those who are not married.[62] Their increasing proportion within the population has also contributed to lower total fertility rates. It is known, for example, that between 2000 and 2015 population growth in OECD countries began to lag behind an increasing average pace: in the Baltic republics, for example, the population fell by 15 per cent in Latvia and Lithuania, and 6 per cent in Estonia. In addition to a reduction in the number of children, as we have seen above, women have disengaged themselves from the reproduction of older adults. Since neither adult males nor young grandchildren have come forward to fill the reproductive voids left by women, the burden of not only looking after themselves, but also that of dealing with continuous processes of change and innovation is weighing heavily, and will continue to weigh more heavily in the future. Aging is a process that changes all phases of life, and new generations play an important role both because they will probably live for longer, and because they will have to establish a new pact between generations.

Third, in the remodelling of the family, women have seized two levers of power through the institution of divorce and the contraceptive pill, which, since the second half of the 1960s, has given sexually active women reliable control over their fertility for the first time in history. The traditional form of engagement has gradually transformed into forms of premarital cohabitation, whereby marriage has become only a

61   United Nations Department of Economic and Social Affairs, Population Division, *World Population Prospects 2022: Summary of Results* (New York: UN DESA, 2022).

62   OECD, *Women at Work in G20 Countries: Policy Action since 2020*, paper prepared for the 2nd Meeting of the G20 Employment Working Group under Italy's Presidency (Paris: OECD, 2021), oecd.org.

formal validation, rather than a stipulation of life as a couple. Fewer and fewer women have decided to get married, so the number of women and men who have decided to be single has increased (but, at the same time, the number of those who live alone because they cannot find a suitable partner has also increased). The number of those remaining single has also increased specifically due to the incidence of older adult women, as women are widowed at a higher rate than men.[63] Fewer and fewer women have decided to get married formally, thus unofficial marriages have increased in number (that is, marriage rites celebrated only to enjoy the ceremony and celebration of commitment, but not to formalise marriage either legally or religiously). Another modality that has increased is long-distance relationships (a togetherness without a shared home). The number of women who do not want to marry but who have not given up on the idea of having children has grown; so too has the number of single-parent families, the majority of which consist in a woman raising one or more children. Generally, it is the woman who, despite being, in many cases, the weaker social subject of the couple form, is the first to request a divorce. Often the separated and divorced – men more than women – rather than swelling the number of single-parent families, remarry and create other families. The general outcome of such recombined families is an extended family. Another important aspect is that separations and divorces no longer involve only young-adult couples, but also older adults. Finally, the number of mixed families, made up of the most varied kinship and non-kinship relationships, has also greatly expanded.

The explosion of family forms has been the result of mass behaviour generated largely by women's self-defence rather than attack. Instead of destroying the family as the basic cell of the capitalist system, these forms of behaviour have tended to modify its composition and connotations, only slightly lowering its level of productivity. It cannot be said that this germination of different types of families has automatically raised the quality of life of its members. There is a large and established body of research showing that blended families resulting from divorce and remarriage or other arrangements often experience problematic

---

63   A prominent 2019 study in the United States counted 8.9 million female widows as opposed to 2.6 million male widowers. Administration on Aging and Administration on Community Living, *2019 Profile of Older Americans* (Washington, DC: Department of Health and Human Services, 2020), acl.gov.

dynamics that are generally not found in traditional families and which have a negative impact on the well-being of children and young people.[64] These dynamics include blurred step-parent roles, ambiguous family boundaries, heightened conflict between children and step-parents as well as between step-siblings and conflicting family cultures; there are also problems resulting from transfers of children and adolescents from one family to another, another factor which may tend to worsen the quality of the parent-child relationship.[65] Children from these families, more frequently than those from traditional families, suffer from higher levels of stress and lower educational achievement.[66]

The drivers that have shattered the family into so many different realities have emerged out of women's frustration and exhaustion from taking on most of the burden of domestic work, given that states, entrepreneurs, political parties and trade union organisations have failed to find effective responses: that is, to assume the economic cost of the direct and indirect economic recompense of women for their housework. This is why women have reorganised the family in many ways and continue to reduce the number of children they have, to make the burden of domestic work a little more bearable. But since the family is the primary cell on which the capitalist state is based, the transformation of the family also has consequences for the structure of society, which has become more diversely articulated and fluid. The regulatory framework, on the other hand, has changed little, making society dysfunctional, as it is based on a family structure that no longer exists.[67] In the European context, Italy's is perhaps the most dysfunctional because, while, in other European nations, the legislation and welfare systems have changed together with the changes in families, in Italy the family form of reference for welfare continues to be the single-income couple with two

---

64   Todd Jensen and Mellissa Lippold, 'Patterns of Stepfamily Relationship Quality and Adolescents' Short-Term and Long-Term Adjustment', *Journal of Family Psychology* 32, no. 8 (2018), 1130–41.

65   Elizabeth Nixon and Kristin Hadfield, 'Blended Families', in Constance L. Shehan, ed., *The Wiley Blackwell Encyclopedia of Family Studies* (Hoboken, NJ: John Wiley and Sons, 2016).

66   Zitha Mokomane, *The Impact of Demographic Trends on Families* (United Nations Department of Economic and Social Affairs [UNDESA] Division for Inclusive Social Development, 2024), 16, social.desa.un.org.

67   On society, see also François Dubet, 'The Return of Society', *European Journal of Social Theory* 24, no. 1 (2020), 3–21.

children. Today this corresponds to only 20 per cent of families. Public policies, which families need more than ever, will necessarily have to take account of these increasingly complex family dynamics.

6. The new division of domestic work in the family

With the increase in the number of women working two jobs, the need to share household chores with other family members had become increasingly urgent over time. Women demand that their husbands, partners, children and brothers share the housework with them. They have also been able to raise their voices because many have brought in a wage or salary from work outside the home – perhaps (though not always) a more modest figure than that of their husbands – which also contributes to the family budget. Disagreements about household chores have been among the main sources of conflict in couples and divorces, since women's unhappiness has exploded in front of husbands or partners who refuse or neglect to do their share, both because such refusals force women into an interminable overall working day and because they express a lack of respect and solidarity. Over time, the perpetuation of a family organisation based on the man/breadwinner and woman/housewife model has become intolerable for women; it no longer makes sense in families where both spouses work and earn. Women's insistence on sharing domestic work has gradually caused husbands/partners and brothers to adopt a greater portion in all industrialised countries, albeit slowly. Men have resisted this change for three reasons: first, because they have had to learn a new job from scratch, which is generally strenuous; second, because taking on household chores after eight hours of work has never thrilled anyone; and finally, because they were reluctant to give up their special privileges.

But this resistance saw significant collapse in the last decades of the 1900s, with most research agreeing that, at the transnational level, there has been a continuous trend towards the greater involvement of men in household chores. It is a global fight that women have won, though not entirely. Data below is drawn from two studies, one concerning the United States and another that examines nineteen European and non-European countries. This is important research, but the findings should be taken with caution, given that domestic work is not considered *real work* and therefore is not regulated within a formal framework for its definition, recognition and quantification. Furthermore, the exclusion of the domestic sphere from the category of recognised work has led to its exclusion from surveys on the employed labour force. Consequently, obtaining accurate estimates of reproductive labour and domestic workers is a daunting task.[68]

The first study compares two series of data in 1965 and 2009-10, and observes that a married woman without children went from performing thirty-four hours per week of domestic work in 1965 to eighteen in 2009–10. If married with children, women went from thirty-six hours per week plus ten hours dedicated to children in 1965, to eighteen hours plus fourteen dedicated to children in 2009–10.[69] Overall, the total average work week of a married woman in this period decreased from thirty-four to eighteen hours (a reduction of sixteen hours per week), but, for women with children, it went from forty-six hours to thirty-two hours per week; a smaller decrease equal to less than fourteen hours per week.

Conversely, the same research tells us that married men have progressively increased the hours of domestic work they perform from five hours per week in 1965 to ten hours in 2009–10; while married fathers went from five hours per week plus three hours dedicated to the children in 1965, to ten plus seven hours dedicated to children in 2009–10. Overall, the total domestic working day of married men has doubled; but if they have children it has more than doubled, from eight to seventeen hours a week in total. At the same time, we should remember that, between 1965 and 1975, the average number of children per family had reached approximately two. As already mentioned however, the housework time and money saved by limiting the number of children has largely been reinvested in a fewer number of children, limiting the benefits for women of any decrease in housework resulting from the drop in births. Parents – especially mothers – have realised that children today require much more energy in the form of love and care than they once did, in order to face an increasingly complex world. The greater

---

68   Malin Nilsson, Indrani Mazumdar and Silke Neunsinger, eds, *Home-Based Work and Home-Based Workers (1800–2021)* (Boston: Brill, 2021).

69   Bianchi, Milkie, Sayer and Robinson, 'Is Anyone Doing the Housework?'; Bianchi, Milkie, Sayer and Robinson, 'Housework: Who Did, Does or Will Do It'.

quantity of love, care, work and money incorporated in future generations, on the one hand, functions well for the capitalist system which is
guaranteed a workforce capable of greater labour productivity, but, on
the other, it helps women and the class in general, because there is
nothing potentially more revolutionary than trying to raise the bar of the
needs and requirements of human civilisation.

Bianchi et al., comparing the total hours worked by men and women,
concluded that there is no longer much difference between them, but
women do more unpaid hours than men.[70] Pupo and Duffy report: 'The
significance of this unpaid labour is documented in various time-budget
studies revealing that over the past half century unpaid work in the
global North has comprised almost half (44.7 percent) of all time spent
"working".[71] This trend can be explained, it can be argued, by noting
that, while the waged male worker had historically been *liberated* from
the work of self-reproduction, this is now much less the case because
women are increasingly demanding that he participate in it, because
there are many divorced fathers who have to take care of their children
directly when they have custody, and because there are more people,
including men, who live alone. The consequence is that the male waged
labour force no longer works only in the sphere of production, but also,
increasingly, in the sphere of domestic reproduction, creating an enormous amount of value, particularly on an immaterial level.

The growth in the male contribution to domestic work has intersected
with another important trend: the concentration of domestic work on
children – that is, on the reproduction of new labour power. In general,
in Western industrialised nations, parents have increased the time spent
in child care since 1965, although such trends have not always been
linear, as was the case in both the United States and France. In addition,
gender differences in time spent by parents caring for children have
narrowed, due to substantial increases in child care time by fathers
coupled with smaller increases in child care time by mothers.[72] It is

---

70   Bianchi et al., 'Housework: Who Did, Does or Will Do It', 55.

71   Pupo and Duffy, 'Unpaid Work, Capital and Coercion', 27.

72   Suzanne M. Bianchi, John P. Robinson and Melissa A. Milkie, *Changing Rhythms
of American Family Life* (New York: Russell Sage, 2006); A. H. Gauthier, T. M. Smeeding
and F. F. Furstenberg, 'Are Parents Investing Less Time in Children? Trends in Selected
Industrialised Countries', *Population and Development Review* 30 (2004), 647–72;
J. Gershuny, *Changing Times: Work and Leisure in Postindustrial Society* (Oxford: Oxford

important to note that, according to these reports, mothers, in order to preserve the time dedicated to housework and care for their children, reduced the time dedicated to household chores, while fathers reduced the time reserved for sleep and entertainment/sports.[73]

Similarly, research conducted in nineteen European and non-European countries showed a progressively greater sharing of domestic work between men and women, but with significant differences between nations as regards both the level and pace of such sharing. It should not be overlooked, however, that there has been a slowdown in the sharing of domestic work since the end of the 1980s in countries where the time devoted by men and women to household chores was already more equal, while the growth of sharing has continued in countries where the gender division of household chores was initially less equal.[74] Naturally, the assumption of a part of the domestic work by the man has upset the narrative of his social role based on diminishing gendered stereotypes. Due to the powerful ideological orchestration that shaped the representation of social roles in the sphere of reproduction, the man with an apron cooking at the stove may have appeared less attractive in the eyes of women used to conceptualising him in other terms. This reorganisation of the relationship between men and women required a period of transition to metabolise this change in the gendered distribution of labour on a cultural level.

The sharing of housework is beneficial not only for women but also, in some ways, for men. For women, because the reduction of their disproportionate responsibility for household chores and child care has given them breathing room, on the one hand, in order to position themselves better on the labour-market (giving them more mobility and work flexibility, for example, and therefore a higher salary), and, on the other hand, because women needed to reduce their involvement in the family more radically in order to recover time from it to devote to

University Press, 2000); L. C. Sayer, S. M. Bianchi and J. P. Robinson, 'Are Parents Investing Less in Children? Trends in Mothers' and Fathers' Time with Children', *American Journal of Sociology* 110, no. 1 (2004), 1–43.

73   Gauthier, Smeeding and Furstenberg, 'Are Parents Investing Less Time in Children?'; L. C. Sayer, 'Gender, Time and Inequality: Trends in Women's and Men's Paid Work, Unpaid Work and Free Time', *Social Forces* 84, no. 1 (2005), 285–303.

74   Evrim Altintas and Oriel Sullivan, 'Fifty Years of Change Updated: Cross-National Gender Convergence in Housework', *Demographic Research* 35 (2016), 455–70.

organising and political mobilisation.[75] For men, it is beneficial because a higher level of paternal involvement in childrearing is associated with a long list of emotional benefits for fathers and their children.[76] Some studies have found that men are happier and less stressed when they do more household chores.[77] Furthermore, in the United States, a less blatantly gendered distribution of predominantly male breadwinners is associated with a lower risk of divorce for couples. Finally, the research is clear on a key point: among couples who share housework, the frequency of sexual intercourse has increased – in other words, sharing reproductive labour is important for the sexual satisfaction of the couple.[78]

But we cannot think that the sharing of domestic work is only a question that can be solved on a subjective level. There are macro-level social structures that influence the distribution of household chores within the family, such as cultural attitudes, corporate cultures and social protection schemes, as well as politics, legislation and the economy.[79] Most work-family policies (e.g. maternity leave and sponsored child care) are designed to equalise the gender division of work in the home by positively influencing women's paid work.[80] Less frequent are policies aimed at strengthening men's caring responsibilities (such as paternity leave). Obviously, the dominant macro-structure is economic, since domestic work is productive work essential for the existence and functioning of businesses, society and the state: the family, the male-female relationship and the division of power between them, the functioning of individual and social reproduction, the unpaid work relationship between woman and capital, mediated by the worker – all are founded

---

75 L. Haas, *Equal Parenthood and Social Policy: A Study of Parental Leave in Sweden* (Albany: State University of New York Press, 1992).

76 M. E. Lamb, 'The Development of Father–Infant Relationships', in M. E. Lamb, ed., *The Role of the Father in Child Development* (Hoboken, NJ: John Wiley & Sons, 1997), 104–20.

77 J. L. Scott and A. C. Plagnol, 'Work–Family Conflict and Well-Being in Northern Europe', in J. L. Scott, S. Dex and A. C. Plagnol, eds, *Gendered Lives: Gender Inequalities in Production and Reproduction* (Northampton, MA: Elgar, 2012), 174–205.

78 Daniel Carston, Amanda J. Miller, Sharon Sassler and Sarah Hanson, 'The Gendered Division of Housework and Couples' Sexual Relationships: A Reexamination', *Journal of Marriage and Family* 78 (2016), 975–95.

79 Mary Noonan, 'The Impact of Social Policy on the Gendered Division of Housework', *Journal of Family Theory and Review* 5 (2013), 124–34.

80 H. Stier and N. Lewin-Epstein, 'Policy Effects on the Division of Housework', *Journal of Comparative Policy Analysis* 9, no. 3 (2007), 235–59.

on it. But the capitalist system structurally cares only minimally whether men or women do the housework. The most important thing is that such work is carried out under the conditions it dictates (unpaid and unregulated).

For women, on the other hand, it is an important victory to have managed to share at least a certain portion of housework with their husbands, partners, children and other family members, because on a tactical level it has made women's lives more liveable, less dominated by their overall work burden. But having achieved this by offloading a part of the housework onto men cannot be satisfying politically. Reducing one's working day by lengthening that of others has no strategic value. The problem is one not simply of sharing domestic work but *destroying it* as a capitalist-labour relationship. The strategic objective is therefore to obtain financial recognition for this work (which largely remains invisible and unpaid) and for anyone who carries it out, of whatever gender. Money is a first step to reducing such labour and subsequently to destroying it as a waged employment relationship. Many more men should now be willing to fight alongside women to obtain a wage for domestic work, because they themselves have become, in part, workers in the sphere of reproduction.

7. The most relevant changes in work outside the home

On the contrary, the fact that women in the capitalist system – as was emphasised in *L'arcano* – have essentially been responsible for housework and the education of children, has never implied the expropriation of their ability to work away from home. The labour-market was conceived, structured and regulated within the Fordist model, which viewed the man as obliged to exchange his labour power on the market with the woman in the marriage market. It was conceived as such for the male workforce, for a free worker, who freely sold his ability to work on the market, without limits on such freedom. With women's entry into the labour-market, they arrived as only *semi-free* to sell their labour power, because many of them were conditioned by their role as wives/mothers. It is true that a growing number of women have decided to favour paid work by remaining unmarried or childless, but a large majority of women are still not willing to give up on having romantic relationships and children to devote themselves to work the same way men do. This decision implied that they could *afford* to work only if they were somehow able to reconcile the world of work outside the home with the world of the home: a far-from-easy undertaking, given that organisations of the male left had seldom felt the need to fight for a harmonisation of family rhythms and times, of kindergarten and school, with those at work.

Although the Fordist labour-market was historically structured for males, paradoxically for the capitalist system, the ability to count on women when necessary was also fundamental. In fact, when it was necessary to replace men at the front in the factories, as during the wars, or to resort to cheap labour, women were systematically called upon to work in the factories, offices, schools and hospitals. Similarly, when the economic crisis led to heavy layoffs, the first to pay this price were women – which also promptly happened with COVID, since, according to the OECD, women still have to fill the employment gaps left open by the pandemic.[81] In particular, the women who are at risk of being left behind by the economic recovery are those with young children, those who work in the sectors that have been most affected by the crisis and those who face violence and physical or psychological harassment.

The partial expropriation of their ability to work in the sphere of commodity production meant that, if necessary, in the husband's absence or if his salary had become too low to support the family, women tried to contribute to the family budget by going to work outside the home. Brandolini underlines how in Italy, for example, the increase in female employment between 1972 and 1992 was also due to the impoverishment and proletarianisation of the middle classes, which forced women of those social classes to go to work outside the home to attempt to maintain prior levels of living and consumption.[82] For other women, going to work outside the home has always been an obligation, such as for example for Black women in the United States, whose families were characterised by a high percentage of mothers with one or more children or by families in which women could not count on the husband's salary.[83]

---

81 OECD, *Women at Work in G20 Countries*.

82 A. Brandolini, 'La disuguaglianza di reddito in Italia nell'ultimo decennio', *Stato e Mercato* 74, no. 2 (2005), 207–29.

83 S. Ruggles, 'The Origins of African-American Family Structure', *American Sociological Review* 59, no. 1 (1994), 136–51.

While the presence of middle and upper-class women has persisted over time in companies, services and professions, with women gaining increasingly better positions and salaries, the mass of women have been offered more subdued work outside the home – the humblest and least-paid tasks – or in workplaces with strong gender segregation, such as nursery, primary and secondary schools, hospitals (as support workers, health workers and nurses) and private and public offices, also accompanied by a subpar salary. Alternatively, they were offered part-time work, with an even lower wage, which did not allow them full personal economic autonomy. To give an idea of the extent of female extra-domestic employment, consider for example that in 1970, just less than half of US women (48 per cent) had an extra-domestic job, while in Europe the percentage was higher in some countries of the North, such as, for example, Finland (65.5 per cent), Sweden (59.4 per cent) and Denmark (58.0 per cent), and significantly lower in some countries of the South such as Spain (29.2 per cent), Italy (29.6 per cent) and Greece (32.1 per cent).[84]

Until the 1970s, women's wages were generally conceived as a supplement to that of the husband and *not* as an instrument of personal economic autonomy. Moreover, women as extra-domestic workers rarely had their hands free, like male workers, because they had to evaluate paid work's compatibility with domestic and care work, which, regardless, they were still required to guarantee.[85] They therefore favoured jobs with flexible or part-time working hours and limited mobility, which usually resulted in lower wages.[86] The hypothesis of paid work as a lever for women's emancipation immediately revealed itself as a failed mass political strategy because women generally ended up doing more than one job (a double exploitation) for less pay.

Where did this vision of women in relation to work outside the home and the related regulatory and organisational framework come from? This

---

84   For the US, see England, Privalko and Levine, 'Has the Gender Revolution Stalled?'; for European figures, see K. L. Brewster and R. R. Rindfuss, 'Fertility and Women's Employment in Industrialised Nations', *Annual Review of Sociology* 26 (2000), 271–96, 276.

85   J. O'Neill, 'The Gender Gap in Wages, circa 2000', *American Economic Review* 93, no. 2 (2003), 309–14.

86   B. Petrongolo and M. Ronchi, 'Gender Gaps and the Structure of Local Labor Markets', *Labour Economics* 64 (2020), 101819.

was a long historical journey, which Sarti, Bellavitis and Martini have helped us to reconstruct.[87] The word 'economy', as they report, was born historically and paradoxically to indicate the management of the house (the Greek *oikos* – economy – refers to the management of the house), and it is only starting from the 1600s that the term took its own autonomous path, from indicating a domestic economy to its parthenogenesis as political economy. From the late eighteenth century onwards, when the work of producing commodities began to leave the home (the primary place of original accumulation for several centuries), the work carried out in houses was marginalised and naturalised. Consequently, even service staff, which included butlers, wet nurses, servants and waitresses, become a sort of servile extension of the employers' family, so they tended to lose the status of true workers. The social configuration of the figure of the housewife, as *a person who does not work* and is maintained by the family, occurred between 1800 and 1900, and, precisely because work is the terrain for the conquest of rights, housewives as supposedly non-working women end up without rights. It is from this historical, social and cultural background that women started when they presented themselves to sell their labour in the non-domestic market. One can easily imagine the compromised contractual position that women, used to labour that is not classified as such and without any rights, have held. The OECD argues that gender inequality in unpaid care work is the missing link in analysing gender gaps in labour force participation, wages and job quality.[88]

This picture was turned upside down due to the initiative of women who demanded a real salary, not a corollary to that of their husband/partner, and who feminised a labour-market that had been built according to a male-only logic. First of all, young women have decided to invest much more in their education. It is precisely in the field of education that women have made the most significant progress in recent decades, thanks to the solidarity of mothers who, to support their daughters, have given up asking them to help them with household chores. As far as Italy is concerned, for example, in the period preceding the growth in the participation of women in the extra-domestic workforce, almost two-thirds of the increase in female employment must be

---

87   Sarti, Bellavitis and Martini, *What Is Work?*.

88   OECD, *Unpaid Care Work: The Missing Link in the Analysis of Gender Gaps in Labour Outcomes* (OECD Development Centre, December 2014).

attributed to the increase in education levels.[89] The generation of daughters who would start the feminist movement of the 1970s was able to develop high-value knowledge, skills and competencies, and consequently to obtain significant economic benefits, such as higher employment and earnings rates and faster earnings progression.[90] The price paid by this generation is that the transmission from their mothers to them of the knowhow related to housework has stalled, so that they may not have learned how to cook or how to stop a newborn from crying. The greater isolation from other women, mothers and relatives, which also occurred following the greater presence of women in the labour-market, has meant a loss in the transmission of knowledge and work experience on which feminine roles are based. This loss is serious because daily life contains an immense wealth of culture. Through new technologies (blogs, specialised sites, social networks), this knowledge has been reconstructed in a more formal and impersonal fashion, but it sometimes becomes more scientific and collective in the process.[91] It was this generation of young women who was more present in the labour-market precisely at a time when the development of the service sector required the female workforce to be channelled into offices. These more educated women managed to express greater bargaining power and therefore to obtain a wage or salary still not equal, but comparable, to that of their husband or partner.

Another factor that has contributed to greater pressure from women on the labour-market is their decision to give up having children or to postpone pregnancy for several years – or to lengthen the interval between the birth of the first and second child to strengthen and stabilise their job position. In particular, the decision to postpone pregnancy has been only partially compensated for by the increase in fertility later in life as demonstrated by the increase in the number of only children. These strategies expressed the willingness of women to reduce the burden of unpaid domestic work, while, at the same time, reducing its

---

89   E. Reyneri, *Sociologia del mercato del lavoro* (Bologna: Il Mulino, 2005).

90   S. Scherer and E. Reyneri, 'Come è cresciuta l'occupazione femminile in Italia: fattori strutturali e culturali a confronto', *Stato e mercato* 83, no. 2 (2008), 183–216; OECD, *Education at a Glance 2018: OECD Indicators* (Paris: OECD Publishing, 2018).

91   Leopoldina Fortunati, 'Women's Knowledge Co–production and Sharing in Online Communities', *Internet Histories: Digital Technology, Culture and Society* 2, nos 1–2 (2018), 75–97.

penalising impact on their work outside the home, which remained the only source of economic autonomy at a personal level.

On the other hand, a factor that has continued to curb the influence of women in the extra-domestic labour-market is the lack of or limited availability of efficient public social services, so that women have had to resort to help from parents and in-laws, or to paid professionals such as babysitters, housekeepers and carers. All these subjects – with their unpaid domestic work in the first case or poorly paid in the second case – allowed women with extra-domestic work, especially if they were mothers with small children, to perform their jobs. With the cuts in social services that Western states have made year after year however, the provision of free domestic work by grandparents and other family members has become increasingly important, particularly because working-class women can rarely afford (from their own extra-domestic salaries) to pay for the work of babysitters, domestic workers and other caregivers. An additional factor that has hindered the influence of women in extra-domestic labour is the increasing average age of adult parents and in-laws. In Italy this obstacle has been overcome, among more affluent women at least, by resorting to immigrant domestic work. In the last two decades of the 1900s, for women from forty-nine to sixty years of age, on whom the heavy task of assisting their parents in old age was burdened more and more, the sharp increase in the employment rate – almost all full time – was made possible by the wide and growing offer of low-cost immigrant home assistants, as highlighted by the amnesty of 2002–3.[92] The use of domestic work by immigrant women has probably played a crucial role not only in allowing access to paid work for Italian women, but also in allowing them to remain in work for a longer period.

A factor that has served to stratify the female extra-domestic workforce further is a type of industrial development – linked to the development of the service sector and new technologies – that has led, at least in Italy, to a profoundly unequal path, in which less-educated women of lower social origins who are more in need of finding part-time work, because they are fully employed at the family level, have been penalised.[93] A final factor to bear in mind is the decision of many women to go to work

---

92   M. Barbagli, A. Colombo and G. Sciortino, eds, *I sommersi e i sanati. Le regolarizzazioni degli immigrati in Italia* (Bologna: Il Mulino, 2004).

93   Scherer and Reyneri, 'Come è cresciuta l'occupazione femminile in Italia', 191.

outside the home, even when their earnings are not essential to the family budget, because they guarantee them economic independence from their husband or partner.[94] These women are also aided in their ability to fully pursue extra-domestic work by their greater possibility of resorting to paid female domestic work, often from immigrants. This decision by women of the middle classes to pursue extra-domestic work, even when they could rely on a husband's wages, proved to be farsighted, because any separation or divorce would have exposed unemployed women, especially those with small children, to becoming poor (given the reluctance of ex-husbands to pay child support expenses established by a judge).[95]

It is equally important to note that, over the last two decades, the growth in the number of women working outside the home has stalled. For example, England, Privalko and Levine write that, in the United States since 2000, the percentage of women working outside the home has declined, stabilised and then declined further during the Great Recession, reaching a low of 69 per cent, before rebounding to 73 per cent in 2018.[96] All subsequent changes have been small, fluctuations between 70 per cent and 75 per cent. At the same time, the division of domestic work between men and women within families has also stalled, as we saw in the previous section. But apart from this stalemate, the entire history of women's employment over the last fifty years has illustrated how the strategy of extra-domestic work as women's empowerment and liberation from domestic work has failed as a political strategy, achieving the exact opposite of its emancipatory goals. It was not work outside the home that freed women from domestic work (which awaited them inexorably when they returned home); rather, it was housework that limited and heavily influenced women's work outside the home, remodelling it so as to make it more reconcilable with the management of the house and the children. Furthermore, the hope of emancipation in the extra-domestic market has generally hit a wall of workplace discrimination. Heymann, for example, showed that women were one and a half times more likely to lose wages to care for

---

94   U. Huws, 'The Reproduction of Difference: Gender and the Global Division of Labour', *Work Organisation, Labour and Globalisation* 6, no. 1 (2012), 1–10.

95   M. Barbagli, *Provando e riprovando. Matrimonio, famiglia e divorzio in Italia e in altri paesi occidentali* (Bologna: Il Mulino, 1995).

96   J. Heymann, *Forgotten Families: Ending the Growing Crisis Confronting Children and Working Parents in the Global Economy* (New York: Oxford University Press, 2006).

a sick child than their male counterparts, and six times more likely to lose a job promotion for the same reason.[97] The difficulty for a woman to find and maintain work outside the home is directly proportional to the number of her children: the more children she has, the more difficult it is for her to work outside the home; while the fewer children she has, the easier it is for her to work outside the home.[98] Women with more than one child are much more likely to have to take part-time or flexible jobs with limited mobility.

Certainly, outside work has given women partial economic autonomy, but it has also forced them into heavy work rhythms that have often left them exhausted, and it has forced many women to pay other women to replace them as workers in the house. The salary that women earn by working outside the home is not only lower overall than that of men, but all the costs that women incur in not being at home must also be deducted from their family budget in the form of private social services, domestic workers and babysitters. In the end, very little remains.

In general, the amount of reproductive housework provided by women has been reduced, but they continue to perform long hours of work per day. While the number of women housewives varies by region, in south European countries this number is still very high and largely represented by women from the poorest strata of the population. These women who go to work have not left their houses unguarded, however: they also continue to work at home, because children, partners and women themselves continue to eat, need clean linen and clothes, and live in an environment with an acceptable level of hygiene.

On the political level, the model of women's emancipation through external work has met with strict limitations – and one, in particular, that is insurmountable. This model assumes the recourse to predominantly female immigrant domestic work – but who does the housework and takes care of the children and older adult relatives of the immigrant women who do housework in other women's homes? This model, in liberating some women, obliges others to leave young children alone at home while they are at work. Is it sustainable as a feminist strategy?

---

97   Esteban Ortiz-Ospina and Sandra Tzvetkova, 'Working Women: Key Facts and Trends in Female Labour Force Participation', Our World in Data, March 2018, ourworldindata.org.
98   Ibid.

8. Social services, or the social reproduction of the workforce

8.1 What are social services?

Social services are where the socialised reproduction of labour power occurs – where a formalised, waged and professionalised type of domestic work takes place. Under capitalism, the state must guarantee a socialised reproduction of the labour force to compliment that which takes place at home. The socialisation of reproduction in the social sphere implies, for capital, having to organise the personnel who work there (mostly women) in a completely different way from the organisation of the sphere of domestic production. In other words, it must organise it in a context of division and cooperation of labour and of wage-labour relations.

As for the first aspect, the organisation of social services increasingly resembles that of the factory, despite resistance from users of such services, who would like more participation and oversight in the way they are run. It is no coincidence that one of the most pressing requests from the relatives of users and patients in public facilities such as kindergartens, care homes and hospitals is to be able to control what happens inside these facilities. On the contrary, the control exercised by social services over the sphere of domestic reproduction, which is indirectly but constantly monitored and controlled, is more effective. Teachers inevitably evaluate the quantity and quality of domestic work incorporated in the children, for example: if the children and students are well fed, well dressed, washed and combed, and if they behave appropriately with other children and with their teachers, it means that the mothers and fathers are doing a good job at home.

As for the second aspect – the salaried employment relationship – working in social services is a source of income, especially for many women, but generally the wages received here are low and the pace of work so high that users and patients end up being seen as a source of trouble, rather than as human beings to be taken care of. In these sectors, the workers live in very stressful conditions, and indeed the phenomenon of the Great Resignation, which spread like wildfire in many countries after the pandemic, has massively affected this type of worker. If one of the purposes of social services is to control domestic reproduction, who has control over the proper functioning of social services? The state seems far from developing effective control strategies within the services, given that every day there is a scandal that some rest home or nursery school fails to correspond to the elementary criteria of care. The state's solution to its lack of control and inability to guarantee the well-being of its communities has generally been to increase surveillance and adminis-tration in every service. The unions have opposed this proposal because it is considered an intolerable way to control the workers, but, so far, no alternative solutions have been proposed.

There has been a great deal of debate within the feminist movement and the left over the role of social services within the capitalist system and whether or not the work done there is productive. My thesis is that this work is productive because it is an extension in the social body of the work of reproduction, which is productive, as *L'arcano* has demonstrated. In fact, work in social services has the purpose of contributing to the reproduction of the workforce, which is the most precious asset for capital.

8.2 The relationship between the family and social reproduction

Social services were generally conceived as a corollary of domestic work, which remains the premise and basis for the reproduction of the labour force. Schools and health and public services provide services comple-mentary to those carried out in homes. Among these services there are those designed with the aim of allowing women to go to work, such as those intended for children such as nurseries and kindergartens, and those intended for older adults, such as care homes. Social services have always served to allow capital to use the female labour force if necessary. They were not designed to free women, whether they engage in extra-domestic work or not, from housework.

What does social reproduction represent for children, the sick and older adults? It represents the transition from an *à la carte* labour of love to an employment relationship organised directly in capitalist terms, which is not part of a loving relationship, but is a salaried one: the exchanging of work for a salary. The point is that social service workers are not expected to love the children and older adults in their care, but to perform their jobs professionally by caring for them responsibly. On the other hand, in public and/or private structures, children and older adults experience secondary socialisation (outside the family) and learn to relate to others and to face all the positive and negative consequences that forced coexistence, outside one's own home and in a social and public place, entails. The weakness of the sphere of domestic reproduction, combined with the lack of real economic recognition, also tends to make social service workers politically and socially weak. Low wages and growing workloads make these workers vulnerable to an increasingly powerful system of exploitation. Consequently, children, the sick and older adults are exposed to all the behaviours that result from the capitalist organisation of work: refusal or resistance to work, or real violence that is unleashed on those the workers are supposed to take care of.

8.3 The evolution of state policy towards social services, from the concept of savings to that of profit

The modern state was born as a guarantor of the production and reproduction of the workforce with respect to the capitalist system. The importance of this function can be seen from the fact that the state budget is basically divided into three areas: the education system, the health system and the army. Public spending on welfare is modelled (shrinks or grows) according to the power relations between the classes but is careful not to cross the line that defines social reproduction as complementary to domestic reproduction. Welfare functions, in fact, as a form of indirect salary to the female workers in the house: as an institutionalised alienation of care work and as a form of social control over the work carried out at home.

The changes that have taken place in the objectives of social services should be carefully analysed.[99] At the beginning, they were created not to make profit, but to offer services that weighed as little as possible on the state budget. Therefore, the watchword was shrewdness in spending and management. About twenty years ago, the system began to adopt an increasingly corporate logic. Now there is a further step: the state is increasingly inclined to hand over many health and educational services to the private sector because this apparently costs them less. The presumed savings that the state would make by pursuing this social policy nonetheless are paid for by children, the sick and older adults, who become a direct source of income and therefore of value extraction. The consequence is that labour power is increasingly devalued in its reproduction, even in the sphere of social reproduction.

---

99   An interesting point of departure is Sara Farris and Sabrina Marchetti, 'From the Commodification to the Corporatization of Care: European Perspectives and Debates', *Social Politics: International Studies in Gender, State and Society* 24, no. 2 (2017), 109–31.

8.4 The mobilisations and struggles of social service workers: where they fit into the class composition

The mobilisations and struggles of social service workers have demonstrated in the practice of their political action that they are situated within the range of the forces in struggle in the sphere of reproduction, both domestic and social. It is no coincidence that social service students have been inspired by, for example, the Montreal Wages for Housework campaign to demand that their internships be paid.[100]

8.5 For the construction of a common political strategy for housewives and social services workers

For a part of the feminist movement, the central moment of the political strategy for women's liberation remains the recourse to extra-domestic work, to which is added a timid request for social services. For another part, the political perspective is the request for social services as a strategy to fight for the radical reduction of domestic work, the presence of which in the working day of women is now considered the greatest obstacle to equality with respect to men. In this perspective, social services are seen as an almost complete form of socialisation of the workforce considered inactive. The children go to kindergarten or school and stay there all day (and night?), while older adults, when they are no longer independent, are sent to care homes where they live permanently.

As strategies of liberation from domestic work and from the historical detriment of women, they have all shown their limits over time. Women who went to work outside the home to free themselves from domestic work have their economic independence and contribute to the family budget, but have found themselves doing double work, often for meagre wages. Women who have focused above all on social services as a strategy of liberation from domestic work have found themselves assuming the complete responsibility for domestic reproduction and its transformation into social reproduction within institutions. Could it be a reasonable political goal to turn all material and immaterial domestic work into work performed by social services? In practice, however, these women found themselves having to face constant cuts in public spending, leading to fewer and fewer social services, year after year, without having the organisational or political strength to counter them.

---

100   Berthiaume et al., *Grèves des stages, grève des femmes*; Simonet, '"Wages for"'.

More or less reformulated, the political discourse on social services is often imprecise, because it confuses an objective of struggle with a political strategy for women's liberation, and, let us add, it is illusory, because it starts from the assumption that the reproductive socialisation of the workforce completely manages to replace the production and reproduction of the workforce of female workers in the house carried out at an individual level. This assumption is wrong because social services (nursery, hospital, school) not only presuppose domestic work at home but constantly require it. Just think of the vital assistance that relatives, generally women, provide to the sick, and which allows hospitals to function, or the fact that, when a child falls ill, nurseries and schools immediately call the parents to pick them up and take them home. Finally, this assumption is wrong because a large part of domestic work cannot be socialised or eliminated by the development of technology. It can and must be destroyed as capitalist labour, freed from the yoke of exploitation and released to the wealth of individual creativity. I refer here to immaterial domestic work (affection, love, consolation and, above all, sexuality), which, among other things, comprise an increasingly important part of domestic work.

To be clear: the goal of a fully socialised reproduction of the labour force does not make sense even as a political programme. In fact, this would imply the liberation of women from indirectly wage-earning domestic work, but at the cost of total state control over everyone's life, including the obligatory factory for every woman and the edu-factory for every child from birth. This is exactly the opposite of what we must aim for. Surely, the struggle for social services is a crucial goal within a feminist strategy, but it must have its rightful place on the political agenda.

9. The technological attack on women

Capital's response to the struggles of women in the sphere of reproduction, as described in the previous sections, and to the workers' struggles in factories and offices, which has managed to wrest substantial wealth since the post-war period, has been tough. On the one hand, capital has used the sphere of reproduction against that of production to erode, little by little, the wealth that the grandparents and parents of current workers had managed to snatch from capital. In Italy, for example, in 2021, according to ISTAT, 18.2 million families, equal to 70.8 per cent of the total, were owners of the house in which they live, while 5.2 million (20.5 per cent) live in rented accommodation and 2.2 million (8.7 per cent) have their home in usufruct or free of charge.[101] Furthermore, Italian households have traditionally had substantial levels of private savings, for a long time among the highest in the developed world, but these have been declining for over twenty years due to practically zero growth in wages (when there has not been a reduction in real terms), and due to very low growth rates of the Italian economy since the 1990s.[102] It is also this workers' wealth that capital targets, when it offers below subsistence wages, or offers young people unpaid, underpaid or precarious work, or offers pensions that are negligible in light of such high inflation. On the other hand, capital has attempted to reclaim its dominance over reproduction through an attack that has used digital technologies as its powerful new weapons. And it is this attack in particular that I will describe below, showing how through digital technologies capital, on the one hand, has directly affected the power of women, attacking them at the level of communication (the first ground for negotiation and mediation in the man–woman relationship) and, on the other hand, has directly colonised immaterial labour.

9.1 The attack on women

How to contain and possibly decrease the social power of women, which has been resistant to any attack? The solution was offered by digital technologies: personal computers, cell phones, digital televisions, home automation, robotics, virtual assistants, chatbots – that is, highly advanced technologies that came from the heart of industrial innovation. This process has been analysed in detail by Fortunati and Edwards, in a work that I resume here.[103] The diffusion of the analogue technologies of the telephone, radio and television in our homes had already allowed states and capitalist systems to overcome the difficulties of

---

101   'Istat: nel 2021 il 70,8% delle famiglie con la casa di proprietà, il 20,5% in affitto', *Idealista*, 16 September 2022, idealista.it.

102   Matteo Ridolfi, 'La sfida del risparmio tra crescita e incertezza', *Econopoly*, 14 November 2022, econopoly.ilsole24ore.com.

103   Leopoldina Fortunati and Autumn Edwards, 'Gender and Human-Machine Communication: Where Are We?', *Human-Machine Communication* 5 (2022): 7–47.

exercising control over the domestic environment.[104] These difficulties emerged from the fact that, having posited the sphere of reproduction as natural, capital was forced to stop at the front door, which sanctioned, on the one hand, the end of the public sphere over which it had direct jurisdiction, and on the other, the beginning of the private sphere, over which it had an indirect jurisdiction and therefore could not directly control.

In fact, control of individuals and of the domestic sphere in the society of capital could only be exercised ex ante, outside the domestic process itself, when the labour force arrived at the gates of factories, offices or schools. Analogue technologies (mass media) and the telephone had already taken a first step, however, putting the outside world in contact with individuals and vice versa, through almost invisible means: through electricity, electromagnetic waves, and so on. Furthermore, they had allowed capital both to reorganise the time discipline and pace of everyday life according to the timetables of TV news and entertainment broadcasts, and to control information and shape the imagination and culture of the public. A further step has been taken since the early 1990s with the introduction of digital and wireless technologies (such as computers, laptops, mobile phones and the market saturation of broadband and wireless internet), which have undergone the same process of commodification which transport, household appliances and the mass media had been subject to previously. Naturally, this solution was not painless, because it meant that these intelligent technologies were then subject to the purchasing power of consumers and therefore to the will of potential buyers to dispose of them as they pleased.

The diffusion of digital technologies was of great importance, because it took place in a particular historical moment in relation to the women's movement. After various waves of feminism, women had reshaped power relations within the domestic sphere and the family more in their favour, strengthening their mastery and control over in-person communication, where the power differential between men and women had diminished, and also communicating confidently in the public sphere.[105]

104   Joshua Meyrowitz, *No Sense of Place: The Impact of Electronic Media on Social Behavior* (New York: Oxford University Press, 1985).

105   For interpersonal communication, see Daniel Canary and Kimberley Hause, 'Is There Any Reason to Research Sex Differences in Communication?', *Communication Quarterly* 41, no. 2 (1993), 129–44; Kathryn Dindia and Mike Allen, 'Sex Differences in

The arrival of digital technologies in the domestic sphere has reversed this situation, undermining the power that women had acquired in terms of communication.[106]

Unfortunately, this capitalist offensive has not been met with unified opposition from women. Understandably, women as domestic workers tended to covet household appliances, which could immediately free them from a certain amount of material fatigue, and to generally neglect electronic and digital devices, which, at the time, were associated more with entertainment or other areas of limited political value. Given the unequal power relations within the family, however, while women's competence in the use of household appliances was perceived as socially irrelevant, the use of information and communication technologies ended up disproportionately empowering men.[107] In this process there has been a crucial step, which has had a particular importance with regard to the issue of gender: the introduction of the computer into the domestic sphere. It is above all through the computer that women's power over communication has been reduced, since this artefact has been designed (even more than the cell phone) by communities of hyper-masculine innovators for young males (intended particularly for the wealthy Western market).[108] Digital technologies are one of those instances where technology has been used against women.

During the first phase of diffusion of these technologies, the percentages of their access, ownership and use by women were lower than by men. In fact, women needed more time to understand and appropriate these devices, which were not in fact designed for them. Through these technologies, men have regained control over communication and information, a control they have tried to keep, even if women have more recently regained possession of communication technologies, especially mobile phones. Among digital technologies, the computer was particularly difficult for women to appropriate, for various reasons, including

---

Self-Disclosure: A Meta-Analysis', *Psychological Bulletin* 112, no. 1 (1992), 106–24; Janet Hyde and Marcia Linn, 'Gender Differences in Verbal Ability: A Meta-Analysis', *Psychological Bulletin* 104, no. 1 (1988): 53–69. For communication in the public sphere, see Fortunati, *Telecomunicando in Europa*.

106   Fortunati and Edwards, 'Gender and Human-Machine Communication'.

107   Ibid.

108   Jessica Lingel and Kate Crawford, '"Alexa, Tell Me about Your Mother": The History of the Secretary and the End of Secrecy', *Catalyst: feminism, theory, technoscience* 6, no. 1 (2020), 2380–3312.

the fact that, when it was first launched, the computer was not marketed or tailored to them. In general, the penetration of these technologies into the sphere of reproduction has entailed a higher level of robotisation of individuals, as we will see below. In terms of the critique of political economy, these technologies have aimed to increase the production of value in the social and individual reproductive sphere, to increase social discipline and to decrease the autonomy of the workforce and its control over knowledge and know-how.

9.2 The direct colonisation of domestic labour

The initiative of capital has not limited itself to reducing the power of women but has also sought to colonise material and immaterial domestic work through these new technologies, albeit to different extents. The attack that has been launched by the capitalist system through digital technologies has favoured immaterial domestic work, because in this area the technologies were easier and less expensive to produce. In relation to material work, capital applied a converse strategy, enforcing the traditional underdevelopment of technologies, which in this context were more difficult to produce and more expensive. Immaterial housework however has been completely reshaped by capitalist strategy with an infusion of machines, platforms and high-level services, which have tried to subsume the part of immaterial housework that women had refused or simply no longer provided. These technologies have reorganised this work in the world of the web, interpellating not only women as new workers of technologically advanced immaterial reproduction but *everyone* (children, men, adolescents and older adults). As a result, immaterial domestic work has become increasingly *mediated, automated, self-reproductive, self-exploited, self-disciplined and dematerialised.*

This strategy was necessary for various reasons: first, to restore a high level of value production in daily life; second, to maintain control over women by dispossessing them of an intangible part of reproductive work; third, to produce a workforce capable of coping with both the complexity of globalisation and the growing share of domestic work no longer performed by women. Through these new technologies, immaterial labour has not only created value in the process of reproducing the workforce by extracting value directly from sociability, friendship, feelings, emotions and so on, but it has also directly generated capital, as I have argued in previous work.[109] While household appliances succeeded in reducing the time spent on some material domestic activities, new technologies have intensified and lengthened the working day in the sphere of reproduction. While household appliances represented a symbolic operation, through which industrial developers proposed a positive image of technological progress after the disasters of the Second World War, new technologies, on the contrary, represented the rationalisation of a sector in which the industrial convergence between two different leading industrial traditions – information technology and media technologies – allowed the restoration and intensification of the productivity of intangible housework.[110] Considering that the use of household appliances was targeted primarily at women, the new technologies (though initially aimed at young, white, wealthy men) have tended to become more ecumenical.

In the domestic sphere today, a great mass of people use 'intellectual' machines.[111] Consequently, in the current capitalist system, the typical user of fixed capital (machines) is no longer the classic factory or office worker, but rather women, children and older adults, as well as the ordinary citizen in the domestic sphere. These machines are now distributed throughout society. Taking a cue from Tronti, it can be said that, faced with the extreme fragility of class consciousness today, people present great homogeneity of a particular technical position: all are users and consumers of these technologies.[112] The new technologies and the various work processes that they support in the domestic environment represent the various parts of a large assembly line, whose workers are women, men, children and older adults – that is, all the subjects who provide, albeit to different extents, domestic work, as well as all individuals as citizens.

Powerful digital technologies, such as the computer, the mobile phone and, more recently, robots, virtual assistants, chatbots and LLMs (large-language models) such as ChatGPT have been brought to market,

---

109   Leopoldina Fortunati, 'Immaterial Labour and Its Mechanization', *Ephemera: Theory and Politics in Organisation* 7, no. 1 (2007), 139–57.

110   Alain Gras, *Grandeur et dépendance: Sociologie des macro-systèmes techniques* (Paris: PUF, 1993); Lev Manovich, *The Language of New Media* (Cambridge, MA: MIT Press, 2011).

111   Thomás Maldonado, *Critica della Ragione Informatica* (Milan: Feltrinelli, 1997).

112   Tronti, *Workers and Capital*.

orchestrated by fierce ideology. These technologies are all about power and the separation of mind and body, and they are authoritarian. In general, in highly industrialised countries, the intellect is the primary centre of the production of value, the crucial tool of contemporary production.[113] Machines, which are now distributed throughout society and throughout the realm of reproduction, specifically automate and standardise immaterial housework, making it uniform and homogeneous. Digital technologies have introduced a double mechanism: on the one hand, machines shape and reshape people; on the other, machines shape and reshape themselves, based on people's habits and practices in their use. The consequences are many: let us try to decipher the most important.

The first consequence was the remodelling of the strategic area of the immaterial domestic sphere through the automation of immaterial labour in the domestic sphere. The immaterial work of the domestic sphere includes many dimensions: from communication to information, from education to entertainment, from affection and emotions to sociality. Each of these spheres has been subsumed within specific platforms: communication, from WhatsApp, Facebook, Instagram, TikTok and so on; information from online newspapers, news sites and discussion forums; education from online teaching and learning, online research, educational robotics; entertainment from YouTube, video games, social networks; affections and emotions from SMS, instant messages, mobile calls and so on; sociability from Badoo, Meetic, Tinder and many others. The second consequence is that digital technologies in the social body have led to the implementation of uniform, undifferentiated and homogeneous social behaviours (which can be more easily influenced, manipulated and controlled) – that is, they have conveyed the development of social automation in many fields such as emotions, tastes, courtship and conversation. Technologies impose on living labour the legacies of the dead labour incorporated in them. This leads to a further alienation: the invasion of the inorganic into the organic, so that, in contemporary society, there are combined tendencies both to machinise human beings and to anthropomorphise objects: the body is assimilated

---

113   Michael Hardt and Antonio Negri, *Empire* (Cambridge, MA: Harvard University Press, 2000); Antonio Negri, 'Kairos, Alma Venus, Multitudo', in *Time for Revolution*, trans. M. Mandarini (London: Continuum, 2003).

to the machine; objects become technological; technologies become *intelligent*. A new order is being born, a new system, where the hybrid is the key figure that passes from the imaginary to the statute of reality. The more technologies penetrate the human body, the more they limit the amount of living labour necessary to produce the body itself and its work capacity, and therefore further devalue individuals and the workforce. The third consequence is that they have also outlined the progressive evacuation of individuals from the communicative sphere, which represents an advanced stage in the progressive isolation of individuals, of which Marx has already written.[114]

This picture of profound transformations in the sphere of reproduction is fully understood only through the lens of globalisation. Faced with the rebellious behaviours described above, by women and the cycle of workers' struggles of the 1960s and 1970s, which had eroded a large proportion of profits in the old industrialised countries, capital responded with globalisation. Globalisation was, on the one hand, a forced process in which capital was compelled to migrate to developing countries to recover a high level of profits by de-industrialising the West.[115] On the other hand, it has turned into an attack, at a higher level, against women, the working class and the proletariat. Since globalised capital has created worlds, communities, organisations and policies without borders to increase its profits, it has, at the same time, had to undermine the new freedom that the fall of borders brought with it, by building walls around each individual.[116] This process has been further strengthened by the spread of digital technologies. Producing new labour power in these conditions of increased social isolation has become increasingly difficult. This physical separation between individuals is an extension to all of society of the separation and isolation that women have always suffered in their homes, with each woman separated from the others, and from all other people. Social isolation has now spread to all individuals,

---

114   Steve Jones, 'People, Things, Memory and Human-Machine Communication', *International Journal of Media and Cultural Politics* 10, no. 3 (2014), 245–8.

115   Ferruccio Gambino, 'Composizione di classe e investimenti diretti statunitensi all'estero', in Ferrari Bravo, ed., *Imperialismo e classe operaia multinazionale* (Milan: Feltrinelli, 1975), 318–59.

116   Leopoldina Fortunati, 'Gender and Identity in Human–Machine Communication', in Andrea L. Guzman, Rhonda McEwen and Steve Jones, eds, *The SAGE Handbook of Human–Machine Communication* (SAGE, 2023), 127–35.

thanks to information and communication technologies – through the evolution of human communication, which has passed from face-to-face communication to telephone communication, to communication via mobile phone, or via computer, to communication between humans and machines. This series of communicative shifts has had the effect of increasingly dissuading human beings from making personal communications and building relationships with each other on a *physical level*. In other words, the transition from face-to-face communication to mediated communication in all its forms outlines a long process of physical distancing between individuals, reaching its apex in communication not through machines but *with* machines.[117] When we talk to Alexa or Google Home, or ask questions of our bank's virtual assistant, we are communicating with machines, not other human beings.

The physical separation that individuals now experience can be seen as a way to weaken and control them more easily. The enormous expansion of social relations that these technologies have opened in virtual space ends up undermining the possibility of creating true solidarity between individuals, and of building a political and trade union consciousness. In other words, it weakens people's political, bargaining and social power. This process of physical separation between individuals describes not only a weakened worker – of whatever gender – but also citizens who are weakened and more easily controlled. In the meantime, these technologies have penetrated the public administrative sphere, radically changing the relationship between the state and the end user (citizen). Citizens have been forced to transform themselves from users into digital workers, as Fortunati and Austin describe.[118]

The fourth consequence is that women today create a different workforce: mobile (for many workers, it is no longer sufficient to sell their working capacity, as Marx affirms, but they must also sell their ability to move), already accustomed to automation and an intimate interaction with machines, more capable of coping with alienation, more socially separated from other workforces (more individualised, less politicised, less unionised, less linked to political parties, with more delocalised networks of relationships), more informed, cosmopolitan and flexible.

---

117   Andrea Guzman, *Human-Machine Communication: Rethinking Communication, Technology, and Ourselves* (Berlin: Peter Lang, 2018).

118   Fortunati and Austin, 'Digital Labour and the Domestic Sphere'.

The fifth consequence is that the boundaries between human beings and machines have become increasingly blurred ontologically. Machines are getting smarter and humans increasingly automated. In particular, the body of individuals and especially that of women is no longer just a natural machine but has hybridised with the machines themselves. The body, a natural machine, attracts and contains artificial machines at a diagnostic level (such as probes), a therapeutic one (pacemakers, radiation, hormone therapies), and at other levels: from the reproductive (for example, in vitro fertilisation), to those of identity (plastic surgery, genetic engineering, sex changes), to those of communication (mobile phone, laptop, pager). But these technologies are not the ones that would be needed to transform the organisation of domestic work in an anticapitalist sense. The body, even if technologised, is left to its difficult domestic activity with little help from technology, and everyday life remains in its pre-industrialised (not pre-capitalist) substrate. The mind, on the other hand, feeds itself electronically in various ways. Sometimes, for reasons of social control, as in post-industrial countries, the nature of work expands to include more communication, organisation and management, becoming more and more intellectual. It is the same old story: technology makes work, in this case domestic work, superfluous, and devalues the human body and the individual. This process is also likely to be persistent.

The sixth consequence is the tendency that has established itself in the capitalist system to conceal the differences between objects and subjects, making cooperation on the part of the public, consumers and people both possible and necessary. How is this cooperation managed? Users collaborate by agreeing to live out this fiction as if it were not fiction. For example, communicating via WhatsApp with your distant grandchild under the illusion of keeping an emotional relationship alive in this way, neglects the fact that you cannot pick him up and kiss him. The diffusion and use of new technologies has produced an important phenomenon: men and women, for one reason or another, are fleeing everyday life. There is a strong impression that the flight from reality is growing because reality is too contradictory, difficult and complex to negotiate and experience. The refusal or incapacity to take care of others, to work to reproduce them, recreate them or recreate with them in a way free from the logic of capital, is the real social problem of the third millennium. Perhaps because they distance themselves from reality, people feel an anxious voracity for reality, which they want to consume in ever greater quantities, even if only on a virtual level. The result is that, beyond the old residual poverty, which also exists in industrialised countries, the new universal poverty is a poverty of first-hand reality: many of us spend all day in front of a screen (computer or mobile phone), and this means that we do not live our lives directly but live rather a second-hand reality.

The economic system is paying a huge price for not recognising the value of domestic work. The detachment from everyday life is also strengthened by the fact that, as we have seen above, we feel a growing desensitisation towards the problems of those who live next to us, while paradoxically we are more sensitive to the problems of the global world as they are conveyed through the mass media. Meanwhile, whole realms of experience are liquidated. Even virtual reality was born in response to the fact that women dismissed the everyday – the sphere of domestic work – because there was no concrete recognition of the value of such work. It was also born as a response by a broad array of classes to the limited choices and programmes that political parties (including those of the left) continued to propose. Finally, it was born from what Virilio calls 'the defeat of facts and events'.

All this has served, as we have seen, to prepare humanity for the acceptance of automation, robotics and artificial intelligence. In particular, it is in the field of reproduction that robots have made an important ontological leap, because, thanks to artificial intelligence, neural networks and machine learning, they are able to perform a vast range of tasks and, above all, communicate and engage in dialogue. While factories have robots, homes have social robots – artificial agents and voice assistants such as Alexa. If, in the industrial sectors, robots imitate human gestures and actions to replace human beings' material capacity for work, in the sphere of reproduction social robots aim to imitate human beings' (*women's*) immaterial capacity for care. Would it be a desirable world, where we can leave all the work to the machines? Would it be a desirable world, where our relationship with reality and our environment is increasingly mediated by machines? Would it be a desirable world, where intelligent machines outnumber human bodies? Not to mention that, as Silvia Federici repeatedly emphasises in conference presentations, digital technologies are eating up the world: as many as fifty of the ninety natural elements existing on the planet are used to produce computers, laptops, smartphones and the various components and peripherals, some of which, such as hafnium, are quickly becoming scarce, with wars being waged for its extraction.[119]

10. Conclusion

From a sphere ancillary to the production of commodities, the sphere of reproduction has been structurally transformed in the past forty years to become dominant because a double production of value has been established here. Consequently, women have emerged as the key subject of class composition. Reproduction has emerged as the field where the bloodiest battles were fought, radically transforming not only the sphere of domestic and care work but social organisation as a whole. This is the result of a mass refusal of the work of reproduction in confrontation with states that continue to ignore the seriousness of the political and economic problem to be solved. So far, there has been a series of back-and-forth debates between state and the capitalist system regarding the importance of domestic work, but no one wants to take charge of it. This blame game must be stopped because, in the meantime, there has been a devastating deterioration in the quality of care, starting with children and ending with older adults.

It is clear that the struggles of women and the working class have been the driving force behind the development of neo-capitalism: without them we would not have the technologies of digital work, smart working, distance learning or social media. Therefore there is also a lot of *us* incorporated in these new technologies – a lot of our creativity, our innovation, as well as our resistance and struggles. Nor would we have the wealth that today is still in the hands of a substantial part of the proletariat, despite all the attempts that capital has made and is making to appropriate it.

The clashes between women, class interests and capital have intensified to the point that they jeopardise the reproduction of the workforce. The problem today is to transform these standardised behaviours into

---

119 Charmaine Pereira and Dzodzi Tsikata, 'Contextualizing Extractivism in Africa', *Feminist Africa* 2, no. 1 (2021), 14–48.

ever stronger, organised struggles, in the North as in the Global South. The label they are given is less important: wages for housework, guaranteed income, universal basic income, welfare rights and so on. On the organisational level, it is not appropriate for women to start their struggles from extra-domestic work, where they are divided into sectors and sub-sectors and separated from women who are not employed in waged labour. Starting instead from the shared burden of domestic work promises to immediately dissolve the waged/unwaged division between women.

Already today, these struggles are taking place frequently in many countries: street demonstrations and general strikes have followed one another for example in Iceland, Italy, Switzerland, several Latin American countries and the United States. Women must organise a global strike and demand money for housework. The important thing is that, all over the world, from North to South, women of any ethnic group and of any religion, find themselves united in demanding money for the work they do and in giving a future to subsequent generations. Money means reappropriating the value that women have produced, which has been stolen from them without any social consideration or respect. And this time, they must be joined in this struggle by men and children, who are also increasingly burdened by this unpaid work. Only in these new solidarities can the grave crisis gripping the sphere of reproduction today be transformed into a new renaissance, capable of bringing love, mutual respect, appreciation and solidarity into this sphere.

Index